# Philip Roth

Manchester University Press

## Contemporary American and Canadian Writers

*Series editors:*
Nahem Yousaf and Sharon Monteith

*Also available*

**Douglas Coupland** Andrew Tate

# Philip Roth

David Brauner

Manchester University Press
Manchester and New York
*distributed exclusively in the USA by Palgrave*

*Published by* Manchester University Press
Oxford Road, Manchester M13 9NR, UK
*and* Room 400, 175 Fifth Avenue, New York, NY 10010, USA
www.manchesteruniversitypress.co.uk

*Distributed exclusively in the USA by*
Palgrave, 175 Fifth Avenue, New York,
NY 10010, USA

*Distributed exclusively in Canada by*
UBC Press, University of British Columbia, 2029 West Mall,
Vancouver, BC, Canada V6T 1Z2

*British Library Cataloguing-in-Publication Data*
A catalogue record for this book is available from the British Library

*Library of Congress Cataloging-in-Publication Data applied for*

ISBN 978 0 7190 7424 0 *hardback*
ISBN 978 0 7190 7425 7 *paperback*

First published 2007

16 15 14 13 12 11 10 09 08 07 10 9 8 7 6 5 4 3 2 1

For my parents, Irène and Jacob Brauner

The artist must know the manner whereby to convince others of the truthfulness of his lies. (Pablo Picasso, quoted in R.B. Kitaj's *First Diasporist Manifesto*)

[W]riting books is a trying adventure in which you cannot find out where you *are* unless you lose your way. (Philip Roth, *The Counterlife*, italics in original)

# Contents

# Series editors' foreword

This innovative series reflects the breadth and diversity of writing over the last thirty years, and provides critical evaluations of established, emerging and critically neglected writers – mixing the canonical with the unexpected. It explores notions of the contemporary and analyses current and developing modes of representation with a focus on individual writers and their work. The series seeks to reflect both the growing body of academic research in the field, and the increasing prevalence of contemporary American and Canadian fiction on programmes of study in institutions of higher education around the world. Central to the series is a concern that each book should argue a stimulating thesis, rather than provide an introductory survey, and that each contemporary writer will be examined across the trajectory of their literary production. A variety of critical tools and literary and interdisciplinary approaches are encouraged to illuminate the ways in which a particular writer contributes to, and helps readers rethink, the North American literary and cultural landscape in a global context.

Central to debates about the field of contemporary fiction is its role in interrogating ideas of national exceptionalism and transnationalism. This series matches the multivocality of contemporary writing with wide-ranging and detailed analysis. Contributors examine the drama of the nation from the perspectives of writers who are members of established and new immigrant groups, writers who consider themselves on the nation's margins as well as those who chronicle middle America. National labels are the subject of vociferous debate and including American and Canadian writers in the same series is not to flatten the differences between them but to acknowledge that literary traditions and tensions are cross-cultural and that North American writers often explore and expose precisely these tensions. The series recognises that situating a writer in a cultural context involves a multiplicity of influences, social and geo-political, artistic and theoretical, and that contemporary fiction defies easy categorisation. For example, it examines writers who invigorate the genres in which they have made their mark alongside writers whose aesthetic goal is to subvert the idea of genre altogether. The challenge of defining the roles of writers and assessing their reception by reading communities is central to the aims of the series.

Overall, *Contemporary American and Canadian Writers* aims to begin to represent something of the diversity of contemporary writing and seeks to engage students and scholars in stimulating debates about the contemporary and about fiction.

Nahem Yousaf
Sharon Monteith

# Acknowledgements

I would like to take this opportunity of thanking all those who have helped me complete this book. I owe a large debt to the editors of this series, Sharon Monteith and Nahem Yousaf, and to Alison Kelly for their careful and sensitive reading of the manuscript. Thanks are due also to various friends and colleagues with whom I have conducted many helpful conversations, both formal and informal, about Roth over the years, in particular Derek Parker Royal, Bryan Cheyette, Catherine Morley and Deb Shostak. Above all, my heartfelt gratitude and love goes to my wife, Anne, always my first and best reader, and to my children, Joseph and Jessica, for reminding me of what really matters.

The author gratefully acknowledges permission to reproduce in altered form portions of 'American Anti-Pastoral: Incontinence and Impurity in *American Pastoral* and *The Human Stain*', published in *Studies in American Jewish Literature* 23 (2004): 67–76, and portions of 'Everyman out of Humour' (review of *Everyman*), published in the *Jewish Quarterly* 202 (Summer 2006): 80–82.

# 1

# Introduction

For so long an *enfant terrible* of the American literary world, Philip Roth may now be considered one of its elder statesmen. He has published eighteen full-length works of fiction in an *oeuvre* that spans high seriousness (*Letting Go* (1962)) and low humour (*The Great American Novel* (1973)), expansive monologue (*Portnoy's Complaint* (1969)) and elliptical dialogue (*Deception* (1990)), spare realism (*When She Was Good* (1967)) and grotesque surrealism (*The Breast* (1972)). In addition to the novels for which he is most renowned, Roth has also published two novellas (*The Breast* and *The Prague Orgy* (1985)), a collection of short stories with a novella (*Goodbye, Columbus* (1959)), two collections of essays (*Reading Myself and Others* (1975) and *Shop Talk* (2001)), a political satire (*Our Gang* (1971)), an autobiography (*The Facts* (1988)) and a memoir of his father (*Patrimony* (1991)), as well as numerous articles, reviews and uncollected short stories. This book offers an overview of the career of Philip Roth, with particular emphasis on his later work, and an assessment of his contribution to contemporary American fiction.

I have been reading Roth for over twenty years and writing about him, on and off, for over a decade, so this book is the product of a prolonged period of research and reflection. Like any long-term relationship, mine with Roth has had its ups and downs, but I have never felt like walking out or giving up. More accurately, perhaps, I have never felt able to withdraw from this intense engagement with his work. For me, Roth is the most gripping of writers. At one point in *The Ghost Writer* Nathan Zuckerman – the author protagonist of many of Roth's novels – is told by his mentor, E.I. Lonoff, that he has 'the most compelling voice I've encountered in years' (Roth 1989: 52) – and this is the key to Roth's power as a novelist. Whether writing comedy or tragedy, satire or epic, fable or farce, when the narrative voice in Roth's fiction speaks, I, like the wedding guest in Coleridge's 'The Rime of the Ancient Mariner' (1798), 'cannot choose but hear' (Coleridge 1985: 47).

Although the style and content of Roth's fiction is extraordinarily diverse, there is always audible a distinctive voice: irreverent yet earnest, questioning yet authoritative, subtle and nuanced yet powerful and passionate; above all, obsessive, compulsive, *driven*. In an interview, Roth once remarked of *The Anatomy Lesson* (1983) that '[t]he book won't leave you alone. Won't let up. Gets too close' (Roth 2001a: 141) and this applies equally to all his work. When Henry Zuckerman complains bitterly that his brother Nathan 'could . . . leave nothing and no one alone!' (Roth 1986: 231) he is also identifying one of the distinguishing features of Roth's work. Roth, too, leaves nothing and no one in his fiction alone. Ira Ringold, the protagonist of *I Married A Communist* (1998), having beaten his adversary 'to a pulp', returns moments later 'to make the victory *total*' (Roth 1998: 300, italics in original), and Alvin, the cousin of the protagonist Philip in *The Plot Against America* (2004), not content with shooting dead a German soldier, 'crawl[s] over to where he was . . . sho[o]t[s] him twice in the head' and finally 'spit[s] on the son of a bitch' (Roth 2004: 150). Like the characters he creates, Roth never rests easy, never feels finished. He tracks down his quarry again and again, revisiting old hunting grounds and breaking into new ones; honing, refining, sharpening and expanding his armoury.

Writing about any living artist presents certain difficulties: the writing is still evolving, the reputation built on that career being revised as each new work appears. Writing on contemporary American fiction is particularly problematic because it is a very crowded field and one which is especially susceptible to the fluctuations of literary-critical fashion; new contenders for the title of 'Great American Novelist' are constantly appearing and, more often than not, soon afterwards, disappearing. Writing a book on Philip Roth entails confronting further obstacles: the fact that he himself is such an eloquent and persuasive critic of his own work, and that other criticism of Roth has become something of a minor (or maybe not so minor) industry, makes the task of finding something new and worthwhile to say about his work a challenging one.[1] The accelerating process of Roth's literary canonisation – symbolised by the reprinting of his collected works in the prestigious Library of America series[2] and his receipt of the four major literary prizes in America (the National Book Critics Circle Award, the PEN/Faulkner Award (twice), the National Book Award and the Pulitzer Prize), as well as the Gold Medal in fiction from the American Academy of Arts and Letters – has ensured that work by Roth and on Roth is receiving more attention within the academy than at any previous time in his career.

During the last decade of the twentieth century and the first of the new millennium, critical accolades for Roth have been growing steadily in number and volume. Although some critics, such as Mark Shechner, have long argued that Roth possesses 'the most distinctive voice in American fiction', his position in the pantheon of classic post-war American authors was for many years somewhat precarious (Shechner 2003: 216). Critical acclaim and controversy came early to Roth and ensured that he was one of the most fashionable American novelists at the end of the 1950s and 1960s, but in the early 1970s his sales and his literary reputation began to decline and he was often regarded as the junior partner of a Jewish-American triumvirate that included Saul Bellow and Bernard Malamud. This trend continued throughout the seventies and most of the 1980s, when younger novelists such as Don DeLillo and Paul Auster, who seemed to owe more to Thomas Pynchon than to Roth, established themselves, and the work of African-American novelists, most notably Alice Walker and Toni Morrison, threatened to eclipse that of their Jewish-American peers. The publication of *The Counterlife* in 1986, however, signalled the beginning of Roth's second coming and over the course of the 1990s he was indeed often treated as the saviour of American fiction, not only resurrecting his own career but redeeming a genre (realist historical fiction) and a generation (those American writers born in the 1930s who made their names in the 1960s) that had seemed to many largely exhausted.[3] Having often been compared unfavourably to John Updike over the previous twenty years, Roth now found himself used as the yardstick by which all his peers, including Updike, were measured. James Wood reflected this shift in the balance of power between these two prolific post-war American novelists by claiming in 1997 that '[t]hose who think John Updike is a great American writer would surrender this illusion if they attended to Roth's greater stringency and intellectual urgency' (Wood 1997: 9). Sean O'Hagan suggested that Roth had nothing to fear from younger rivals either, pointing out that '[w]hile newer talents such as . . . Jonathan Franzen have been praised for their attempts to create the Great American Novel for our times, Roth, without fuss or fanfare, has written four of them in the last decade' (O'Hagan 2004: n.p.). The reviews of *The Plot Against America* (2004) yielded an especially rich crop of tributes to Roth's pre-eminence. For example, his fellow novelist, the South African two-times winner of the Booker Prize, J.M. Coetzee, compared him to the greatest figure in English literary history, suggesting that 'at his very best he reaches Shakespearean heights' (Coetzee 2004: 6); Greil Marcus argued that 'his supremacy as the most commanding novelist of his time' was now unchallenged (Marcus 2004: 1); Alan Cooper felt that Roth had moved 'into a realm of narrative seldom attained', displaying a mastery at which '[m]ost professional writers will just gape' in awe (Cooper 2005: 252); David Herman called him 'a great writer, one of the best writers of the second half of the twentieth century' (Herman 2004: 76) and *Esquire* magazine went one better, awarding Roth the tag of 'the greatest fiction writer America has ever produced' (cited on the official Roth website of Houghton Mifflin). Finally, Blake Morrison considered that, 'given the extraordinary late blooming of an already illustrious career . . . the word genius doesn't seem excessive' and finished his review by posing the rhetorical question: 'Isn't it time they gave him the Nobel?' (Morrison 2004: 2).

Given that his literary stock has never been higher, and looks likely to retain or even increase its value, Roth would seem now to represent a safe investment for any critic. Unlike many of his contemporaries, he has stayed the course, and seems likely to be read and taught on college courses for many years to come. Yet writing about Roth remains in many ways a risky venture. Roth's critical reputation has not always been stable; over the years it has fluctuated considerably. In his introduction to a collection of essays on Roth's work in 1982, Sanford Pinsker observed that '[n]eutral criticism hardly exists where Roth is concerned . . . critics . . . either love his work or hate it' (Pinsker 1982: 2–3). In fact, for the first twenty years or so of Roth's career, the hate was more in evidence than the love, often manifesting itself in personalised polemics that offered little insight into the work itself, being more concerned with the morality of its author. Few contemporary authors (with the obvious exception of Salman Rushdie) have inspired such animus: Jeremy Larner accused Roth of being 'a liar' (Larner 1982: 28), John Gross was offended by his 'intolerable knowingness about lubricants and deodorants, menstruation and masturbation' (Gross 1982: 41) and Robert Alter accused him of harbouring 'a kind of vendetta against human nature' (Alter 1982: 45).

An extraordinarily vicious, *ad hominem* attack was published in 1972 in *Commentary* (a journal devoted to Jewish-American culture that had published a number of Roth's early stories), by the influential Jewish-American critic, Irving Howe, who had written an enthusiastic review of Roth's first book *Goodbye, Columbus*. Howe charged Roth with, among many other things, 'not behaving with good faith', displaying a 'failure in literary tact' and a 'need to rub our noses in the muck of squalid daily existence' (Howe 1982: 234, 238). *Goodbye, Columbus* and *Portnoy's Complaint*, Roth's first and fourth books, excited most controversy and I will have more to say about their reception in the following chapter, but some later novels were also condemned in unusually emotive terms. Joseph Cohen, for example, dismissed *The Anatomy Lesson* as 'merely a spewing forth of venom' (Cohen 1992: 197) and Philip Hensher denounced *Operation Shylock* as 'a dishonest and wicked book' and 'an immoral misuse of fiction' (Hensher 1993: 11). Morris Dickstein described *Sabbath's Theater* as 'ugl[y]', 'deliberately offensive', 'a work of profound self-loathing', 'a bitter retrospective . . . [that] smells of panic and hatred', and 'an execration in the face of critics who had long since stopped criticizing, a gauntlet thrown down to feminists who had long since stopped caring' (Dickstein 2002: 225, 228).

Even among his ostensible supporters, admiration for Roth during the first half of his career tends more often than not to be tempered with a certain distaste for (what was perceived as) his own bad taste. Most of the authors of early books on Roth seemed slightly embarrassed by their choice of subject and often took him to task: Sanford Pinsker felt that Roth is too 'self-indulgent' a writer (Pinsker 1975: 73); Bernard Rodgers that Roth's 'persistent flaw has been a tendency towards diffusiveness' (Rodgers 1978: 148) and Judith Jones and Guinevera Nance that he was guilty at times of 'exhibitionism' (Jones and Nance 1981: 72). When praise was forthcoming, its faintness was sometimes damning: George Searles, for example, in the introduction to his book on Updike and Roth, offered a half-hearted endorsement, averring that Roth had 'contributed several decidedly superior works that are quite likely to endure' (Searles 1985: 7). The first monograph on Roth seriously to redress this critical imbalance and to begin to do justice to the richness and complexity of Roth's work was Hermione Lee's study, in which she makes a powerful case for Roth as 'a writer of remarkable virtuosity and adventurousness' (Lee 1982: 82). Though now of course rather outdated, Lee's slim book remains one of the best to have been published on Roth and its author one of the few early critics of his work to move beyond parochial debates about whether or not Roth was a good thing for the Jews towards a more sophisticated analysis of his work in terms of its aesthetic value and formal qualities.

The ten years between Lee's book and Jay L. Halio's *Philip Roth Revisited* (1992) was, as Halio's title implies, a relatively quiet period in Roth criticism, broadly coinciding with the nadir of his critical reputation. It was a period in which Roth seemed to many observers to have become 'increasingly self-contained, writing beautifully poised sentences in a vacuum of ingenuity; a writer's writer, writing about a writer writing about a writer writing' (Brown 2000: 67). From the mid-1990s onwards, however, writing on Roth 'exploded', as one of the best of a younger generation of Roth critics, Derek Parker Royal, puts it (Royal 2004b: 145), so that now, in the words of one of the best of the older generation, Mark Shechner, '[y]ou can drown in Roth criticism' (Shechner 2003: 245).[4] Unlike the earlier criticism, most of this later work is both more sympathetic to its subject and more rigorous in its analysis.

Alan Cooper's book *Philip Roth and the Jews* (1996), though at times guilty of reading Roth's works as too narrowly personal, nonetheless represents an important advance on the much cruder, reductive biographical criticism to which Roth's earlier books were often subjected. The argument of Steven Milowitz's book, *Philip Roth Considered: The Concentrationary Universe of the American Writer* (2000) – that Roth's fiction is best understood in terms of its engagement with the Holocaust – is at times tendentious, often tenuous and occasionally perverse, but it contains some very thoughtful, original readings of selected texts. Mark Shechner's book, *Up Society's Ass, Copper* (2003), consists largely of material that has appeared before, with some 'second' and sometimes 'third' thoughts appended, but is nevertheless a useful reminder of the fact that its author has been one of the most consistently perceptive and entertaining critics on Roth for four decades. The most important of the later books on Roth, however, is Debra Shostak's *Philip Roth: Countertexts, Counterlives* (2004). Shostak's central thesis – that 'Roth's books talk to one another as countertexts in an ongoing and mutually illuminating conversation, zigzagging from one way of representing the problems of selfhood to another' – is not entirely original,[5] but she develops it in greater detail and with greater tenacity than anyone else has. Hers is the first book to make extensive use of the Library of Congress collection of Roth papers and the first to do justice to the implications of his work for the larger questions of how we read and how we think about identity. Shostak's Bakhtinian reading of Roth as a 'dialogical' writer demonstrates persuasively that his work is much more open-ended and diverse than has generally been acknowledged.

What Shostak does with Roth she does extremely effectively. She is, however, guilty of two notable sins of omission. Firstly, in her insistence on the ways in which Roth's texts read each other, she neglects to consider the ways in which they read, and are read by, other texts and consequently gives the impression, at times, that Roth's work is somewhat insular, produced and consumed in isolation from his predecessors and contemporaries. Secondly, although she expertly teases out the intellectual, philosophical and psychological complexities of Roth's fictions, she doesn't have that much to say about Roth as a stylist. Indeed, the efflorescence of Roth criticism in the early years of the new millennium notwithstanding, there has been little attention paid to these aspects of Roth's work – a situation that this book seeks to redress. Whereas authors of books on Roth used to complain with some justice that 'Roth's work has suffered the fate of being either misread or misused' (Wade 1996: 130) or, in more charged terms, that Roth has been the '[v]ictim of gross misreadings' (Milowitz 2000: ix), the work of Shostak and others has moved the nature and level of the debates on Roth on and up. However, there are still many aspects of Roth's large and ever-expanding oeuvre that remain neglected.

The task of the Roth critic should no longer be to defend the embattled author but rather to recognise and examine the ambiguities, ambivalences and paradoxes that make Roth's fiction demand and amply repay repeated readings. In the chapters that follow, I engage in detailed analysis of texts and suggest a number of contexts in which these texts can be situated, reading them in terms of their relation to each other but also juxtaposing them with work by some of Roth's contemporaries. I am interested primarily not in questions of influence but in the possibilities for mapping intertextual connections that such juxtapositions offer. Rather than attempting to survey all of Roth's work, I concentrate on the second half of his career, from the publication of *The Ghost Writer* (1979) to *The Plot Against America* (2004).[6]

In the first chapter I argue that the four books that comprise the *Zuckerman Bound* series – *The Ghost Writer, Zuckerman Unbound*

(1981), *The Anatomy Lesson* (1983) and *The Prague Orgy* (1985) – represent a detailed exploration of the ethical and aesthetic conflicts faced by the post-war Jewish-American writer. Focusing on Roth's use of legalistic language in these fictions, I suggest that the trials (the tests and ordeals) which Nathan Zuckerman (the protagonist of all four books) undergoes not only reflect Roth's paradoxical responses to the critical reception of his earlier work by Jewish readers but also function as metaphors for the ways in which, historically, Jews have often judged, and been judged, by themselves and others. The second chapter considers some of the ways in which Roth's generic experimentation, which I trace from his early novel *My Life as a Man* (1974), through *The Counterlife, The Facts* (1988), *Deception* (1990) and *Operation Shylock* (1993), appropriates, complicates and finally parodies aspects of both realism and postmodernism, making connections between these texts and works by Nathaniel Hawthorne, Thomas Pynchon, Tim O'Brien and Bret Easton Ellis. In the third chapter, I discuss Roth's treatment of morality, mortality and masculinity in what I consider to be his masterpiece, *Sabbath's Theater* (1995), comparing it with a short story by Stanley Elkin and a novel by Howard Jacobson that share many of its themes. The fourth chapter develops work that I began in my previous book, *Post-War Jewish Fiction* (2001), exploring Roth's use of what I call the 'anti-pastoral' mode in his 'American Trilogy' of novels. Whereas in earlier work, I looked at the anti-pastoral primarily in terms of 'nature anxiety', here I apply the term in a more metaphorical sense to define Roth's deconstruction of the Utopian dreams and rituals of purification with which many of the characters in *American Pastoral* (1997), *I Married A Communist* (1998) and *The Human Stain* (2000) delude themselves and deceive others. In the last chapter I look at *The Plot Against America* alongside Jonathan Safran Foer's novel *Extremely Loud and Incredibly Close* (2005) as studies of the relationship between history and fiction, trauma and imagination. Finally, in Afterword, I examine Roth's *Everyman* (2006) and assess Roth's critical reputation fifty years into his career and indicate some of the directions that I would like to see future criticism take. The thread running through all the different sections of the book is the idea of paradox, both as a rhetorical device of which Roth is particularly fond, and also as an organising intellectual and ideological principle that inflects all of his work. In the remainder of this introduction I will establish some of the ways in which Roth's writing and its reception have been characterised by paradoxes, identifying three key areas of debate that cut across all the chapters of this book and all the books of Roth's *oeuvre*.

## Autobiographical fiction or fictional autobiography?

Roth has, from the start of his career, been labelled an autobiographical novelist. Although his third novel, *When She Was Good* (1967), a tragic tale of a mid-Western girl crushed by the mediocrity of the men surrounding her and by her own inflexible sense of moral rectitude, seemed as far removed from Roth's own experiences as anyone could imagine, its lukewarm reviews confirmed for many the suspicion that it had, arguably, been designed to disprove: that Roth could only write (successful) fiction based on his own life. In the introduction to their edited collection of essays, *Reading Philip Roth* (1988), Asher Milbauer and Donald Watson lamented the fact that 'critical responses' to Roth's fiction 'are permeated by a constant confusion of tale and teller' (Milbauer and Watson 1988: ix). Certainly, Roth's detractors have often seemed either unwilling or unable to distinguish between Roth's narrators and their creator, notably in the case of novels such as *Portnoy's Complaint* and *Sabbath's Theater*, in which the eponymous protagonists are particularly outspoken and outrageous. Hence Irving Howe denounces 'a spilling-out of the narrator which it becomes hard to suppose is not also the spilling-out of the author' in *Portnoy's Complaint* (Howe 1982: 234). This view is shared by George Searles, who claims that Portnoy's 'strident denunciations constitute . . . a fictive expression of the author's feelings' (Searles 1985: 13). In a similar vein, David Zucker announces that 'Sabbath is more or less an artistic "stand in" for Roth-the-artist' (Zucker 2004: 140) and Morris Dickstein asserts, confusingly, that '[i]t would be absurd to identify Sabbath with Roth but equally absurd not to see him as a projection of Roth' (Dickstein 2002: 228). Even critics sympathetic to Roth have sometimes suggested that his work is not as fully imagined as that of other great novelists. Mark Shechner, for example, comments that '[if] Roth's books are not precisely autobiographies, neither are they wholly fictions as, say, Tolstoy's or Dickens's novels are fictions' (Shechner 2003: 76). Others argue that it is impoverished by its introspection, as in the case of Jonathan Yardley, who identifies Roth's 'fixation on self' as 'the greatest weakness in his work, one that has kept him from fully realizing his amazing literary gifts because it personalizes and narrows everything it touches' (Yardley 2004: 2).

Still other critics have challenged this view. Michael Wood, for example, is emphatic that 'Roth's project is . . . an explanation of his world, not his person' and that his 'novels are not variable confessions but different worlds, and different instruments of understanding' (Wood 2004: 3). Louis Menand insists, enigmatically, that 'Zuckerman is the Roth who is not Roth' as part of his argument that Roth is deliberately subverting the conventional distinctions between the two, 'daring his readers to guess which part is the fact and which part is the act' (Menand 1997: 88).

Roth's own response to this critical debate about his work has been characteristically paradoxical. In his fiction since *Portnoy's Complaint*, as I discuss in detail in chapters 1 and 2, he has endowed many of his fictional protagonists with biographical details that closely resemble his own, and in a number of novels has even given these protagonists his own name. In interviews and essays, however, he has repeatedly expressed his exasperation with (mis)readings of his work that deny its imaginative autonomy. At times he represents such interpretations as the product of a naïve misunderstanding of the very nature of fiction:

> If all . . . readers can see in my work is my biography, then they are simply numb to fiction – numb to impersonation, to ventriloquism, to irony, numb to the thousand observations of human life on which a book is built, numb to all the delicate devices by which novels create the illusion of a reality more like the real than our own. (Roth 2001a: 112)

Strident as this defence of fiction as artifice is, it nonetheless relies on a paradox (the phrase 'a reality more like the real than our own') that potentially compromises, or at least complicates, the clarity of the statement as a whole. Elsewhere, Roth concedes that his novels are only partially invented, resulting from a process of 'concocting a half-imaginary existence out of the actual drama of my life' (Roth 2001a: 123). In an interview in 1981, Roth portrayed himself as a hermit, dedicating himself with monastic discipline to his art, and he dismissed the idea of writing an autobiography on the grounds that such a book 'would consist almost entirely of chapters about me sitting alone in a room looking at a typewriter', its 'uneventfulness' making 'Beckett's *The Unnamable* read like Dickens' (Roth 2001a: 100). Yet seven years later he published an autobiography called *The Facts* (1988) which, if hardly sensational, nonetheless exposed this portrait of the artist as a reclusive ascetic as itself a fiction. If Claire Bloom's account of her years with Roth, *Leaving A Doll's House* (1996), is anything to go by, Roth's life has in fact been far from uneventful.

## Jewish American or American Jew?

As with the question of autobiographical influences on Roth's work, so with the issue of ethnicity: almost as soon as he started to publish, Roth was classified as a Jewish writer and he has spent much of the rest of his career trying to tear the tag off with one hand, while refusing to relinquish it with the other. When he first came to prominence, Roth was often associated with Saul Bellow and Bernard Malamud as part of a putative Jewish-American literary movement. Bellow had indeed been a major influence on the young Roth (an influence acknowledged in Roth's miscellany *Reading Myself and Others*, first published in 1975, which is dedicated to the older writer), not least because he functioned as a role model for a generation of Jewish authors who wished to establish themselves in American letters. In his essay 'Rereading Saul Bellow', published in the later miscellany *Shop Talk: A Writer and His Colleagues and their Work* (2001), Roth recalls that Bellow had once confessed to him that '"somewhere in my Jewish . . . blood there were conspicuous traces of doubt as to whether I had the right to practice the writer's trade"' (Roth 2001b: 142). Roth's admiration for Bellow seems to be based at least partly on the way in which he triumphantly overcame this (Jewish) self-doubt and blazed a trail into the heartland of American literature:

> Going where his pedigreed betters wouldn't have believed he had any right to go with the American language, Bellow was indeed Columbus for people like me, the grandchildren of immigrants, who set out as American writers after him. (Roth 2001b: 143)

Alluding to the opening and closing lines of Bellow's third novel, *The Adventures of Augie March* (1953), whose Jewish hero begins the novel by announcing 'I am an American' and ends it by proclaiming himself 'a sort of Columbus of those near-at-hand', Roth pays tribute to Bellow by implying that he discovered – and colonised – a part of the American literary landscape that other Jewish writers were subsequently able also to inhabit (Bellow 1966: 3, 536). Yet this process of colonisation works both ways: if Bellow and his Jewish-American followers were able to claim a part of American culture as their own, in doing so they were also claimed by that national culture, as is suggested by the fact that

Roth uses the word 'American' twice in the passage above while omitting the word 'Jewish' (opting instead for the less ethnically specific term 'immigrant').

In spite of the debt that Roth owes Bellow, the differences between the two writers, and between both of them and Malamud, are more striking than the similarities. Arguably, they most closely resemble each other in their resentment of the way in which they were often lazily lumped together as exponents of a Jewish-American school of writing, an idea that Roth peremptorily dismisses with the paradoxical observation that the three writers 'constitute a Jewish school . . . only in the odd sense of having each found his own means of transcending the immediate parochialism of his Jewish background' (Roth 2001a: 108). Nonetheless, the label stuck for many years, becoming something of a critical commonplace. Even as late in the day as 2003, with Malamud dead and Bellow in declining health, Harold Bloom, in his introduction to a volume of critical essays on Roth, instinctively describes Roth's preoccupations as a writer in terms of his (Jewish) relationship to these two writers. Bloom concludes that 'Roth . . . is a Jewish writer in the sense that Saul Bellow and Bernard Malamud are not . . . because his absolute concern never ceases to be the pain of the relations between children and parents, and between husband and wife, and in him this pain invariably results from the incommensurability between a rigorously moral normative tradition whose expectations rarely can be satisfied, and the reality of the way we live now' (Bloom 2003: 2). Bloom's definition of Jewish writing here seems to me little more than a tired journalistic cliché (surely an 'absolute concern' with family relationships and with the tension between traditional moral frameworks and contemporary social mores is no more the peculiar stamp of Jewish writing than it is of Italian or Greek or Scottish writing) and moreover somewhat perverse, since it applies more to Malamud's fiction than Roth's. Beyond the specific details of Bloom's criteria for classifying Jewish writers, however, the very fact that he is so keen to admit Roth to his Jewish canon, and to do so by measuring his Jewishness against that of Bellow and Malamud, says more about the contemporary obsession in the American academy with identity politics than it does about Roth, Bellow or Malamud.

With the advent of multiculturalism, Jewish-American writing, so fashionable in the academy during the 1950s and 1960s, found itself marginalised once again, all but eclipsed by the enthusiasm for African-American, native American, Hispanic American, and Asian American writing.[7] Although Irving Howe had predicted in 1977 that the genre of Jewish-American fiction was in its death throes, the subsequent three decades have in fact seen the emergence of a third generation of Jewish-American novelists and short story writers whose work is often much more explicitly concerned with Jewishness than that of Bellow's or Roth's generation ever was.[8] With a few exceptions, however, these writers have received little critical attention, and Roth has, consequently, been either represented as the solitary survivor of a moribund literary sub-genre, or relocated in the mainstream American tradition. Frederick Karl adopts the former position, observing that 'the impetus which gave energy to the so-called "Jewish novel" is no longer there' and that '[o]nly Philip Roth still mines' this 'exhausted' 'vein' (Karl 2002: 20). Mark Shechner takes up the latter position, claiming that 'Roth is now, willy-nilly, an American writer, Jewish variant, and he shares a readership not with Amos Oz or David Grossman [Jewish Israeli novelists] but with John Updike and Richard Ford' (Shechner 2003: 211). Robert Alter, ingeniously, tries to reconcile the two identities – Roth as minority Jewish writer and as fully-fledged American writer – by arguing that 'Roth may in fact be thought of as an exemplary American novelist if one keeps in mind the essentially hybrid character of American society, its shifting composition as an uneven patchwork of immigrant groups and of regional, ethnic, and racial subcultures' (Alter 2002: 25). In other words, Alter argues, with Rothian paradoxical logic, that it is Roth's very marginality and ethnicity that makes him quintessentially American.

Roth's own position with respect to his ethnic identity is similarly paradoxical. When Roth discusses his upbringing, he often emphasises its Jewishness. In *Reading Myself and Others* he describes how, as a boy, he 'lived in a predominantly Jewish neighborhood and attended public schools where about 90% of the pupils and the teachers were Jewish' and how at the age of seventeen he 'went off to a small college in rural Pennsylvania' because he 'wanted to find out what the rest of "America" was like. America in quotes – because it was still almost as much of an idea in my mind as it had been in Franz Kafka's' (Roth 2001a: 106, 105). The impression created by statements such as these is that the young Roth grew up in a parochial, insular Jewish enclave – a ghetto, to all intents and purposes – which he felt was in America, but not really a part of it. Yet elsewhere he claims that 'for me being a Jew and being an American are indistinguishable, the one identity bound up and given shape by the other' (Roth quoted in Brent 1992:

231). For Roth, there is no contradiction between these two positions. When he recalls his childhood bond with other local Jewish kids, he observes that '[i]t would have seemed to us strange *not* to be Jewish' but that 'simultaneously, this intense adolescent camaraderie was the primary means by which we were deepening our *Americanness*' (Roth 1988: 31, italics in original). Again, Roth employs paradox to reconcile two apparently opposing ideas: he argues that one of the defining aspects of his and his comrades' Jewishness was their shared sense of themselves as American. His use of italics in this passage, however, reveals a certain rhetorical strain that reflects the ideological struggle to hold the identities of 'Jew' and 'American' together. Indeed, the tensions between these two aspects of Roth's identity are clearly visible in his own shifting stance on the question of how his writing should be defined and in which tradition it can best be accommodated.

At times Roth has been all too happy to acknowledge the importance to his development as a writer of his relationship with his Jewish readership, conceding that 'the relationship with an attentive audience may . . . shape one's conduct . . . as a writer' and that 'conflict with my Jewish critics was as valuable a struggle as I could have had at the outset of my career' as it gave his writing 'a direction and emphasis that it might not have had otherwise' (Roth 2001a: 69, 68, 115). At other times, however, he has deliberately distanced himself from the idea that his work addresses or responds to the concerns of a particular audience, claiming that he never has in mind 'any special-interest group whose beliefs and demands one either accedes to or challenges' (Roth 2001a: 15). In an interview with George Plimpton in 1969, Roth commented that 'the historic predicament of being Jewish' was a blessing for a writer, since it was 'a complicated, interesting, morally demanding, and very singular experience' (Roth 2001a: 17–18). Thirty-six years later, however, he responded tetchily to Martin Krasnik's suggestion that he might be 'seen as an American-Jewish writer', announcing that 'I know exactly what it means to be Jewish, and it's really not interesting. I'm an American' (Roth 2005: 15). In 1973, in a self-interview conducted to promote *The Great American Novel* (whose title itself stakes a claim, albeit with its tongue firmly in its cheek, to the status of a national literary classic), Roth was keen to point out that 'the dreadful comic fantasies of persecution and humiliation' depicted in his short story 'On the Air' were 'decidedly Jewish' (Roth 2001a: 75). When Krasnik describes *The Plot Against America* as 'Roth's great Jewish history', however, Roth launches into a tirade:

> Jewish? . . . It's my most American book. It's about America. About America . . . I don't accept that I write Jewish-American fiction. I don't buy that nonsense about black literature or feminist literature. Those are labels made to strengthen some political agenda. (Roth 2005: 14–15)

If, earlier in his career, Roth saw (or claimed to see) no tension between the identities designated by the adjectives 'Jewish' and 'American', here they seem to have become almost mutually exclusive. The repetition of the words 'American' and 'America' is clearly intended to negate, rather than simply refine or qualify, the word 'Jewish', and Roth's distaste for the idea that the two identities might be yoked together to form a hyphenated, hybrid genre – 'Jewish-American' fiction – is unequivocal. Bryan Cheyette has argued that 'the cosmopolitan Roth' of the 1980s has 'been replaced by an Americanized Roth of recent years who is finally writing the "great American novel"' and that this shift in emphasis 'represents a narrowing or Americanization of his previous extraterritorial reach' (Cheyette 2004a: 48). Certainly the passage above might be adduced as evidence of this process of 'Americanization', but then again *The Great American Novel* itself was published when Roth was heavily under the sway of European modernism in general and Franz Kafka in particular, and the later novels which explicitly advertise their concern with the state of the nation (*American Pastoral* and *The Plot Against America*) are, among other things, parables about the dangers of Americanization. In fact it seems clear to me from the way in which he moves swiftly from disowning the idea of Jewish-American fiction to denouncing the 'political agenda' that he believes lies behind all such labels, that Roth, in common with Cheyette, is dismayed by what he sees as the narrow dogmatism of identity politics operating in contemporary American literary studies, and in the larger society. It is this ideological opposition to what he sees as the division of literature into special interest groups – to the politicisation of literary studies – as much as any 'Americanization' of his work, that accounts for Roth's increasing resistance to any attempts to read him as a Jewish writer.

## Conservative radical or radical conservative?

The question of where Roth's political affiliations lie and how politically engaged his fiction is, has become an area of increasing controversy in Roth studies. Early in his career Roth published *Our Gang* (1971), an ebullient satire on the cynical machinations of Richard Nixon (pre-Watergate), as well as three other explicitly political pieces ('The

President Addresses the Nation', 'Cambodia: A Modest Proposal' and 'Our Castle') collected in *Reading Myself and Others.* However, it is his later work, particularly *American Pastoral* and *The Plot Against America,* that has generated most debate about the nature and extent of Roth's political commitments. I will have more to say about the political dimension of the latter novel in the final chapter of the book, but here I want to concentrate on the former.

For many critics, the 'American Trilogy' represents a turning point in Roth's fiction. Derek Parker Royal argues that whereas history tended to operate in the background of Roth's earlier fiction, in these novels Roth 'has taken on history . . . as his fictional foreground', exploring the ways in which 'identity is not only a product of, but also a hostage to, the many social, political, and cultural forces that surround it' (Royal 2004a: ix). Laura Tanenbaum, similarly, observes that '[w]hat is new in the trilogy is not the presence of history per say [sic] but its ability to subdue the voices of Roth's famously fluent characters to its own purposes and the recognition of what might be at stake in the postwar world' (Tanenbaum 2004: 41). In an interview with Roth in 2001, Jean-Louis Turlin describes *American Pastoral, I Married A Communist* and *The Human Stain* as an 'obliquely political trilogy' (Turlin 2001: 4), but for other critics its engagement with American politics is not oblique enough. Lorrie Moore complains that *The Human Stain* 'indulges in the sort of tirade against political correctness that is far drearier and more intellectually constricted than political correctness itself' (Moore 2000: 8) and many reviewers of *I Married A Communist* felt that the novel was too didactic to be aesthetically compelling.[9]

However, it is the first novel in the trilogy, *American Pastoral,* that has attracted most controversy for its representation of radical politics in the 1960s. Laura Tanenbaum suggests that it is 'less a novel of political ideas than an account of changing historical mores' (Tanenbaum 2004: 47), James Wood that '[t]he reason why this book is so distinguished is that Roth's vision is not, in the end, political, but insistently philosophical' (Wood 1997: 9) and D.J. Taylor that it is concerned with 'the complete inability of late-20th Century humanism to come to terms with the conditions in which late-20th Century life is lived' [sic] (Taylor 1997: 36). Most critics, however, read the novel as a deliberate intervention on Roth's part in contemporary debates about the legacy of the 1960s in American culture and political life. Typically, however, they disagree fundamentally about Roth's political position.

Some argue that the novel is essentially consistent with the political liberalism that Roth has always espoused. Louis Menand, for example, feels that the novel is not so much a critique of sixties radicalism as 'a story of how the spirit born out of the victory over Fascism was destroyed by Vietnam and Watergate' (Menand 1997: 93). Others, such as James Wood, argue that 'Roth was never politically radical' (Wood 1997: 9). For most commentators, however, the novel appeared to signal a reactionary shift in Roth's politics: Mark Shechner describes it is an unequivocally 'anti-sixties book' (Shechner 2003: 157), G. Neelakantan accuses Roth of 'stereotyping the sixties revolution as one run by the misplaced enthusiasm of neurotic adolescents' (Neelakantan 2004: 58) and Robert Boyers complains that it fails as a novel because it does not pay serious attention to the grievances of the politically marginalised and hence is 'not an adequate study of social disorder' (Boyers 1997: 40–1).

These critics tend to focus their attack on one particular aspect of the novel: Roth's presentation of Merry Levov, the daughter of its protagonist, Seymour. Todd Gitlin, the title of whose review of the novel, 'Weather Girl' (alluding to the notorious dissident group known as the Weathermen), left no room for doubt as to the political nature of his response, finds fault with the historical details of Roth's narrative, pointing out that Merry's acts of terrorism do not fit convincingly into the actual chronology of the period (Gitlin 1997). Others, however, take offence at what they see as a failure of imaginative sympathy on Roth's part. Mark Shechner characterises Merry and her fellow radical activist Rita Cohen as a pair of 'cartoon insurrectionists' (Shechner 2003: 159), a criticism echoed in Robert Boyers' comment that Merry Levov is a 'cartoon of adolescent rebellion . . . utter puerility and one-dimensionality' (Boyers 1997: 38, 39), in Tanenbaum's complaint that Merry's 'political convictions . . . emerge as clichés and slogans that are never fully formed' (Tanenbaum 2004: 45), and in Neelakantan's judgement that Roth 'portrays Merry . . . as bereft of sensitivity or intelligence' (Neelakantan 2004: 58).

In his article 'The End of Identity: Philip Roth's *American Pastoral*', however, Timothy Parrish proposes a more dignified role for Merry Levov. Parrish argues that she is a 'more extreme version' of the novel's narrator, Nathan Zuckerman, pointing out that '[t]hey share as distinguishing character traits a relentless commitment to transformation and the desire to disrupt all pretensions to complacency' (Parrish 2000: 91). Parrish is on to something here, but whereas he sees Merry's 'relentless commitment to transformation' as part of Roth's ongoing project to redefine the parameters of identity – a movement away 'from the postmodern decentring of the self that has been one of the hallmarks of his fiction' – I believe that it has more radical implications for the relationship between the personal and the political in Roth's work (Parrish 2000: 93).

In his review of *The Plot Against America*, Michael Wood observes that '[p]olitics is for Roth what makes private life possible'. But the opposite is equally true: it is private life that makes politics possible in Roth's work (Wood 2004: 3). Paradoxically, Merry is both a contemptible, contemptuous caricature and a portrait of the artist. Her decision to detonate a bomb at the local Post Office store is pathetic in both senses of the word: a futile, destructive, self-destructive, attention-seeking expression of adolescent self-righteous indignation and a powerful, poignant, radical statement of political opposition. In this respect, Merry functions not simply as Zuckerman's surrogate, but as Roth's. In an interview with Walter Mauro in 1974, reprinted in *Reading Myself and Others* as 'Writing and the Powers That Be', Roth denies that his fiction is politically committed, observing that 'whatever serious acts of rebelliousness I may have engaged in as a novelist have been directed far more at my imagination's systems of constraints and habits of expression than at the powers that vie for the world' (Roth 2001a: 12). Yet in the same interview he describes, in terms that anticipate closely Merry Levov's evolving political consciousness in *American Pastoral*, his feelings of political alienation during the Vietnam War: 'One . . . began to use the word "America" as though it was the name . . . of a foreign invader that had conquered the country and with whom one refused . . . to collaborate. Suddenly America had turned into "them"' (Roth 2001a: 11). Furthermore, one of Roth's favourite metaphors for his own methods of composition is that of the artist as insurrectionary, the book as incendiary device. In his self-interview of 1973, Roth described Gabe Wallach, Alexander Portnoy and David Kepesh (the protagonists of *Letting Go*, *Portnoy's Complaint* and *The Breast*, respectively) as 'three stages of a single explosive projectile that is fired into the barrier that forms one boundary of the individual's identity and experience' (Roth 2001a: 74). In another interview some twenty years later he returned to this theme:

> Portnoy wasn't a character for me, he was an explosion, and I wasn't finished exploding after *Portnoy's Complaint*. The first thing I wrote after *Portnoy's Complaint* was a long story called 'On the Air' . . . I looked in

> the arsenal and found another dynamite stick, and I thought, 'Light the fuse and see what happens.' I was trying to blow up more of myself . . . blowing up a lot of old loyalties and inhibitions, literary as well as personal. (Roth 2001a: 133–4)

Like Merry, whose bomb is a means both of personal emancipation and of public protest, Roth's metaphorical sticks of dynamite – his books – are acts of self-liberation and also of definitive rupture with a larger community. On the one hand, Roth figures the conflict as an internal battle between conflicting impulses, the writer's intellectual arsenal being used to explode his block(ade): 'It was as though I were blasting my way through a tunnel to reach the novel I couldn't write' (Roth 2001a: 138). On the other hand, he acknowledges that 'behind [the] book' was the 'the rage and rebelliousness', the 'angry defiance and hysterical opposition' that were 'in the air' in 1960s America, particularly its manifestations in violent opposition to the Vietnam War (Roth 2001a: 136). Just as Merry's personal rebellion against what she sees as her father's complacent conformity – his bourgeois, assimilationist patriotism – finds expression in her political acts of terrorism, her private rage detonating in a public space, so Roth's private struggle to liberate himself as a writer is facilitated by the political *zeitgeist* and is discharged publicly in the form of an inflammatory book that ignites a cultural firestorm.

Roth, then, is the most paradoxical of writers. At once sincere and disingenuous, introspective and imaginative, serious and hilarious, his work is, at the stylistic level, full of oxymorons, incongruities and reversals that reflect and enact an intellectual and ideological restlessness, a relentless determination to confront the ambiguities and inconsistencies of life and fiction. It is this, above all, that makes Roth such a difficult and such a rewarding writer to read and to write about, and it is the purpose of this book to wrestle with some of the difficulties and illuminate some of the rewards presented by Roth's later work.

## Notes

1 Roth now has a scholarly journal – *Philip Roth Studies* – devoted exclusively to his work, and keeping up with the criticism published on him elsewhere is a full-time job. The success of the Philip Roth Society, founded by Derek Parker Royal in 2002, is another indication that Roth's career is, as Royal himself puts it, 'at the apex of its trajectory' (Royal 2005c: 5).

2 Roth is only the third writer to be accorded this honour during her or his lifetime (Saul Bellow and Eudora Welty are the others).
3 In an essay published in 1967 entitled 'The Literature of Exhaustion', John Barth diagnosed what he saw as a malaise in American fiction, which he argued had become stale and 'used-up' by comparison with the vital experimentation of European modernists such as Joyce and Beckett and South American contemporaries such as Borges (Barth 1967: 29). Barth's essay was taken up as a manifesto for postmodernist fiction and it became de rigeur in criticism of the field throughout the 1970s and 1980s to cite it approvingly.
4 For an excellent summary of the developments in Roth criticism over this period, see Royal 2005b and 2005c.
5 See, for example, Brauner 1995: 24–36.
6 There are two exceptions: I include one earlier text, *My Life as a Man* (1974), because I see it as anticipating some of Roth's later work in a number of ways and I exclude *The Dying Animal* (2001), because I find it the least interesting work of Roth's last phase. I also discuss *Patrimony* (1991), Roth's memoir of his father, only in passing, primarily because of the constraints of space. For my views on Roth's most important early novel, *Portnoy's Complaint* (1969), see Brauner 2000 and Brauner 2005.
7 For a detailed discussion of the uneasy relationship between Jewish writing and multiculturalism, see Biale et al. 1998 and Furman 2000.
8 See Howe 1977 and Furman 2000.
9 See, for example, Stone 1998 and Wood 1998.

# 2

# The trials of Nathan Zuckerman, or Jewry as jury: judging Jews in *Zuckerman Bound*

> 'This is now the club they use on Jews – you the prosecutor, you the judge, *you* shall be judged, judged in every infraction to the millionth degree!' (Roth 1986: 170)
>
> 'For me the books count . . . where the writer incriminates *himself*.' (Roth 1978: 139, italics in original)
>
> Writers always have a third eye that's watching, a third ear that's listening, a judge who seems to be working for the writer in you [.] (Roth quoted in Sarnoff 1992: 209)

Trials, literal and metaphorical, real and imagined, are ubiquitous in the work of Philip Roth. From Peter Tarnopol's lengthy divorce litigation in *My Life as a Man* and the fantastical indictment of Alexander Portnoy at the end of *Portnoy's Complaint*, to Mickey Sabbath's arraignment on charges of obscenity in *Sabbath's Theater*, to the historical court case of John Demjanjuk that dominates the opening of *Operation Shylock*, the trial is one of Roth's favourite tropes. Frequently employing a confessional mode in his fiction, Roth noted early in his career that 'the question of who or what shall have . . . jurisdiction over one's life' was central to his work and that his fiction was a crucible for self-interrogation: 'I have greatly refashioned my attachments through the effort of testing them, and over the years have developed my strongest attachment to the test itself' (Roth 2001a: 73–4, 9). Of all these 'attachments', arguably the most abiding and tenacious has been his preoccupation with Jewish identity and, indeed, in his work Jewishness is intimately bound up with, and often figured in terms of trials, both in the sense of tests and ordeals.

The association of Jews with the law has a long history. The Hebrew Scriptures have often been represented, not least in the New Testament, as excessively legalistic, placing justice above mercy. This tradition underlies, and is perpetuated in, Shakespeare's *The Merchant of Venice* (1596), in which Shylock (repeatedly referred to generically as 'the Jew') initiates court proceedings in order to claim the 'pound of flesh' that Antonio is obliged to forfeit, having defaulted on the repayment of his loan, only to find himself indicted for attempted murder and forced to convert to Christianity. In the nineteenth century, the trial of Alfred Dreyfus, a French Jewish army officer, polarised public opinion and precipitated an unprecedented debate on the nature of anti-Semitism throughout Europe. In the twentieth century, a number of trials of Jews became international *causes célèbres*: Mendel Beiliss was accused, as a result of the agitations of an anti-Semitic organisation known as the Black Hundred, and eventually acquitted of the ritual murder of a twelve-year-old boy in Russia in 1913; Leo Frank, wrongfully convicted of the murder of a young girl, was subsequently abducted and executed by a gang of anti-Semitic vigilantes in the United States in 1914; and Ethel and Julius Rosenberg were executed by the American government for passing State secrets to the Russians in 1953. Each of these cases has been fictionalised in novels by Jewish-American authors: Bernard Malamud's *The Fixer* (1966), David Mamet's *The Old Religion* (1997) and E.L. Doctorow's *The Book of Daniel* (1971), respectively. The trials in Israel of Adolf Eichmann (tried and executed in 1961) and John Demjanjuk (initially sentenced to death in 1988, but subsequently acquitted on appeal in 1993) for war crimes against Jews also received intense media coverage globally and provoked considerable controversy.

Older even than the history of Jews being prosecuted as the result of anti-Semitic myths – and tenacious enough to survive the more recent examples of Jews prosecuting others for anti-Semitic crimes – is the tradition of Jews judging themselves and each other. According to the Anglo-Jewish writer Dan Jacobson, 'the sense of being forever on trial' dates back to biblical times and is 'one of the consequences of the apparent arbitrariness of the claim to have been specifically chosen' (Jacobson 1982: 48). Given the recurring pattern in the Hebrew Scriptures of the Jews being subjected to a trial of their faith, which they fail, and for which they are subsequently punished, before being forgiven again, it is hardly surprising if the psychological scars of this process of perpetual probation are visible even among Jews for whom its theological origins are now obscure. Over many centuries, the sense of being on trial has given rise to a tradition of self-censure. It is this tradition that Aharon Appelfeld, the Israeli novelist, has in mind when he tells Philip Roth that '[t]he ability of Jews to internalize any critical and condemnatory remark and castigate themselves is one of the marvels of human nature' (Roth 2001b: 37). It might also partly explain why Franz Kafka's novel *The Trial* (1925) is often referred to by critics as the most quintessentially Jewish of texts, in spite of the fact that Jewishness is mentioned nowhere in this, or indeed in any of this secular Jewish modernist's tales of existential guilt.

The influence of these traditions on Roth's work – particularly the example of Kafka, who became for Roth something of an obsession in the 1970s – should not be underestimated. In an interview, conducted 'After Eight Books', reprinted in *Reading Myself and Others,* Roth quotes from a passage near the end of *The Trial* that he has 'always been drawn to' in which the novel's protagonist, K., looks hopefully at a priest delivering his sermon:

> If the man would only quit his pulpit, it was not impossible that K. could obtain decisive . . . counsel from him which might . . . point the way, not toward some influential manipulation of the case, but toward a circumvention of it, a breaking away from it altogether, a mode of living completely outside the jurisdiction of the Court. (Roth 2001a: 93)

Roth goes on to comment 'Enter Irony when the man in the pulpit turns out to be oneself' and to pose the rhetorical question: 'How to devise a mode of living completely outside the jurisdiction of the Court when the Court is of one's own devising?' (Roth 2001a: 93–4). If the hope of 'living completely outside the jurisdiction of the Court' is remote in Kafka's novel, as the series of conditionals ('If . . . would . . . could . . . might . . .') and the double negative formulation 'not impossible' in the passage suggests, it is even less tenable, Roth implies, if you are your own prosecutor and judge. However, the strain of self-incrimination and self-recrimination that runs through Roth's work can also be traced back to his own experience as a writer who has found himself on trial in one sense or another ever since he began writing.

In the 'Author's Note' to the 2001 edition of *Reading Myself and Others,* Roth reflects that the 'opposition' that he encountered 'almost immediately' as a fledgling writer ensured that he 'felt called upon . . . to defend my moral flank the instant after I had taken my first steps' and, indeed, the book that follows is partly an extended apologia for his own convictions, and an attempt to exonerate himself from the crimes for which others (mostly Jewish others) seek to convict him (Roth 2001a: xiii). Legal metaphors permeate the prose of *Reading Myself and Others*. Whether reflecting wryly on his quiescent adolescence in Newark – 'I obediently served my time in what was, after all, only a minimum-security institution, and enjoyed the latitude and privileges awarded to the inmates who make no trouble for their guards' – or more bitterly on 'the alimony and court costs incurred for having served two years in a childless marriage', Roth instinctively frames his life with sentences (4, 129). In a footnote to 'Writing American Fiction', for example, Roth recalls being 'cross-examined' by the US broadcaster Mike Wallace after having won the National Book Award (170). In 'Imagining the Erotic: Three Introductions', Roth speculates playfully on whether his friendship with fellow Jewish-American novelist Frederica Wagman 'should have constrained me from accepting her publisher's invitation to write a preface to the French edition of *Playing House* [Wagman's first novel]', before deciding that, in spite of the fact that the issue is likely 'to be taken up by Guardians of Literary Standards', he will proceed 'until that court hands down its verdict' (246). Discussing the origins of *Portnoy's Complaint* with George Plimpton, Roth recalls that in the early stages of writing he 'was teaching a lot of Kafka' in a course that 'might have been called "Studies in Guilt and Persecution"' (19). In yet another interview (on *Our Gang*) Roth records the impact on him of the 'chilling, depressing' transcript of the trial of two Soviet writers published in translation in America in 1966 with the title *On Trial* (47). Explaining his decision to include in *Reading Myself and Others* an indignant letter that he wrote (but never mailed) to the critic Diana Trilling in response to an unfavourable review of *Portnoy's Complaint*, Roth points out that 'the reviewer, critic, or book journalist generally finds himself in the comfortable position of a prosecution witness who, having given his testimony, need not face cross-examination by the defense' (22). In the letter itself he writes that he 'is not looking to be acquitted [. . .] of having some sort of view of things', but insists that readers would not 'be doing [him] . . . justice' if they assumed, along with Trilling, that Roth's fiction articulates a 'position' held by its author (26). Nevertheless, in an interview with Alan Lelchuk, Roth concedes that his novella *The Breast* 'has the design of a rebuttal or a rejoinder' that proceeds 'by attempting to answer the objections' that 'might be raised . . . by its own fantastical premise'

(59, 58). Many years later, when Roth spoke of an article in which he was accused by 'a woman activist' of misogyny, he observed that '*My Life as a Man* was the most damaging evidence brought against me by the prosecution' and he complains that his 'Jewish critics [. . .] would tell you that I bend over backwards not to make the Jewish case' (101, 109).

It is this sense of being judged not simply as a writer, but as a *Jewish* writer – of being constantly subjected to ideological, as well as aesthetic, scrutiny – that comes to haunt Roth's work. In *The Facts* (the title of which, Alan Cooper points out, carries the 'implication of . . . clarification for the record in a legal proceeding') (Cooper 1996: 53), Roth describes how, as an undergraduate at Bucknell University, he was 'admonished by the Dean of men' and 'brought before the Board of Publications for censure' after publishing a satirical attack on the student newspaper. This reprimand for a juvenile misdemeanour prefigures the accusations of much more serious crimes that the adult Roth was soon to face (Roth 1988: 66). In 'Writing About Jews', in *Reading Myself and Others*, Roth describes the storm of indignation that broke out in certain sections of the Jewish-American community over the publication of *Goodbye, Columbus*. He deals at length with some of the letters from Jewish readers 'accusing' him of being anti-Semitic and 'self-hating', as well as with attacks by a number of rabbis, one of whom 'express[ed] regret over the decline of medieval justice', since Jews of that era 'would have known what to do with him [Roth]' (Roth 2001a: 193, 204). In *The Facts* he recounts a particularly traumatic experience at a seminar at the Yeshiva University in New York, where he was subjected to relentlessly hostile questioning from the audience. Shortly after the publication of *Goodbye, Columbus*, Roth accepted an invitation to participate – along with Ralph Ellison and an Italian author, Pietro di Donato – in a symposium entitled 'The Crisis of Conscience in Minority Writers of Fiction'. He was taken aback when the question-and-answer session rapidly evolved into a *de facto* inquisition: 'The trial (in every sense) began after di Donato, Ellison, and I had each delivered twenty-minute introductory statements' (Roth 1988: 127). In spite of Roth's 'determin[ation] to take every precaution against being misunderstood', he finds himself 'being grilled' and then listening to 'one denunciation after another', moving 'beyond interrogation to anathema', so that the beleagured writer begins to envision a scenario in which the 'inquisitorial pressure' would culminate in his being 'stoned to death' (Roth 1988: 128). When the 'tribunal' delivers its 'final verdict', Roth comments that it was 'as harsh a judgement as I ever hope to hear in this or any other world' and he vows to '"never write about Jews again"' (Roth 1988: 128, 129).

Although his second book, *Letting Go*, did in fact feature two Jews – Gabe Wallach and Paul Herz – as its protagonists, it did not excite the controversy that *Goodbye Columbus* had, and his third book, *When She Was Good*, was indeed Jewless. With the publication of *Portnoy's Complaint*, however, the allegations of self-hatred made against Roth earlier in his career resurfaced, this time not simply from the pulpits of synagogues or the students of Orthodox Judaism, but from some literary critics. Writing in *Reading Myself and Others* about a particularly intemperate example of such attacks by Marie Syrkin, who had claimed that passages from Roth's novel issued 'straight from the Goebbels/Streicher script', Roth observes wryly that '[h]ad she not been constrained by limits of space, Syrkin might eventually have had me in the dock with the entire roster of Nuremberg defendants' (Roth 2001a: 278). However, it was Irving Howe's scathing attack on him (in an essay entitled 'Philip Roth Reconsidered') that stung most, both because Howe had been an early admirer and because – unlike most of the authors of the ill-informed invective that had come Roth's way in the past – Howe was someone whose literary taste and judgement Roth had respected.

Roth's response to Howe was characteristically paradoxical. Initially, he decided, effectively, to say 'fuck you' by producing a series of increasingly outrageous fictions in the years immediately following the publication of Howe's essay. As Roth put it: 'I set myself the goal of becoming the writer some Jewish critics had been telling me I was all along: irresponsible, conscienceless, *unserious*' (Roth 2001a: 76). According to Roth, this phase of his career (encompassing 'On the Air', *Our Gang*, *The Breast* and *The Great American Novel*) constituted a rebellion not simply against self-appointed Jewish arbiters of good taste like Howe, but also against his own internalised censor, whom he represents as a judge. Whenever this phantom prosecutor 'rose responsibly in his robes to say, "Now look here, don't you think that's just a little too – "', Roth 'would reply, "Precisely why it stays! Down in front!"' (Roth 2001a: 96–7). At the same time as he was playfully baiting his critics in his fiction, however, he continued earnestly and vigorously to defend himself in his non-fiction. In the latter part of the 1970s and throughout the 1980s, Roth's fiction veered away from the 'sheer playfulness' of his post-*Portnoy* work and he produced a sequence of novels in which he subjected his protagonists (and by implication himself, since they were designed deliberately to resemble their author) to a process that I have called elsewhere 'fiction as self-accusation'.[1]

There is a certain self-punishing tendency in some of his earlier work: the protagonist of 'The Love Vessel', for example, has to remind himself that 'this was no time to be whipping himself' (Roth 1959b: 51), and the eponymous hero of 'Novotny's Pain' has 'premonitions of his court-martial and his internment in the stockade' (Roth 1980b: 271). However, this becomes increasingly explicit in his later work. In *Deception*, for example, the protagonist (named Philip and credited with authorship of Roth's books) is cross-examined by his lover on the subject of his alleged misogyny: '"Can you explain to the court why you hate women?"/"But I don't hate them."/"If you do not hate women, why have you defamed and denigrated them in your books? Why have you abused them in your work and in your life?"' (Roth 1990: 109). In *Operation Shylock*, the narrator (who presents himself as Roth the author) poses as a French journalist whom he impulsively – and mischievously – names Pierre Roget, interrogates the man who is impersonating him (whom he later names Pipik), and reminds him that 'You are a Jew . . . who in the past has been criticized by Jewish groups for your "self-hatred" and your "anti-Semitism"' (Roth 1993a: 41). It is, however, in the three novels and novella that make up *Zuckerman Bound* that Roth investigates in forensic detail the various charges of internalised anti-Semitism, or self-hatred; of betraying his family and his tribe; of immorality and obscenity, that had been brought against him by other American Jews.

In *The Ghost Writer* (1979), *Zuckerman Unbound* (1981), *The Anatomy Lesson* (1983) and *The Prague Orgy* (1985), re-published in a single volume entitled *Zuckerman Bound* (1989), Roth revived Nathan Zuckerman, a character who had first appeared as the fictional alter-ego of Peter Tarnopol (himself apparently a fictional alter-ego of Roth's) in *My Life as a Man* (1974), exposing him to experiences which echoed Roth's in many ways.[2] Like Roth, Zuckerman achieves fame and fortune with the publication of a scurrilous, sexually explicit novel. The reputation of *Carnovsky* (the name of Zuckerman's fictional novel, playing on the word 'carnal') mirrors that of Roth's *Portnoy's Complaint*; and Zuckerman is constantly equated with his fictional hero, Gilbert Carnovsky, just as Roth was with Alexander Portnoy. Zuckerman receives some vehement criticism from those in the Jewish community who feel that his fiction perpetuates anti-Semitic stereotypes and constitutes a betrayal of his tribal origins and a contamination of the moral tradition of Jewish literature. In *The Anatomy Lesson*, Roth actually quotes verbatim from Irving Howe's vituperative essay 'Philip Roth Reconsidered', attributing his words to a fictional critic he calls Milton Appel.

In spite of these correspondences between Nathan Zuckerman's life, as it unfolds in *Zuckerman Bound*, and Roth's own career, there are also some crucial divergences between author and protagonist. Chief among these is the reaction of the writers' families to their work and the notoriety that it engenders. At the end of his family memoir, *Patrimony* (1991), Roth describes having a dream in which his recently deceased father rematerialises to rebuke him: 'I should have been dressed in a suit. You did the wrong thing' (Roth 1991: 237). Pondering the significance of the dream, Roth decides that his father 'had been alluding to this book, which, in keeping with the unseemliness of my profession, I had been writing all the while he was ill and dying' (Roth 1991: 237). He concludes that '[t]he dream was telling me that, if not in my books or in my life, at least in my dreams, I would live perennially as his little son, with the conscience of a little son, just as he would remain alive there not only as my father but as *the* father, sitting in judgement on whatever I do' (Roth 1991: 237–8). In life, Herman Roth (together with Roth's mother and the rest of his family) staunchly defended the author against accusations that he had exploited or misrepresented them, but it is clear from the conclusion of *Patrimony* that Roth refuses to acquit himself so unequivocally. Instead, he tries and retries his proxy, Nathan Zuckerman, imposing on him in *Zuckerman Bound* a succession of ordeals and tribulations that constitute a sustained cross-examination of his own values, a thorough review of the ethical dilemmas of the Jewish writer and a prolonged meditation on judging Jews, both in the sense of Jews who judge, and Jews who are judged.

## *The Ghost Writer*

In *The Ghost Writer* Nathan Zuckerman, now a well-established author in his forties, recounts the seminal events that took place when, at the age of twenty-three, he visited his literary hero, E.I. Lonoff, the once-fashionable author of 'unsettling stories [. . .] where the pitiless author seems [. . .] to teeter just at the edge of self-impalement', now peremptorily dismissed by 'the jury at [Zuckerman's] first Manhattan publishing party' (Roth 1989: 11, 3). Relishing the recent publication of his first short stories but reeling from an argument with his father about his reworking of an 'old family feud' in which Zuckerman's father 'had played peacemaker for nearly two years before the opponents ended up shouting in court', Zuckerman resolves 'to submit myself for candidacy as nothing less than E.I. Lonoff's spiritual son, to *petition* for his moral sponsorship and to win . . . his *advocacy* and his love' (58, 7, my italics). Zuckerman hopes to find in Lonoff a mentor, a father/confessor, a benign judge who will acquit him of all charges of betraying his real father and exploiting his family history for the purposes of furthering his career.[3] However, in attempting to adopt, and be adopted by, Lonoff, he is, of course, compounding his crime, effectively replacing his biological father with a spiritual surrogate. The irony is deepened by his subsequent betrayal of Lonoff, for in telling the story that is *The Ghost Writer* (an act that Lonoff himself anticipates at the close of the novel when he tells Zuckerman 'I'll be curious to see how we all come out someday. It could be an interesting story'), Zuckerman exposes unedifying aspects of the reclusive novelist's life, just as he had revealed the dysfunctionality of his own family in the story that precipitates the rupture with his father (129).

The terms of the debate between Zuckerman and his father over Zuckerman's story 'Higher Education' echo those between Roth and the Jewish critics of his early short stories 'Epstein' and 'Defender of the Faith'.[4] Doc Zuckerman (as Nathan's father is known), a chiropodist who might have realised his ambition to become a medical doctor but for the quota system that capped the number of Jewish entrants to medical schools in the U.S. in the pre-war years, is a dedicated family man, who takes great pride in his son's intellectual achievements. However, when Nathan sends him a copy of 'Higher Education', hoping for the usual 'admiration and praise', Doc Zuckerman is shocked to discover that it relates episodes that constitute for him 'the most shameful and disreputable transgressions of family decency and trust' (58, 59). Like many of the Jewish critics of Roth's early stories, Doc Zuckerman fears that 'Higher Education' will fuel the fires of anti-Semitism. He tells Nathan that 'you don't know what Gentiles think when they read something like this', explaining that they will read it not in aesthetic terms, as 'a great work of art', but in sociological terms, 'judg[ing] the people in your story' as 'kikes [. . . who] love [. . .] money' (68). When Nathan returns to college, having defended his right to write 'this kind of story', he leaves behind a 'bewildered father [. . .] thinking himself and all of Jewry gratuitously disgraced and jeopardized by [Nathan's] inexplicable betrayal' (69). Soon after this contretemps, Zuckerman receives a letter containing 'TEN QUESTIONS FOR NATHAN ZUCKERMAN' from Judge Leopold Wapter, one of Newark's 'most admired' Jews, from whom Doc Zuckerman had elicited a letter of recommendation to support Nathan's application to college some years previously (74, 70). Many of the judge's questions, including the final one ('Can you honestly say that there is anything in your short story that would not warm the heart of a Julius Streicher or a Joseph Goebbels?'), are lifted almost verbatim from hostile reviews and correspondence that Roth had received (75). Alan Cooper observes that 'the critic, like the rabbi or the parent, is a necessary opponent who calls the artist to account for his betrayals', but the fact that the implied allegations of anti-Semitism here are voiced *not* by a critic or a rabbi but by a judge acting on behalf of a *father* who is himself symbolically passing judgement, makes Roth's intentions all the plainer (Cooper 1996: 180).

When Nathan arrives at Lonoff's rural Berkshire retreat, Doc Zuckerman is still 'waiting for some enlightened sign of contrition for the offenses I had begun to commit against my greatest supporters' (58). When he finally sits down at Lonoff's desk to compose a letter 'explaining myself to my father', Zuckerman compares his predicament, somewhat self-importantly, to that of famous literary precursors: 'Hadn't Joyce, hadn't Flaubert, hadn't Thomas Wolfe [. . .] all been condemned for disloyalty or treachery or immorality by those who saw themselves as slandered in their works?' (79). In much the same way, in many of the essays in *Reading Myself and Others*, Roth had responded to such allegations by allying himself with illustrious forbears.[5] Zuckerman's attempts at self-exoneration are soon interrupted, however, by the sound of 'muffled voices coming from above my head' (84). Aware that he is 'committing [. . .] a sordid, callow little indecency', Zuckerman nonetheless eavesdrops on the conversation, which turns out to be an anguished exchange between Lonoff and a young woman, Amy Bellette, who had been introduced to Zuckerman as an ex-student of the older writer's, a librarian at Harvard, visiting Lonoff in order to sort through his manuscripts with a view to depositing them at the university (84, 18). Zuckerman hears Bellette trying to persuade Lonoff to elope with her to Florence and is astounded, so that his 'shame at the unpardonable breach of his trust' pales beside 'the frustration [he] soon began to feel over the thinness of [his] imagination' (86). He wishes, paradoxically, that he 'could invent as presumptuously as real life', but at the same time recognises that such audacity would only deepen the rift between him and his father: '[W]hat then would they think of me, my father and his judge?' (86).[6] The implicit irony is that Zuckerman is presenting as a humbling reality that highlights the pusillanimity of his imagination, a fiction that actually demonstrates its boldness. Far from being outdone by the reality of the domestic drama being played out in the Lonoff household, or inhibited by the prospect of inciting further disapproval from his father and Judge Wapter, Zuckerman proceeds to imagine a scenario far more daring – and, for his Jewish critics, provocative – than the satire of Jewish middle-class mores in 'Higher Education'.

In an essay entitled '"I Always Wanted You to Admire My Fasting"; or, Looking at Kafka', written in 1973, Roth had hypothesised what might have happened to Kafka had he survived the bout of tuberculosis that killed him in 1924, and the horrors of the Second World War. In Roth's alternative version of history, Kafka (his writing unknown) emigrates to America, where he becomes the young Roth's Hebrew teacher and briefly courts his Aunt Rhoda. Having imaginatively reincarnated his greatest literary hero, Roth now (through Zuckerman) revives Anne Frank, 'the most famous' of 'all the Jewish writers, from Franz Kafka to E.I. Lonoff', in the form of Amy Bellette (109).

Zuckerman begins to weave exotic and erotic fantasies around the figure of Amy from the moment he first lays eyes on her. 'Immediately assum[ing] that she was his [Lonoff's] daughter', Zuckerman compares Amy to a Spanish infanta painted by Velázquez and soon envisages himself 'married to the *infanta* and living in a little farmhouse of our own not that far away' (12). Later, instead of projecting his fantasies into a fictional future in which he and Amy are living in domestic bliss in Lonoff's beneficent paternal orbit, Zuckerman rewrites Amy's past. He imagines that she is actually Anne Frank, who survives the camps unbeknownst to her father and whose new names derive from the sobriquet – 'Little Beauty' – given her by the nurses in the British field hospital where she gradually recovers from her ordeal in the camps, and from 'an American book she had sobbed over as a child, *Little Women*' (90). (What Zuckerman doesn't say about the name is that it is also a play on 'belles lettres'). Assuming that she is the sole survivor of her family, she decides to emigrate to America, on the basis that 'it might be best to put an ocean the size of the Atlantic between herself and what she needed to forget' (91).

When she hears of the publication of her diary and realises the impact that it is having on readers around the world, Amy/Anne resolves not to identify herself as its author, reasoning that '[w]ere *Het Achterhuis* known to be the work of a living writer, it would never be more . . . than a young teenager's diary', whereas 'dead [. . .] she had written [. . .] a book with the force of a masterpiece to make people finally see' (104–5). For this reason – placing her responsibilities as a writer above her filial duty in a way that reflects and refracts Zuckerman's breach with his father – she also decides not to contact Otto Frank, though she goes to bed every night 'begg[ing] forgiveness for the cruelty she was practicing on her perfect father' (95). Zuckerman's version of Anne/Amy's history functions both as self-exculpation and self-indictment. On the one hand, her decision to preserve her anonymity, even at the expense of her father's grief, is taken partly for the sake of her art (to ensure that her work retains the status of a 'masterpiece'), which seems to justify Zuckerman's resolve that he will publish 'Higher Education', on the grounds that withholding it would compromise his integrity as an artist. On the other hand, Zuckerman sacrifices his father's feelings and refuses to accept his and Judge Wapter's argument that he has to take responsibility as a post-Holocaust Jewish writer for the influence that his representation of Jews might have on a Gentile audience, whereas Amy sacrifices her own feelings for the sake of didactic power. She believes her diary can 'make people finally see', opening the eyes of a Gentile audience to the horrific inhumanity of anti-Semitism.

Zuckerman's ambivalence about his duties as a Jew and a writer also manifests itself in the denouement to this alternative history of Anne Frank, in which, as in his fantasy of her as Lonoff's daughter, Amy marries him. For Zuckerman, such an alliance represents the ultimate vindication of his character in front of his Jewish judges, Amy serving as his 'unassailable advocate', his 'shield against their charges of defection and betrayal' and 'exonerat[ing]' him from the 'idiotic indictment' of the 'outraged elders' (122). No one, Zuckerman reflects complacently, would 'dare accuse of such unthinking crimes the husband of Anne Frank' (122). Yet, this vision of a triumphant homecoming is soon undermined by Zuckerman's realisation that his redemptive fantasy, 'far from acquitting me of their charges' would 'seem to them a desecration even more vile than the one they had read [i.e. 'Higher Education']' (122). His very willingness to entertain this means of reconciliation with his Jewish judges, Zuckerman recognises, paradoxically, only emphasises the gulf between his position and theirs: enlisting the aid of Anne Frank, the most sacred of Jewish icons, in his dispute with the elders of the community, would exacerbate rather than mitigate his sins in their eyes.

## *Zuckerman Unbound*

In Roth's subsequent novel, *Zuckerman Unbound*, Zuckerman has indeed scandalised the Jewish establishment once more and earned a fortune and national notoriety in the process, through the publication of the obscene bestseller *Carnovsky*. In *Zuckerman Unbound*, Zuckerman is accused by Alvin Pepler – an embittered former winner of a popular television quiz show, later disgraced when it turns out that he and other contestants have been given the answers prior to transmission – of having 'stole[n]' his life (243). Zuckerman wonders at one point whether Pepler's manic stalking of him is some kind of '[t]ribal retribution' for his alleged betrayals of his Jewish origins: like Zuckerman – and Roth – Pepler hails from Newark and, in common with many of Zuckerman's antagonists throughout Roth's later fiction, claims to represent the interests of 'the Jewish people' (245, 146).[7] Zuckerman also has to confront the consequences for his family of his new-found fame when he begins to receive anonymous phone-calls threatening the kidnapping of his mother. The climax of the novel comes when Zuckerman, attending his father's deathbed, hears his father's final word, 'bastard', '[b]arely audible, but painstakingly pronounced' (270). Although Zuckerman notes that Doc Zuckerman is looking 'into the eyes of the apostate son' as he makes his enigmatic final utterance, he gradually convinces himself that his father was either alluding to someone else ('Lyndon Johnson? Hubert Humphrey? Richard Nixon?') or that what he actually said was 'Faster', 'Vaster' or 'Better' (270, 274). Zuckerman is soon forced to forgo these consoling alternatives when his brother, Henry, confirms his initial fears: 'He did say "Bastard", Nathan. He called you a bastard' (287). Henry goes on to add his fraternal seal to this damning paternal verdict:

> 'You *are* a bastard. A heartless conscienceless bastard . . . To you everything is disposable! Everything is *exposable*! Jewish morality, Jewish endurance, Jewish wisdom, Jewish families – everything is grist

> for your fun machine . . . You killed him, Nathan. With that book.' (287, italics in original)

In spite of the apparent implausibility of Henry's accusations, Zuckerman concedes that he had 'known when he was writing' *Carnovsky* and that 'he'd written it anyway' (287). What exactly he'd 'known' is not specified (that the book would upset his father? offend him? enrage him? 'kill' him?), but when his father suffers his stroke it seems 'like a blessing' to Zuckerman, who claims to have 'thought he had beaten the risk. And beaten the rap' (287). Once again, Zuckerman deploys an idiom from the American legal system: by speaking of 'beating the rap' he casts himself in the role of a guilty criminal hoping to evade justice. In this light, the fact that Zuckerman ends the novel being driven around the old Jewish neighbourhoods of Newark by an armed chauffeur takes on an additional significance. Although he hires the chauffeur ostensibly to protect himself from the unwanted attentions of stalkers such as Alvin Pepler, there is also the sense that Zuckerman now feels himself to be, albeit metaphorically, a fugitive on the run, a man who requires protection not so much from outlaws as from the law itself. This idea is reinforced by Zuckerman's fascination with the weapon his driver carries (he asks the chauffeur to show him the gun and asks whether it has been '[f]reshly cleaned' and '[f]reshly fired') and by the ambiguity of the phrase he uses to describe the final severing of his links with his childhood haunts in Weequahic: 'I've served my time' (290, 291).

## *The Anatomy Lesson*

If, at the end of *Zuckerman Unbound*, Zuckerman hopes that he has already been sufficiently punished for his crimes – which now apparently include parricide – then the third novel in the sequence, *The Anatomy Lesson*, brutally disillusions him. Far from liberating him from the bonds of Jewish responsibilities, the death of his father binds Zuckerman ever more closely to them; instead of diminishing, the trial tropes intensify and proliferate. The novel begins with Zuckerman prostrate as the result of chronic neck pain, the origins of which remain mysterious. Unable to identify any physiological cause for his suffering, Zuckerman turns to a psychoanalyst who suggests that his pain may be his 'judgement on [him]self and that book [*Carnovsky*]', a self-inflicted punishment by 'the atoning penitent, the guilty pariah' (312). So indignant is Zuckerman that he promptly decides to 'terminate' the therapy and walks out (312). Zuckerman admits that he is 'weary of the fight' with his Jewish critics but insists that 'it didn't follow that his illness represented capitulation to their verdict. It wasn't punishment or guilt that he was expiating' (440). Nevertheless, the rest of the novel provides much evidence to support the analyst's theory.

Alongside the physical discomfort of his neck pain, Zuckerman spends much of the novel tormented by the contents of a hostile article reviewing his career by an eminent Jewish-American critic, Milton Appel. Zuckerman's friend, Ivan Felt, 'tak[ing] his comrade by the arms . . . and, only half-mockingly, pronounc[ing] judgement', diagnoses '[b]uried anger, troves of it' towards Appel as the source of Zuckerman's affliction (353). Zuckerman, only half-mockingly, pins the blame for his suffering on the critic and the Jewish elders he represents, complaining that 'it's these Appels who've whammied my muscles with their Jewish evil eye' (409). Just like Irving Howe, an early admirer of Roth's work who recanted spectacularly, Appel, having reviewed 'Higher Education' positively, '[f]ourteen years on, following the success of Carnovsky . . . reconsidered what he called Zuckerman's "case"' (344). Ironically, Zuckerman sees in Appel's intemperate attack on him the very self-hatred that Appel accuses him of: 'this is what you know about someone you have to hate: he charges you with his crime and castigates himself in you' (351). Zuckerman is so enraged at what he sees as Appel's inconsistency, hypocrisy and sanctimony that he retaliates, first by 'por[ing] over' Appel's own writings 'like a professional litigant' for evidence of his duplicity, then by ringing him up at home and berating him for displaying 'the inquisitor's passion for punishing verdicts' and for disguising the moral rigidity of a 'Hanging Judge' beneath a veneer of 'judicious reappraisal', and finally (under the influence of a cocktail of drink and drugs intended to numb his neck pain) by assuming Appel's name and purporting to be the 'most notorious pornographer in America', the owner of a hardcore magazine entitled *Lickety Split* and producer of 'Supercarnal' films (357, 361). He is delighted when he discovers that Appel is unwell, construing his malady as a form of poetic justice for Appel's own compulsion to pronounce judgement, his 'addiction to scolding': 'All the verdicts, all the judgements . . . finally it's poisoning him to death' (414).

In spite of all this indignation and thirst for vengeance, it is clear that at one level Zuckerman feels that Appel's criticisms are not entirely groundless. The very fact that Zuckerman expends so much time and energy in attempting to rebut Appel's arguments suggests that the critic has struck a raw nerve; at one point Zuckerman admits that 'even the worst criticism contains some truth' and that Appel is 'one of the few of them [critics] who make any sense at all' (367). Moreover, when Zuckerman insists that Appel is '*not my father's deputy*', we might suspect him of protesting too much, for Appel's critique clearly echoes Doc Zuckerman's fears about the reception of 'Higher Education' (409). The critic's paranoid conviction (expressed in a letter to Ivan Felt) that 'the whole world is getting ready to screw the Jews' recalls Doc Zuckerman's admonition to his son in *The Ghost Writer* about 'how very little love there is in this world for Jewish people' (356, 67, italics in original). Indeed, Zuckerman observes that Appel's letter (which Felt has forwarded to him) 'could have come from his own [. . .] father' (357). He denounces Appel as a 'sententious bastard' whose 'bloodthirsty essay' 'pervert[s]' and 'distort[s]' Zuckerman's work in order to pass 'moral judgement' on him, and resolves to make '*no further appeals to the Court of Appels*' because '*[t]he father who called you a bastard from his deathbed is dead, and the allegiance known as Jewishness beyond their moralizing judgement*', but he prosecutes himself throughout the rest of the novel as zealously as he defends himself to Appel (415, 409, italics in original).

At times Zuckerman incriminates himself implicitly, by comparing his confinement in his apartment due to his neck pain to a prisoner's incarceration in his cell: for example, he claims that he has 'sentenced myself to house arrest' and observes that just as '[t]he jailhouse lawyer stores his well-thumbed library under the bed and along the cell walls; so does the patient serving a stretch to which he thinks himself illegally sentenced' (444, 398). At other times, he explicitly places himself in the dock, most notably when he is recovering in hospital from surgery to reconstruct his jaw. So excruciating is the pain, that Zuckerman desperately devises strategies to distract himself from the agony:

> One of the maneuvers he adopted to get from one minute to the next was to try calling himself Mr Zuckerman, as though from the bench [. . .] you have granted jurisdiction over your conscience to the wrong court [. . .] It appears, Mr Zuckerman, that you may have lost your way since Thomas Mann last looked down from the altar and charged you to become a great man. I hereby sentence you to a mouth clamped shut. (494)

Once again, Roth is exploiting the connections between literary and legal discourses here, so that when Thomas Mann 'charge[s]' Zuckerman to become a great man, the word denotes 'command' but also carries with it the connotations of making a formal accusation in a court of law. Conversely, when the judge (Zuckerman) pronounces his 'sentence' on himself, the primary meaning of the word is the announcement of the punishment for a convicted criminal, but its grammatical meaning (a sequence of words making autonomous sense) offers an additional irony: the sentence that Zuckerman passes on himself is that he be prevented from pronouncing any sentences. Paradoxically, this sentence is itself unspoken, since Zuckerman's mouth is already clamped shut, so that he can only dramatise this courtroom scene silently, in his imagination. Finally, the crime that Zuckerman is accusing himself of here – namely that of betraying his vocation as an artist, symbolised by the moral gravity of the great German novelist Thomas Mann – is, as ever in the series of Zuckerman novels, bound up with more personal betrayals.

Zuckerman is in hospital recovering from facial injuries inflicted by his female chauffeur, Ricky, who intervenes when Zuckerman threatens to strangle his friend's father. Prompted partly by a desire to escape from his physical pain, and partly by a desire to escape from his identity as the celebrity author of *Carnovsky* (fantasies that are yoked together by the pun on 'corpus' with which Roth concludes the novel),[8] Zuckerman flies to Chicago with the plan of enrolling as a medical student with the aid of his old college friend, Bobby Freytag, an eminent physician. Freytag is, naturally, deeply sceptical about Zuckerman's motives, even though Zuckerman explains that his fame as a writer has resulted in him becoming a recluse who has 'sentenced [him]self to house arrest' and that, paradoxically, '[t]here's nothing more wearing than having to go around pretending to be the author of one's own books – except pretending not to be' (444). However, Zuckerman is persistent and attempts to ingratiate himself by offering to take Freytag's recently bereaved father to visit his wife's grave. At the cemetery the old man confesses his resentment of the fact that his son's 'brilliance [is] locked in his genes' (Bobby is infertile as a result of contracting mumps as a young man), while his adopted grandson is 'a piece of contempt who gets on the phone with his father and tells him to go eat shit' (483). Working himself up into a rage, Freytag vows to 'kill that little bastard', whom he accuses of exploiting his family's 'Jewish love'. At this point Zuckerman's own repressed rage erupts:

> Zuckerman . . . pounced upon the old man's neck. *He* would kill – and never again suppose himself better than his crime: an end to denial; of the heaviest judgement guilty as charged. (483, italics in original)

What precipitates Zuckerman's homicidal rage, it appears, is Freytag's assumption that Bobby's adopted son behaves as he does because he has not inherited his father's (Jewish) genes. As Zuckerman's hands are 'frantically straining to throttle [Freytag's] throat', he cries 'Our genes! Our sacred little packet of Jewish sugars', before launching into a parody of the Ten Commandments: 'Honor thy Finkelstein! Do not commit Kaufman! Make no idols in the form of Levine! Thou shalt not take in vain the name of Katz!' (484). Half-crazed as he is at this stage of the narrative because of the alcohol and medication that he has been recklessly consuming in a futile attempt to dull his neck pain, Zuckerman's attempt to enact literally the crime which he was accused of committing metaphorically in *Zuckerman Unbound* – the murder of a Jewish father – reveals the extent to which he has accepted the legitimacy of the charge and internalised the guilt of the crime. That his mother dies at the beginning of *The Anatomy Lesson* (her death possibly hastened by that of her husband and by the burden of being constantly identified with the fictional mother in *Carnovsky*)[9] exacerbates Zuckerman's sense of guilt but also emboldens him to acknowledge the ambivalence of his feelings for his father:

> Who that follows after us will understand how midway through the twentieth century, in this huge, lax, disjointed democracy, a father – and not even a father of learning or eminence or demonstrable power – could still assume the stature of a father in a Kafka story? No, the good old days are just about over, when half the time, without even knowing it, a father could sentence a son to punishment for his crimes, and the love and hatred of authority could be such a painful, tangled mess. (497)

Characteristically, Zuckerman contextualises his own troubled relationship with his father in literary terms (alluding to Kafka's representations of paternal tyranny) and socio-historical ones (seeing his generation as the last one for whom the authority of the father will prove to be such a vexed question). This attempt to extrapolate from the particular to the general – the movement from personal experience to objective analysis – cannot disguise the fact that in the *Zuckerman Bound* novels it is not so much that Doc Zuckerman represents a type of the Jewish (or American) father as that all Jewish men of his generation (E.I. Lonoff, Judge Wapter, Milton Appel, Mr Freytag) represent surrogates for, or alternative versions of, him. Zuckerman's parricidal impulse towards 'Poppa Freytag', as he takes to calling him, like his manic fury towards Milton Appel, is an echo of his murderous feelings towards his own father. Freytag's dismay at the betrayal of his paternal Jewish genetic legacy by his adopted Gentile grandson, like Appel's 'overwrought polemic[s] for endangered Jewry', cuts Zuckerman to the quick because it arouses in him the 'love and hatred', the paradoxical, 'painful, tangled mess' of his feelings towards his father's Jewish judgements. And this is the key point: Zuckerman's aggression towards Freytag and Appel is not simply the re-enactment of an Oedipal conflict with his father, a Freudian urge to usurp paternal potency. Zuckerman's desire to punish these judging Jewish patriarchs is in fact also a desire to punish himself, as his decision to *become* Appel (that is, assume the name of his old adversary) and his masochistic behaviour while in that guise confirm.

During the days leading up to his attack on Freytag, Zuckerman as Appel has been persistently goading his chauffeur, Ricky, 'a good-natured girl of twenty-seven, only a few years out of rural Minnesota' (458), in a series of manic monologues, regaling her with stories of his tribulations and, of course, his trials:

> I can tell people a thousand times that I'm a serious person but it's hard for them to take at face value when the prosecution holds up *Lickety Split* and on the cover is a white girl sucking a big black cock and simultaneously fucking a broom. It's an unforgiving world . . . Those who transgress are truly hated as scum. (435)

Here Zuckerman is taking revenge on Appel by representing the urbane literary critic as the purveyor of the most vulgar, sexually explicit trash. He is also parodying his own (and, by extension, Roth's) predicament as a 'serious' writer struggling to live down a popular reputation as the author of a supposedly pornographic novel, *Carnovsky* (*Portnoy's Complaint*). At the same time he is baiting Ricky, deploying increasingly obscene imagery in an attempt to flush out her own values. Later he offers her a permanent job as his chauffeur, persisting in spite of her demurrals, on the basis of the 'well-known pornographical paradox: one has to esteem innocence highly to enjoy its violation' (458).

When she finally kicks him in the face with her 'ominous powerful sleek splendid boots that would have prompted caution in his bearded forbears too', Ricky is not simply stepping in to protect Freytag, but wreaking vengeance on Zuckerman/Appel for all the crimes that he has confessed to – or rather boasted of – over the course of the preceding days (484). As the allusion to the historical victimisation of Jews by uniformed thugs implies, whether the boots belong to Russian cossacks or Nazi officers, they have become a symbol of State oppression of Jews. Zuckerman ironically engineers a scenario in which (his version of) Appel becomes the victim of precisely the kind of anti-Semitic violence that the original Appel's paranoid imagination conjures up (Zuckerman makes Appel's Jewishness a keynote of his invented identity as the porno tycoon by referring to himself as 'the wild Jew of the pampas') (453). However, it is Zuckerman, rather than his intended victim, Appel, who bears the scars of this attack. Zuckerman may have assumed Appel's name but he does not inhabit his body: one of the anatomy lessons that he must learn is that he cannot 'unchain himself from . . . the corpus that was his' (505). Whether or not his neck pains are psychosomatic, Zuckerman ensures that he does receive physical punishment for his crimes: his chauffeur may have carried out the sentence, but it is Zuckerman's own verdict on himself that she executes.

In the final section of *The Anatomy Lesson* Zuckerman, weary of forever 'answering charges, countering allegations' and of paradoxically 'sharpening the conflict while earnestly striving to be understood', decides to abandon his career as a writer and retrain as a medical doctor (501). While convalescing, he receives a letter from the editors of the University of Chicago student newspaper, who want 'to interview him about the future of his kind of fiction in the post-modernist era of John Barth and Thomas Pynchon', which seems to confirm his own sense that his time as a novelist is over and that he has exhausted the possibilities of fiction (497). Included with the letter is a ten-part questionnaire whose form and contents (for example '*1. Why do you continue to write? 2. What purpose does your work serve?*') echo the questionnaire compiled by Judge Wapter and his wife in *The Ghost Writer* (497, italics in original). Like the Wapters' questionnaire, this one encourages Zuckerman to consider the personal motives and the social utility of his work. But, whereas he had responded with defiance to the earlier challenge, he now feels that his writing has become an 'endless public deposition . . . a curse!' (501).

*The Anatomy Lesson* ends with Zuckerman's trial of himself adjourned, the jury undecided – disillusioned with his career as a novelist, but unable to 'escape the corpus that was his' – but the fourth and final book in the *Zuckerman Bound* series, an 'epilogue' to the preceding trilogy entitled *The Prague Orgy*, provides Zuckerman with at least a temporary reprieve from his perennial 'search for the release from self' (504, 492). It also provides a new perspective on the theme of the writer on trial. In *The Anatomy Lesson* an increasingly solipsistic Zuckerman comes to feel that he is imprisoned in his own ego – '[a]ll of you an enclosure you keep trying to break out of', as he remarks to himself – but in *The Prague Orgy* he becomes more concerned with the literal infringements of fellow writers' liberties in Communist Czechoslovakia than with his figurative self-incarceration (442). Indeed in this novella, the prevailing metaphor of the preceding three books in *Zuckerman Bound* becomes political reality. When Zuckerman travels to Prague in the hope of salvaging the manuscripts of an unknown Jewish writer, he discovers that surveillance, interrogation, arrest, trials and even imprisonment are routinely deployed as weapons by the State against authors accused of being dissidents.

## *The Prague Orgy*

The book opens with a conversation between Zuckerman and Sisovsky, a Czech-Jewish writer living in exile in the United States. Sisovsky, the author of a book that has been banned in his native country as a result of the 'outright ideological fanaticism' of the political establishment, expresses sympathy for the 'scandalous' response to Zuckerman's 'masterpiece', *Carnovsky*, claiming that '[t]he weight of the stupidity [of the criticism of the book] you must carry is heavier than the weight of the banning' (510). Zuckerman's response is to point out that Sisovksy has 'been punished in the harshest way. Banning your book, prohibiting your publication, driving you from your country – what could be more burdensome and stupid than that?' (511). When Sisovsky explains that he 'could not write [. . .] without being taken in for interrogation' by the Czech authorities, and his partner, formerly one of the most admired actresses in Czechoslovakia, tells Zuckerman that after she left her husband, a favoured son of the Party, for Sisovsky, she found herself being asked by the Vice-Minister of Culture to account for her decision 'to play the role of the Jewess Anne Frank', it is clear that the leitmotif of judging Jews will continue in this final instalment of the *Zuckerman Bound* series (512, 517).[10]

Persuaded by Sisovsky to retrieve from his ex-wife's apartment in Prague the unpublished works of his father, 'a great Jewish writer that might have been', 'a Jew writing about Jews [. . .] Semite-obsessed all his life', Zuckerman commits himself to another symbolic act of reconciliation with another symbolic father and another mission of salvation for another surrogate self. Like Lonoff in *The Ghost Writer*, Sisovsky's father represents a Jewish cultural patrimony for Zuckerman (a literary legacy that he can claim as his own), but his situation also mirrors Zuckerman's, since his preoccupation with judging Jews has led to him falling out of favour with the authorities. The difference is that Zuckerman alienates the elders of his own community through what they see as his hostile judgements of Jews, whereas the fiction of Sisovksy's father would be regarded as too sympathetic in its portrait of Jewish life by the pathologically anti-Zionist Communist regime.

Having written fiction in which national politics tended to take a backseat to domestic politics, sexual politics and identity politics, in *The Prague Orgy* Roth places Zuckerman in an arena where public policy and private lives cannot be separated, a country in which half the population 'is employed spying on the other half' (523, 520). Here reality seems to imitate the most paranoid fictions of the most famous of Czech-Jewish writers, Kafka. Bolotka, one of the writers Zuckerman encounters in Prague, describes how a fellow writer, in an attempt to curry favour with the authorities, agrees to spy on him but produces reports that 'missed the point of everything [Bolotka] said and got everything backwards about when [he] went where' (538). Far from feeling embittered by his colleague's actions, Bolotka comes to his aid, proposing, paradoxically, to 'spy on [him]self', writing reports on his own activities that his colleague can 'submit . . . as [his] own' (538). Yet, for all the potential for grotesque black humour in the vein of Kafka, or indeed of the Roth of *Zuckerman Unbound* and *The Anatomy Lesson*, there are very serious dangers involved in being a writer in this political climate, as Zuckerman soon discovers.

Zuckerman has barely arrived in Prague before he is warned by a Czech student of his work, Oldrich Hrobek, that the Czech authorities 'are building a case' against him and planning to arrest him on charges of espionage, as an 'ideological saboteur' (546). Sure enough, Zuckerman is apprehended, lectured by the Minister of Culture on the responsibility of writers to display 'moral leadership' and finally deported from the country, branded as a 'Zionist agent' (564, 569). Reflecting ruefully on his motives for accepting Sisovsky's mission, Zuckerman realises that his actions have been driven, at least in part, by a desire to atone for his own fortuitous escape from recent Jewish history ('[b]ecause Sisovsky claimed to be my counterpart from the world that my own fortunate family had eluded didn't mean I had to prove him right by rushing in to change places') and sardonically pronounces one last judgement on himself: 'Guilty of conspiring against the Czech people [. . .] Thus I conclude my penance' (563). The final irony of the book, then, is that, having been accused of callously disregarding the legacy of Jewish history and having accused himself of betraying the bonds of the Jewish family throughout *Zuckerman Bound*, Zuckerman ends by being accused of acting on behalf of the Jewish State and by accusing himself of sentimentally attempting to restore a piece of Jewish family history and to rewrite Jewish literary history.

The four books that make up *Zuckerman Bound* were published individually over the course of six years (from 1979 to 1985) and vary a great deal formally. *The Ghost Writer* and *The Prague Orgy* are first-person narratives, *Zuckerman Unbound* and *The Anatomy Lesson* third-person. *The Ghost Writer* is a tightly structured, coolly ironic, perfectly poised tragicomedy; *Zuckerman Unbound* and *The Anatomy Lesson* are frenetic, indignant, sardonic, self-lacerating satires and *The Prague Orgy* is a political parable and an obscene, elegaic homage to a lost culture. Yet they share not just a protagonist – Nathan Zuckerman – but also a sensibility informed thematically by the trope of the Jewish writer on trial both as a writer and as a Jew, and stylistically by the persistent use of paradox as a way of attempting to do justice to the complexities of such a predicament. Cumulatively, these books construct an extraordinary, sustained metaphor of the process of writing as a trial in all the different senses of that word (the German term for trial – as in the title of Kafka's novel – is *Der Prozess*). In the series of books that follow this tetralogy (or trilogy and epilogue), Roth's predilection for paradox also becomes a marker of generic experimentation; a tool for yoking together apparently incompatible ideas at the semantic level that reflects the dismantling of the barriers between conventional definitions of different fictional modes at the structural level.

## Notes

1 See Brauner 1998.
2 In this chapter, all quotations are taken from the *Zuckerman Bound* volume.

3 In the event, Zuckerman confides to Lonoff not his problems with his father, but rather his recent split with his girlfriend. Again, he couches his account of the end of the affair in self-implicating terms, describing how, in the aftermath of the parting, '[i]n a fit of penitential gloom, [he] fled from New York to Quahsay', where he 'managed to absolve myself of the sin of lust and the crime of betrayal' (27). Later, having witnessed Lonoff maintain a dignified silence while his wife, the ironically named Hope, smashes some crockery in a fit of despair at Lonoff's refusal to acknowledge his desire for Amy, Zuckerman reflects that '[i]f only I had thought to take his approach when Betsy had gone wild', he might have salvaged something from their relationship. He asks himself: 'why didn't I? Because I was twenty-three and he [Lonoff] was fifty-six? Or because I was guilty and he was innocent?' (39). This theme is continued in *Zuckerman Unbound*, when Zuckerman composes a long letter in which he assumes the voice of his most recent girlfriend, Laura, in order to condemn his part in their recent split. Having persuasively presented the evidence of his own guilt, he comments that '[h]e could only hope that she wouldn't be able to make the case against him as well as he himself could' (248).

4 For a detailed discussion of the reception of these stories, see Roth's essay 'Writing About Jews' (Roth 2001a: 193–211).

5 In 'Writing About Jews', he quotes from a letter from an irate reader who sets Roth a series of questions about his story, 'Epstein', including: '"Is it [adultery] a Jewish trait?"' Roth replies '"Who said it was?" Anna Karenina commits adultery with Vronksy [. . .] Who thinks to ask, "Is it a Russian trait?"' (Roth 2001a: 196).

6 Again, there is an echo here of one of Roth's essays, 'Writing American Fiction', in which he claims that 'much of American reality . . . is . . . a kind of embarrassment to one's . . . meager imagination' (Roth 2001a: 167).

7 For a detailed discussion of this aspect of *Zuckerman Unbound*, and its echoes in *The Counterlife* (1986) and *Operation Shylock* (1993), see Brauner 2001: 154–70.

8 In the final words of *The Anatomy Lesson*, Roth observes that 'Zuckerman . . . still believed that he could . . . escape the corpus that was his', meaning that he hopes to break free both from the limitations of his physical body that is constraining him from functioning as he would like to, and from the body of work that is narrowly defining his identity.

9 Zuckerman characteristically presents the case for both the prosecution and the defence, conceding that he could be characterised as '[a] nasty, nothing fellow, surreptitiously vindictive, covertly malicious, who behind the mask of fiction had punished his adoring mother for no reason' but that '[i]n a school debate, he could have argued persuasively' either for the truth or the fallacy of such a description (343).

10 This detail recalls the role of Amy Bellette in *The Ghost Writer* and of Caesara O'Shea, an actress with whom Nathan Zuckerman has a brief affair in *Zuckerman Unbound*, who also makes her name playing Anne Frank in an Irish stage adaptation of the *Diary*.

# 3

# The 'credible incredible and the incredible credible': generic experimentation in *My Life as a Man*, *The Counterlife*, *The Facts*, *Deception* and *Operation Shylock*

> The burden isn't either/or, consciously choosing from possibilities equally difficult and regrettable – it's and/and/and/and/and as well. Life *is* and: the accidental and the immutable, the elusive and the graspable, the bizarre and the predictable, the actual and the potential, all the multiplying realities, entangled, overlapping, colliding, conjoined – plus the multiplying illusions! (Roth 1986: 306)

> It's a bit like looking at the world through a kaleidoscope. You can look at the same scene but find it different every time you turn the viewer. Writing is what I'm talking about. Writing as a way of life. It's a kind of obsessive-compulsive disorder. A requirement to keep trying different ways to describe something that urgently needs describing even if you aren't entirely sure what it is. (Diski 2005: 35)

> 'That's life for you. Always slightly askew fiction.' (Roth 1990: 191)

Over the past forty years or so, critics of contemporary American fiction have tended to fall into two camps: those who write about – and champion – postmodernist fiction, and those who focus on – and defend – more realist forms of fiction. This ideological polarisation has resulted in the creation of two, largely discrete canons of contemporary American fiction: a postmodernist canon that includes Thomas Pynchon, Kurt Vonnegut, John Barth, Donald Barthelme, Robert Coover, Don DeLillo, Paul Auster and Bret Easton Ellis; and a realist canon that includes Saul Bellow, Bernard Malamud, John

Updike, Richard Ford, Alison Lurie, Jayne Anne Phillips, Anne Tyler and Carol Shields. There are of course a number of writers who don't fit easily into these categories, or who straddle the two. Many ethnic minority American women writers, for example Toni Morrison, Alice Walker, Gloria Naylor, Louise Erdrich and Maxine Hong Kingston, write fiction that has certain affinities with the magical realism popularised by South American writers such as Isabel Allende and Gabriel Garcia Marquez. Others, such as Joyce Carol Oates, Annie Proulx and Cormac McCarthy, seem to have more in common with the Southern Gothic tradition exemplified by Flannery O'Connor or with the modernism of William Faulkner. Others still, such as E.L. Doctorow, Jane Smiley and Tim O'Brien, seem to inhabit a different genre with each new work.

In spite of this diversity, critical debate has tended to revolve around a dichotomy (perhaps more perceived than actual) between realism and postmodernism. For enthusiasts of postmodernism, the fiction of writers such as Pynchon and DeLillo is innovative, challenging, subversive, philosophically profound and intellectually rich; according to its detractors it is wilfully obscure, nihilistic, arid and elitist. Conversely, the work of the realists is either subtle, thoughtful, morally challenging and socially relevant; or naïve, nostalgic, reactionary and banal, depending on which authority you consult. The very terms 'postmodernist' and 'realist' have become heavily loaded. For sceptics, postmodernism is a fashionable tag, applied 'indiscriminately to a variety of cultural, intellectual and social practices' (Smyth 2001: 10), a word that intrinsically 'carries a suspicion of trickery, for how can anything already acknowledged as existing, postdate the modern, if we take "modern" to mean contemporary?' (Alexander 1990: 3). Moreover, the fiction that it describes is, according to Eberhard Alsen, ' so difficult that very few people enjoy reading it'. Alsen laments what he sees as 'the emphasis [in academic writing] on this kind of fiction' which, he claims, 'marginalizes the work of more widely read authors' (Alsen 1996: 2). Similarly, the term 'realism' can seem naïve or reactionary: at best the expression of a simplistic, deluded belief in the ability of language to represent mimetically an objective, external reality; at worst, a tool deployed by ideological state apparatuses (schools, colleges, the media) to reinforce the political status quo, promoting an idea of normative values that underpins the Capitalist system. In the last decade of the twentieth century and the first of the twenty-first, attempts have been made to bridge this chasm: Robert Siegle posits the existence of a 'two way corridor' or 'permeable membrane' in contemporary American fiction, implying reciprocal exchange and fluid movement, rather than fixed, hermetically sealed positions (quoted in Durante 2001: 3); Alan Wilde argues for the existence of a 'midfiction' that occupies the middle ground between realism and metafiction (Wilde 1987: *passim*); Tom LeClair proposes a subgenre of contemporary American fiction – the 'systems novel' – that he sees as 'a useful alternative' to the 'dualisms' implied by the opposition of realism and postmodernism (LeClair 1989: 20); and Robert Durante identifies a body of fiction that he sees as 'both realistic and metafictional' (Durante 2001: 7).

Where does Philip Roth fit into this picture? Roth has been both lauded and criticised for what John McDaniel (in the first monograph on Roth, published in 1974) calls his 'commitment to social realism' (McDaniel 2003: 43). According to McDaniel, Roth's realism is part of a moral vision that indicates 'an abiding respect for life': McDaniel praises Roth for having the 'courage' to continue 'putting his finger on our cultural predicament . . . sending us a secular news report, however grotesque the facts of "life itself" may be' (McDaniel 2003: 53). George J. Searles, writing a decade after McDaniel, also sees Roth as 'essentially a social realist' whose work combines acute observation of 'manners' with 'conscious stylistic artistry' (Searles 1985: 2, 120). Other early critics of Roth felt that (what they saw as) his fidelity to realism was holding him back: Irving Malin, for example, opines that Roth's 'loyalty to social realism is unfortunate', while Max Schultz argues that Roth's 'stringent realism' betrays a lack of 'radical sophistication' (quoted in McDaniel 2003: fn 11). Jerome Klinkowitz, a polemical supporter of the fiction of postmodernist writers such as Barthelme, Vonnegut, Jerzy Kosinski, Ronald Sukenick, Raymond Federman and Gilbert Sorrentino, cites Roth in the preface to the second edition of *Literary Disruptions: The Making of a Post-Contemporary American Fiction* (1980) as an example of all that is 'worst' in the mainstream realist tradition (Klinkowitz 1980: n.p.).

By no means all critics associate Roth with realism, however. Thomas Pughe, although he claims to have 'no interest in engaging in debates over why . . . Roth may or may not be [one of the] post-modernists', implicitly places him in that category throughout his book *Comic Sense: Reading Robert Coover, Stanley Elkin, Philip Roth* (1994); Stephen Wade suggests that although 'in Roth one may discover vestiges of realism . . . he is notoriously metafictional in the widest sense' (Wade 1996: 15) and Lilian Kremer claims that 'Roth's best work combines Hebraic moral conscience with postmodern artifice' (Kremer 2002: 49). Some critics see Roth's postmodernism as a decisive shift away from the more conventional fiction of his early career: Robert M. Greenberg notes that since *Zuckerman Bound* 'postmodern conceptions of the self have become dominant' in Roth's fiction (Greenberg 2003: 81), and Morris Dickstein similarly believes that Roth's 'determin[ation] to show how he embroidered his memories with dramatic projections . . . led him belatedly into the company of [the] . . . postmodernists' (Dickstein 2002: 223). Andrew Furman, on the other hand, maintains that Roth's adoption of 'an overtly postmodern aesthetic' is the logical culmination of his lifelong 'fascination with the slipperiness of Jewish identity' (Furman 2000: 28), while Timothy Parrish senses a reversal of this trajectory, arguing that 'Roth in his late phase is distancing himself from the postmodern decentring of the self that has been one of the hallmarks of his fiction' (Parrish 2000: 93). Elaine B. Safer locates Roth unequivocally within the postmodernist tradition, asserting that '[f]or Philip Roth, as for other metafictionalists, the medium is the message' (Safer 1999: 177) and that Roth's 'metafictional preoccupation with the creative process' places him in the company of American 'postmodern writers' (Safer 2003a: 102).

The most detailed discussion of this question to date is to be found in Debra Shostak's excellent book *Philip Roth: Countertexts, Counterlives* (2004). Shostak argues that 'Roth challenges the ideologies of both realism and postmodernism precisely by his commitment to mimetic narratives that celebrate the discursiveness of identity' and that '[e]ven when Roth is most engaged in the play of postmodern narrative form and epistemologies of identity . . . he clearly strives for verisimilitude' (Shostak 2004: 18, 170). For her, Roth 'openly invites questions about how to place the work', while carefully eluding all attempts to do so, 'maintain[ing] a delicate balance [between realism and postmodernism] that has resisted both emphasis on a single mode and a full synthesis of opposing modes' (Shostak 2004: 190). This is well put, yet Shostak's own critical discourse does not always reflect this 'delicate balance', tending to highlight and celebrate the postmodernist rather than the realistic aspects of Roth's fiction and, indeed, at times representing that fiction as paradigmatically postmodernist. According to Shostak, Roth's fiction evolves from an early concern 'with the singular, embodied, and ethnically determined self, through an indeterminate self at play in the public spaces of confession . . . to a self wedged in by historical trauma'. However, her primary interest clearly lies not in the 'ethnically determined self' or the 'self wedged in by historical trauma' but in the 'indeterminate self at play' (Shostak 2004: 15). Shostak's readings of Roth's fiction are often refracted either through the theories of Freud and his interpreters (notably Peter Brooks and Jacques Lacan), or those of Bakthin and his followers (such as Michael Holquist). She cites most frequently and most approvingly those other critics on Roth – such as Patrick O' Donnell and Hillel Halkin – for whom Roth's characterisation is always subordinate to his experiments in narratology, even though she herself insists that Roth's 'reflexiveness . . . remains at the service of a deeply psychological, mimetic conception of character' (Shostak 2004: 188).[1] Shostak's avowed intention is to demonstrate 'the ways in which an apparently "mainstream" American "realist" . . . has complicated and resisted th[is] categor[y] by taking the transgression against norms and borders as the subject and mode of his fiction' (Shostak 2004: 19). But, because she removes Roth both from the American realist tradition and from the context of other contemporary American postmodernist fiction, preferring to read his fiction in dialogue with itself rather than with other fiction, she can give the impression at times that Roth is writing in a literary-historical vacuum.[2] When she argues that 'in textualizing the self . . . Roth recovers metafiction from the implicit nihilism and anxiety of the postmodern decentred or indeterminate self' (Shostak 1991: 198–9), for example, the implication seems to be that his is a lone voice of affirmation in a postmodern wilderness of negativity.

If Shostak makes Roth's work seem more *sui generis* than it really is, Sanford Pinsker, conversely, attributes the postmodern turn in Roth's fiction to opportunism, or at least to Roth's competitive instincts, suggesting that 'from *My Life as a Man* onwards, Roth's novels began to glance uneasily over their shoulders at who, or what, might be gaining on them . . . they became increasingly self-conscious about the very act of writing fiction and about fictionality itself' (Pinsker 1990: 138). Whereas Shostak arguably underestimates the extent to which Roth's fiction intersects with, and partakes of, larger patterns of fictional discourse by suggesting that he single-handedly recuperates postmodernism, Pinsker does Roth a disservice by implying that he jumps onto the postmodernist bandwagon because he is anxious about being left behind. In fact, Roth is by no means the only contemporary

American writer who manages to combine characteristics conventionally associated with postmodernist writing (metafictionality, self-reflexivity, intertextuality, plurality, the indeterminacy and instability of both text and self)[3] with many of the attributes identified with realist fiction (an investment in the psychology of character, a commitment to the ideals of liberal humanism, an assertion of the existence of a socio-historical reality external to, and independent of, the text).[4] At the same time, his most experimental works – *My Life as a Man* (1974), *The Counterlife* (1986), *The Facts* (1988), *Deception* (1990) and *Operation Shylock* (1993) – are distinctive, not least in the way that they repeatedly cannibalise and regurgitate themselves and each other. In the rest of this chapter, I will explore both this self-referential aspect of the works – the ways in which they read and reread each other and themselves – and suggest some affinities with works by a number of Roth's contemporaries: Thomas Pynchon, Tim O'Brien and Bret Easton Ellis. I will also suggest that the generic hybridity and stylistic ambiguity of some of Roth's texts can be traced back to the nineteenth-century romances of Nathaniel Hawthorne.

## *My Life as a Man*

> The idea is to turn flesh and blood into literary characters and literary characters into flesh and blood. (Roth 2001a: 122)

Philip Roth's early work is very much in the classic realist tradition. Although his first novel, *Letting Go*, alternates between an omniscient third-person narration and a first-person narration by the protagonist of the novel, Gabe Wallach, and his third novel, *Portnoy's Complaint*, is formally more complex and adventurous than has generally been recognised,[5] it was only in the post-Portnoy period of his career, in the 1970s, that Roth began to experiment radically with different narrative modes. In the long short story 'On the Air' (1970), the political satire *Our Gang* (1971), the novella *The Breast* (1972) and *The Great American Novel* (1973), Roth produced a series of works characterised by grotesque, surreal humour and a freewheeling, at times free-associating, narrative voice that was, by turns, facetious, ferocious and frenzied. Absurd scenarios abound: a mentally retarded boy with an ice-cream scoop for a hand finds that it eventually becomes stuck in the rectum of a violently anti-Semitic policeman; Tricky Dixon (Roth's name for Richard Nixon in *Our Gang*) suffocates inside a plastic bag and then gets back on the campaign trail in Hell, trying to overthrow

Satan; a professor of literature is transformed into a mammoth mammary gland; the star player of an itinerant baseball team becomes a secret service double agent, precipitating a war between the U.S. and Denmark. Roth's prose (with the exception of *The Breast*, where it is curiously sober and muted, perhaps in order to compensate for the absurdity of its scenario) is extravagant, playful and pyrotechnical, punctuated by ubiquitous exclamation marks, italics and capitals. The psychologically detailed, realistic characterisation of the early fiction gives way to portraits of caricatures and grotesques (again with the exception of David Kepesh, the narrator/protagonist of *The Breast*), whose names – Erect Severehead, Word Smith, Gil Gamesh – unambiguously identify them as satirical devices. Yet if this period of Roth's career certainly marked a move away from the conventions of realism, it was less clear that it amounted to a move towards postmodernism. None of these books had much in common with the paranoid proliferation of plots and preoccupation with modern technology of Thomas Pynchon, or the metafictional games of John Barth. Although, as I have argued elsewhere, *The Breast* advertises its intertextuality explicitly,[6] and *The Great American Novel* features numerous parodies and pastiches of great American novelists, from Melville to Hemingway, it was not until the publication of *My Life as a Man* that Roth seemed truly to have entered postmodern literary territory.

From the outset, *My Life as a Man* announces itself as a novel that will operate on several different levels of reality. In the paratextual material that precedes the novel proper, there is a dedication – '*To Aaron Asher and Jason Epstein*', followed by a 'NOTE TO THE READER', informing us that '*The two stories in part I, "Useful Fictions," and part II, the autobiographical narrative "My True Story," are drawn from the writings of Peter Tarnopol*' (Roth 1985: n.p., italics in original). This in turn is followed by an epigraph – 'I could be his Muse, if only he'd let me' – attributed to the 'diary' of 'Maureen Johnson Tarnopol' (Roth 1985: n.p.). This material raises a number of questions about the status of the work that it prefaces. Publishing conventions suggest that any material outside the main narrative can usually be attributed to the author of the book and is factually accurate, unless it is part of a critical edition with an editor, or clearly intended parodically, as, for example, with John Ray Jnr's 'Preface' to Vladimir Nabokov's *Lolita* (1955). Prefaces, or notes to readers, preceding the main narrative usually conclude with the author's initials, as well as the date and location of their composition. Yet here we have an unattributed note informing the reader that the main contents of the book are 'drawn from the writings of Peter Tarnopol', when in fact it is clear – from the cover of the book if not from any other source – that the book's author is Philip Roth. Tarnopol, it emerges, is Roth's fictional protagonist, himself supposedly the author of the two stories that comprise the first section of the novel, 'Useful Fictions', in which he explores the same material that, in the second section of the novel, he claims to write as autobiography under the title 'My True Story', through another fictional protagonist, Nathan Zuckerman, who is himself a writer and a thinly-veiled surrogate for Tarnopol himself. The 'Note to the Reader' must surely be read then as part of the fiction that follows it. Yet if this is so, what is the purpose of the further note to the reader (this time initialled P.T. and identified as having been composed at Quahsay, Vermont in September of 1967) at the start of *My True Story*, in which Tarnopol, writing of himself in the third person, announces that *'Presently Mr Tarnopol is preparing to forsake the art of fiction . . . and embark upon an autobiographical narrative*'? (100, italics in original). Surely, if Tarnopol had been the author of the earlier note, then this note would be redundant, or, alternatively, the original note would be superfluous? Then there is the awkwardness and ambiguity of the phrase 'drawn from the writings of' (which might imply the intervention or mediation of an editor) and the fact that the dedication is clearly authored by Roth (Asher and Epstein are both editors who worked with Roth, as anyone interested in his biography might ascertain).

Roth's use of paratexts here to collapse the distinction between author and protagonist, fiction and reality, anticipates Tim O'Brien's strategy in his novel *The Things They Carried* (1990). O'Brien's fourth book, like two of his previous works – *If I Die in a Combat Zone* (1973) and *Going After Cacciato* (1979) – deals with the Vietnam conflict in which O'Brien served as an American soldier. Whereas *If I Die in a Combat Zone* appears to be a work of non-fiction (it takes the form of a journal recording O'Brien's experiences during his year's tour of duty) and *Going After Cacciato* is clearly a novel (albeit one that draws on O'Brien's biography), the generic status of *The Things They Carried* is more ambiguous. Most of its titled sections were published separately, as stories, prior to their inclusion in the book. Yet, when placed together in one volume, it is possible to read these either as parts of a short-story cycle, or as chapters in a novel, rather than a collection of miscellaneous pieces about the war. More fundamentally, the question of whether the book is to be read as autobiography, fiction, autobiographical fiction or fictionalised autobiography is raised, as it is in *My Life as a Man*, even before the main narrative begins.[7]

In the pages that precede the first section of the book, O'Brien includes what appears to be a standard disclaimer: 'This is a work of fiction. Except for a few details regarding the author's own life, all the incidents, names and characters are imaginary'. Yet two pages later there is a dedication 'to the men of Alpha Company, and in particular to Jimmy Cross, Norman Bowker, Rat Kiley, Mitchell Sanders, Henry Dobbins, and Kiowa' (O'Brien 1991: n.p.). These are all names of characters in the fiction(s) that follow, so it appears directly to contradict the assertion that the 'characters' who appear in the book are 'imaginary'. Are we to understand that the book is dedicated to the real-life people on whom these characters are based? If so, then the correspondences between the two must be considerable (that is to say, each character must closely resemble an actual individual, who presumably will be able to identify himself with/as one of these names), and it follows that, while the names in the book may indeed be imaginary, many of the 'incidents' in the narrative are likely to be based on events that occurred to these dedicatees. Alternatively, we must assume that O'Brien has 'lovingly dedicated' his book to the products of his own imagination – a curiously narcissistic gesture.

This confusion – or conflation – of fact and fiction continues throughout the book. The one name that O'Brien clearly hasn't changed is his own; yet the relationship between the Tim O'Brien who appears as a character in *The Things They Carried* and the author of the book is by no means straightforward. On the one hand, O'Brien encourages his readers to assume that the two are one and the same. He often adopts an intimate, confessional tone. 'On the Rainy River', for example, begins: 'This is one story I've never told before. Not to anyone. Not to my parents, not to my brother or sister, not even to my wife' (O'Brien 1991: 39). By apparently confiding to the reader truths that even his nearest and dearest have not been privy to, O'Brien the narrator makes an implicit claim to profound sincerity and autobiographical authenticity. However, the book also includes episodes which any reader interested in O'Brien's biography can easily establish as fictional, such as those sections ('Ambush' and 'Field Trip') in which the narrator reports conversations that he has with a daughter, Kathleen (the author has no daughter). At various points in the narrative, O'Brien confronts these contradictions explicitly, most notably in the brief section entitled 'Good Form', in which he draws a distinction between what he calls 'story-truth' and 'happening-truth', explaining that the former can, paradoxically, be 'truer' than the latter (O'Brien 1991: 179). He illustrates the point by returning to a story that he has already told three versions of, in the sections entitled 'Spin', 'The Man I Killed' and 'Ambush': the story of a Vietnamese 'slim . . . almost dainty young man of about twenty' whom he may, or may not, have killed (O'Brien 1991: 179). In this fourth telling of the tale, the narrator concedes that the O'Brien of his book is a fictionalised version of himself: 'I invent myself' (O'Brien 1991: 179). Yet, paradoxically, he presents this confession as evidence of his own truthfulness: the narrator begins the chapter with the bold declaration that 'It's time to be blunt' and proceeds to defend himself, implicitly, from accusations of postmodernist slipperiness by insisting that his self-fashioning is 'not a game' – a retreat from reality into an abstract realm of pure discourse – but rather a strategy that enables him 'to look at things I never looked at' as a young soldier, to represent reality more clearly and faithfully (O'Brien 1991: 179). However, the chapter ends with an exchange between the narrator – in his guise as the older author who has supposedly come clean about his (mis)representation of his younger self – and the fictional daughter (whose questions had prompted the earlier descriptions of the dead man) that seems to pull the rug out from under our feet once more:

> 'Daddy, tell the truth,' Kathleen can say, 'did you ever kill anybody?' and I can say, honestly, 'Of course not.'
> Or I can say, honestly, 'Yes.' (O'Brien 1991: 180)

Whether O'Brien is playing postmodernist linguistic tricks here – deconstructing his own narrative in a series of self-cancelling rhetorical moves – or whether he is trying to find a 'form' that can do justice to the moral ambiguities in which his experience of combat implicated him, is open to interpretation. What is clear is that, unlike, for example, the repeated descriptions of the death of Snowden in Joseph Heller's *Catch-22* (1961), which gradually reveal more and more detail, like a jigsaw being assembled piece by piece, until finally the full picture emerges, the revisiting of the young Vietnamese man's dying expression in O'Brien's novel results in the disintegration, rather than the creation, of a coherent narrative. Rather than clarifying the ambiguities of its prefatory paratexts, then, the main body of *The*

*Things They Carried* only deepens them, and the same is true of *My Life as a Man.*

The opening section of Roth's novel, 'Salad Days', which recounts the 'puppyish, protected upbringing' of Nathan Zuckerman, his college education and his sexual initiation, is truncated, halting abruptly with Zuckerman doing his military service, on the cusp of literary fame. Saved by an administrative error from seeing action in Korea, Zuckerman is assigned instead to a quartermaster unit in Kentucky, where he is given the job of clerk/typist to an anti-Semitic officer who takes pleasure in driving cotton golf balls at Zuckerman's nose. The narrator records that 'each time a golf ball careened softly off his flesh . . . he seethed with indignation', but then reminds us that, humiliating though this experience was, it is not 'what is meant in literature, or even in life, for that matter, by suffering or pain' (Roth 1985: 30). He then ends the narrative by explaining that the pain that was to come Zuckerman's way later in life is a subject too close to the bone for him to treat with the necessary objectivity:

> The story of Zuckerman's suffering calls for an approach far more *serious* than that which seems appropriate to the tale of his easeful salad days . . . or maybe what that story requires is . . . just another author . . . who would see it too for the simple five-thousand-word comedy that it might very well have been. Unfortunately, the author of this story, having himself experienced a similar misfortune at about the same age, does not have it in him . . . to tell it briefly or to find it funny. (31)

Like the earlier note to the reader, this direct authorial intervention raises more questions than it answers. In one sense, it is a preface to, and an explanation of, the following section of the narrative, 'Courting Disaster (or, Serious in the Fifties)', in which Nathan Zuckerman becomes the narrator of his own story: the tale of his disastrous marriage to Lydia Ketterer, her sudden death, and his subsequent marriage to her daughter, Monica, with whom he lives in exile in Italy. Yet in spite of the shift at the end of 'Salad Days' from the third person to the first, the 'author of this story' conspicuously fails to identify himself. Are we to assume that the authorial voice is Tarnopol's? If taken at face value, the note to the reader would support this supposition, and when, in the final section of the novel, 'My True Story', Tarnopol explicitly assumes the narrative reins, his authorship of 'Salad Days' is apparently confirmed. Yet if he is also the author of 'Courting Disaster' (simply using Nathan Zuckerman as a mask or persona), as the paratext and the text of 'My True Story' again claim, then no actual change of author has taken place, merely a shift of rhetorical strategy. If, however, we take the authorial voice that intrudes at the close of 'Salad Days' to be Roth speaking *in propria persona* then what Debra Shostak calls 'the moral and aesthetic question of whether a writer can or should gain "proper distance" or "detachment" from the details of his past' (Shostak 2004: 161) becomes not simply the fictional Tarnopol's fictional problem, but either the real-life Roth's real-life problem with the fiction that we are reading, or the real-life Roth's fictional problem with the fiction we are reading – or both.

Interpreted in this way, the three sections that make up *My Life as a Man* become both the story of a fictional writer's struggle to write his story as fiction and autobiography and the record of a process of a real writer's attempts to transform his life into fiction: first in the form of another writer's (Tarnopol's) fiction about another writer's (Zuckerman's) fiction, then in the form of another writer's (Tarnopol's) fictionalised version of another writer's (Zuckerman's) autobiography, and finally in the form of a fictionalised version of another writer's (Tarnopol's) autobiography. There is another possibility. What if the author of 'Salad Days' is in fact Zuckerman, a Zuckerman who initially narrates the events of his early life in the guise of an objective third-person narrator, then emerges from behind his mask to tell his own story in 'Courting Disaster' and then assumes another mask – that of Peter Tarnopol – for the final section, 'My True Story'?[8] This reading may at first seem rather speculative, but gains more credence in the context of later developments in Roth's fiction: it is, after all, Nathan Zuckerman (albeit with a somewhat different biography from the two versions which appear here) who goes on to become the narrator and/or the protagonist of eight further books: *The Ghost Writer, Zuckerman Unbound, The Anatomy Lesson, The Prague Orgy, American Pastoral, I Married a Communist* and *The Human Stain.* Peter Tarnopol, on the other hand, is never heard from again.

In other words, there are at least three levels of narrative reality co-existing in *My Life as a Man*: the level at which all the sections in the book, including the section purporting to be Tarnopol's 'true' story, are Roth's 'useful fictions'; the level at which Tarnopol is the author of all three sections, the first two being fictionalised versions of his life and the third his 'true' autobiography; and the level at which Zuckerman is the autobiographical narrator of 'Courting Disaster', the unnamed fictional narrator of 'Salad Days' and the narrator (in the guise of Tarnopol) of a fictionalised autobiography. If this vertiginous proliferation of narrative perspectives makes the novel seem rather solipsistic and self-regarding, this would be a misleading impression. Unlike many postmodern metafictions, this novel is embedded in a recognisable social and historical context, the importance of which is implied by the subtitle of 'Courting Disaster' ('Serious in the Fifties') and by Tarnopol's invocation of the cataclysmic political events of the 1960s in 'My True Story'.[9]

Far from abandoning realism in this novel, then, Roth retains a realistic sociohistorical framework while at the same time interrogating the nature both of literary realism and of the reality it purports to represent. Rather than elevating literature above life, or using life to measure the worth of literature, *My Life as a Man* constantly juxtaposes the two in ways that accentuate, and at the same time dissolve, the distinction between them; it interprets life as a text and reads texts as lives; finally, it reads and revises itself, not in a self-consuming, nihilistic manner but as a means of illustrating the infinite, life-enhancing possibilities of fiction, and the fiction-enhancing possibilities of life.

Whoever the narrator of 'Salad Days' may be, his warning that Nathan Zuckerman's tribulations at the hands of the sadistic Captain Clark are not 'what is meant in literature, or even in life, for that matter, by suffering or pain' anticipates one of the dominant preoccupations of 'Courting Disaster' and 'My True Story': namely, the relationship between literature and life and the problem of defining these terms (30). The fact that the narrator of 'Salad Days' refers first to literature, and only second, as a qualifying afterthought, to life, in his attempt to calibrate Zuckerman's pain, prefigures the way in which the Nathan Zuckerman of 'Courting Disaster' instinctively looks for the origins of his debilitating migraines not in his own body but rather in a body of literature about illness: 'I could not resist reflecting upon my migraines in the same supramedical way that I might consider the illnesses of Milly Theale or Hans Castorp or the Reverend Arthur Dimmesdale' (55).[10]

Zuckerman eventually resolves 'to stop worrying about the "significance" of my condition and to try to consider myself . . . to be . . . living tissue subject to the pathology of the species, rather than a character in a novel whose disease the reader may be encouraged to diagnose by way of moral, psychological, or metaphysical hypotheses', only because he is frustrated by his inability to 'endow my predicament with sufficient density or originality to satisfy my own literary tastes' (57). He rejects his attempts to 'read' his own condition as though he were a character in a realist work of fiction not because of any scepticism about the idea that his illness might be psychosomatic, but on the grounds that his explanations of his own unconscious motives lack sufficient complexity and subtlety to be aesthetically satisfying: 'I could not imagine myself *writing* a story so tidy and facile in its psychology, let alone living one' (56, italics in original). Later, after he has eloped with, and subsequently married, Monica Ketterer, his step-daughter whom he calls 'Moonie' (a plot that, of course, knowingly echoes Nabokov's *Lolita*, a novel often seen as an ur-text of postmodernism), Zuckerman consoles himself by claiming: 'I do not think that Moonie is as unhappy in Italy as Anna Karenina was with Vronksy, nor . . . have I been anything like so bewildered and disabled as was Aschenbach because of his passion for Tadzio' (83). Although these references to the grand tragic passions of some of the most famous figures in European literature might be read as at least partly self-satirical in tone, and Zuckerman's and Tarnopol's fondness for drawing analogies between their own predicaments and those of famous fictional characters might be seen as Roth delivering a series of metafictional nudges and winks to his readers, it seems to me that, cumulatively, these moments amount to more than simply a tissue of literary allusions or a prolonged postmodern joke (the characters define themselves against the literature they have read, unaware that their only existence is as part of the very literary discourse that they refer to).

Both Zuckerman and Tarnopol measure out their lives in, and by, books. Tarnopol repeatedly tries to dignify the events of his life with Maureen by invoking the suffering of the protagonists of the literature he teaches. When Maureen informs him that she is pregnant, he is incredulous, but at the same time cannot believe that she would 'deceive me about something as serious as fatherhood' (192). Torn between his instinctive resistance to being 'blackmailed' into a 'union . . . of recrimination and resentment', and his conviction that it is his manly duty to marry Maureen, Tarnopol reflects that 'it was indeed one of those grim and unyielding predicaments such as I had read about in fiction' and at the same time marvels at 'how different it had all been . . . when it was happening to Lord Jim and Kate Croy and Ivan Karamazov instead of to me' (193). Yet the nature of this difference is elusive. Just as Zuckerman insists that the shame endured by the hero of Kafka's *The Trial* cannot be compared with his own, since 'I am not a character in a book . . . I am real' and the Ketterers 'were to me like figures out of the folk legends of the Jewish past – only they were real', so Tarnopol convinces himself that Maureen must be telling him the truth about her pregnancy, since she 'was not a character out of a play by Strindberg or a novel by Hardy, but someone with whom I'd been living on the Lower East Side of Manhattan, sixty minutes by subway and bus from Yonkers, where I'd been born' (86, 94, 192).

What Zuckerman and Tarnopol fail to realise, however, is that life can often be more outrageous, more improbable – less realistic – than fiction. At the start of his career, in 1960, Roth had written, in an essay entitled 'Writing American Fiction', of the difficulty for contemporary American novelists of making '*credible* much of American reality', but this is a lesson that the narrators of *My Life as a Man* have yet to learn (Roth 2001a: 167, italics in original). Whereas the Zuckerman of *Courting Disaster* has the uncanny sensation that he is 'living *someone else's life*' and that 'my life was coming to resemble one of those texts upon which certain literary critics of that era used to enjoy venting their ingenuity', the Tarnopol of 'My True Life' is plagued by the sense that his biography is too bizarre even to pass muster as fiction, let alone convince as autobiography (84, 72, italics in original). Repeatedly, he bemoans the lack of verisimilitude in what he nonetheless insists is his faithful account of his life's story. Because he himself can barely give credence to Maureen's actions – 'I simply could not believe that anybody like her could exist' (216) – Tarnopol despairs of rendering them convincing in his writing. No matter how many times he wrestles with the narrative of Maureen's confession that she substituted a pregnant stranger's urine for her own, he 'cannot seem to make it credible' (208). Regardless of all his attempts to do justice to the complexity of his situation, it begins increasingly to resemble a soap opera, and he himself seems to have 'no more sense of reasonable alternatives than a character in a melodrama' (125). Apparently fatal to Tarnopol's enterprise is Maureen's serendipitous death in a car accident. Having recounted the circumstances of her unexpected demise, Tarnopol concedes that it beggars belief: 'If in a work of realistic fiction the hero was saved by something as fortuitous as the sudden death of his worst enemy, what intelligent reader would suspend his disbelief? . . . Maureen's death is not True to Life' (112). At this point Tarnopol ostensibly concedes defeat. Although he has promised to deliver his 'True Life Story', Maureen's death seems so convenient, so transparently the product of authorial wish-fulfilment, that it cannot be regarded as 'True to Life' (113). Yet, paradoxically, its very improbability – its failure to adhere to the conventions of realism – becomes its greatest claim to authenticity. It is precisely because no writer of realist fiction worthy of the name would dare to present this episode or that of Maureen's deception with the urine specimen within the framework of a novel that they ring so true here – and indeed turn out to be events lifted almost without alteration from Roth's own life.[11] Echoing Roth's own frequent protests against the assumption that all his fiction is thinly-veiled autobiography, Tarnopol insists that his novel *A Jewish Father* was 'not "about" my family . . . It may have originated there, but it was finally a contrivance, an artifice, a *rumination* on the real . . . I do not write "about" people in a factual or historical sense' (250, italics in original). However, he also concedes that he 'could no longer have a real conversation with him [his own Jewish father] that did not seem to me to be a reading from my fiction' (271).

Paradoxically, *My Life as a Man* was both Roth's most autobiographical fiction, and in a literal sense therefore his most realistic, but also his most postmodernist in its relentless interrogation of the nature of reality and its own fictional status. This is a novel that obsessively seeks to articulate the 'true story', while acknowledging the contradiction implicit in that phrase: namely, that the attempt to tell the truth is always compromised by the very narrative form it takes; all stories are implicated in, and complicated by, the processes of their telling. To tell stories, as young children are often told, is always to lie. *My Life as a Man* explores these ambiguities implicitly and explicitly, with one eye clearly on contemporary debates about the nature and purpose of fiction. At one point in *Courting Disaster*, Zuckerman, recalling his experiences teaching the creative writing class in Chicago where he first encounters Lydia Ketterer, observes that '[t]hey [the students] judged the people in one another's fiction not as though each was a collection of attributes . . . to which the author had arbitrarily assigned a Christian name, but as though they were discussing human souls' (65). This might be read as a reflection on the naivety of the students. But in the light of what we know about Zuckerman's own old-fashioned liberal humanism (he admits to having had trouble kicking an 'addiction' to the word 'human' in his own undergraduate essays), it seems more likely to be a swipe at the modish (at the time) structuralist view of characterisation as simply an artificial linguistic construction, a series of artful lexical choices (17). Yet *My Life as a Man* offers plenty of evidence for the structuralist (and poststructuralist) scepticism about characterisation, notably in the form of two authorial interventions – in 'Courting Disaster' and 'My True Story' – that echo the one that occurs at the close of 'Salad Days'.

In the first of these, Nathan Zuckerman, now living in exile in Italy with Monica Ketterer, breaks off from a nostalgic reminiscence of his undergraduate days – 'reading from the European masters in my bachelor bed before sleep . . . Mann, Tolstoy, Gogol, Proust, in bed with all that genius' (86–7) – to resume his story:

> To conclude, in a traditional narrative mode, the story of that Zuckerman in that Chicago. I leave it to those writers who live in the flamboyant American present, and whose extravagant fictions I sample from afar, to treat the implausible, the preposterous, and the bizarre in something other than a straightforward and recognizable manner. (87)

The sly, satirical reference to the 'extravagant fictions' of his contemporaries, which is contrasted with his own 'traditional narrative mode', manages to nail Zuckerman's colours to a realist mast while at the same time demonstrating precisely the sort of self-reflexive awareness that is usually associated with those postmodernists in opposition to whom Zuckerman is apparently defining himself. Like the passage that concludes the previous section of the novel, this might be seen as one of those moments when the author's mask slips, or rather when the puppeteer allows us to see that it is he pulling the puppets' strings. Equally, it might be Zuckerman speaking of himself (an *earlier*, more innocent self) in the third person to emphasise the difference between his present identity and circumstances and those of '*that* Zuckerman in *that* Chicago' [my italics].

The third of these self-reflexive interjections comes towards the end of Tarnopol's reply to a critical essay that he imagines his ex-student and ex-lover, Karen Oakes, might have written on the two 'useful fictions' that make up the first part of *My Life as a Man*:

> Tarnopol, as he is called, is coming to seem as imaginary as my Zuckermans anyway, or at least as detached from the memoirist – his revelations coming to seem like still another 'useful fiction', and not because I am telling lies. I am trying to keep to the facts. Maybe all I'm saying is that words, being words, only approximate the real thing . . . all I can do with my story is tell it. And tell it. And tell it. (231)

Here again the integrity of Roth's framing devices – the narrative hierarchy in which Roth employs Tarnopol as his authorial surrogate, who in turn employs Zuckerman as his alter ego – seems to be deliberately threatened, not simply because Tarnopol's status as a fictional character is explicitly acknowledged, in a part of the narrative that is supposed to be his true story, as told by himself, but because of the strain that is being put on the whole narrative edifice by the very context in which these remarks are being made. Tarnopol is responding here to a response (his own, ventriloquised through Karen Oakes) to the two earlier fictions of the novel, which are themselves a response to each other, and to which this whole section of the novel ('My True Story') is also a response. The process of perpetual revisioning, in which each successive version does not so much displace, supplant or usurp its predecessors, as superimpose itself on each of them, creating a palimpsest, anticipates the even more complex and adventurous experiments in narrative that Roth was to conduct in *The Counterlife*.

## *The Counterlife*

> 'Nathan Zuckerman is an act.' (Roth 2001a: 123)

At one point in *My Life as a Man* Peter Tarnopol, writing to his sister Joan, reports a conversation between himself and his editor, in which the latter, having read 'Salad Days' and 'Courting Disaster', asks the former whether he is 'planning to continue to write Zuckerman variations until you have constructed a kind of full-length fictional fugue?' (Roth 1985: 113). As I have argued above, *My Life as a Man* can itself be read as a series of variations on a single theme: although the names of the protagonists change, as do some of their biographical details, the essentials of Nathan Zuckerman/Peter Tarnopol's story remain the same.[12] In *The Counterlife*, published thirteen years later, Roth plays variations on a number of different stories, involving two protagonists – Nathan and his brother Henry – who are at the same time alternative versions and antitheses of each other.[13]

*The Counterlife* is divided into five chapters. The first chapter, 'Basel', takes place at Henry's funeral and tells the story of how he came to die. Rendered impotent by drugs that regulate a heart condition, Henry opts to undergo surgery in order to resume carnal relations with his dental assistant, Wendy, with whom he has been having an adulterous affair. The title of this section of the novel alludes to an earlier extra-marital affair that Henry had had with a Swiss woman, Maria, with whom he dreamed of eloping. In the second chapter of the novel, 'Judea', Nathan goes to Israel in an attempt to discover why a perfectly healthy Henry has abruptly abandoned his life in Newark in order to fulfil what he now sees as his historical destiny: helping religious Jews reclaim their ancient homeland in Judea. In the third chapter, 'Aloft', on board a flight from Israel to England, Nathan broods over the events related in 'Judea', composes a letter to Henry, reads a letter addressed to him from an old Israeli journalist friend, Shuki Elchanan, and finally gets caught up in the insane attempt of Jimmy Ben-Joseph (a self-confessed fan of Zuckerman's fiction who had first accosted the author during a visit to the Wailing Wall recounted in 'Judea') to hijack the El-Al plane and demand the closure of Yad Vashem, the Israeli memorial to the victims of the Holocaust. The fourth chapter, 'Gloucestershire', is itself divided into three sections and begins with Nathan suffering from the same heart problem that had afflicted the Henry of 'Basel'. Like Henry, he decides to risk life-threatening surgery rather than suffer the side-effects of the medication; in Nathan's case he wishes to rediscover his potency in order to consummate his relationship with an unhappily married English novelist, Maria, with whom he hopes to have a child. Nathan's first-person narrative ends abruptly thirty pages or so into this section, to be succeeded by a third-person narrative in which it emerges that Nathan, again like the Henry of 'Basel', has died in the operating theatre. This section of 'Gloucestershire' is devoted to Nathan's funeral, focusing on the feelings of his estranged brother Henry (the brothers having fallen out after Henry blamed Nathan for precipitating the deaths of both their parents, a rupture that had been dramatised in Roth's earlier novel, *The Anatomy Lesson*). It concludes with Henry ransacking Nathan's papers and disposing of those manuscripts (including one that seems to be the first chapter of *The Counterlife*) that purport to deal with his life. (Henry also finds a piece of writing entitled 'Christendom' – which he leaves in Nathan's flat – that turns out to be the final chapter of the novel.) The last section of 'Gloucestershire' takes the form of a dialogue between an unidentified interviewer and Maria, in which she answers questions about her affair with Nathan. Finally, in 'Christendom', Nathan reappears (resurrected in the same way as the Henry of 'Judea' after his apparent death in 'Basel'), now married to Maria who is pregnant with his child and planning to settle with her in a house by the side of the Thames in London. This part of the novel deals with Nathan's difficulties coming to terms with the anti-Semitism of Maria's mother and sister and culminates in a row between Maria and Zuckerman, after which Maria decides to leave both Zuckerman and the book she believes him to be writing, in which she is a character (and which may or may not be *The Counterlife* itself). The novel finishes with an exchange of letters between Maria and Nathan in which they discuss their relationship in terms of its representation in the novel we are reading.

As will be apparent from this summary, there is much more going on in *The Counterlife* than in *My Life as a Man*, and in many ways it is more of a sequel to the *Zuckerman Bound* series than to the earlier novel featuring Nathan Zuckerman. On the other hand, in its metafictional self-consciousness and its blurring of the line between art and reality, *The Counterlife* undoubtedly echoes, and amplifies, the concerns of *My Life as a Man*. There is, however, a subtle shift of emphasis between the two novels: whereas in *My Life as a Man* lives are read as texts and texts as lives, in *The Counterlife* life is represented as a series of improvised performances; acting as not an imitation of life, but, paradoxically, as its only authentic expression. At the end of 'Gloucestershire', when Maria is being cross-examined about her relationship with Nathan, and the events leading up to his death, she notes that he 'intensified and heightened his illness, too, as though it were taking place in a novel . . . Maybe he wanted that operation for copy too, to see what the drama was like [. . .] Life as an act' (Roth 1986: 250–1). In this instance, Maria aligns textual referents ('the novel, 'copy') with theatrical ones ('drama', 'act'), but it is the metaphor of life as act(ing), rather than as text, that is dominant in the novel.

In notes made during the composition of *The Counterlife*, Roth wrote that 'acting and being are inseparable – acting *is* being' (quoted in Shostak 2004: 131) and Debra Shostak has written brilliantly about what she calls 'the impulse to *impersonate* selves' in Roth's work, the 'conviction that the *performance* of subjectivity is the closest approximation to essence available to the individual self' (Shostak 2004: 112, italics in original). I share Shostak's interest in Roth's construction of the subject as improvisational rather than essential, but what I find particularly striking about *The Counterlife* are the ways in which the various realities that the novel depicts, and the very processes of that depiction, are dramatised in theatrical and metatheatrical tropes. In this novel the act of writing the novel becomes just that: an act, a public performance, an improvised show. Like *My Life as a Man, The Counterlife* scrutinises its own composition, but whereas the earlier novel presents a series of alternative versions of the same story from essentially the same perspective – a painstaking, and painful, working-through of a particular fictional problem – the later novel constantly shifts perspectives, and realities, revelling in, rather than attempting to resolve, the fictional puzzles it poses. To put it another way: whereas *My Life as a Man* says 'it was like this *or* like this *or* like this', *The Counterlife* says 'it might have been like this *and* like this *and* like this'.

When Nathan visits the Wailing Wall, in 'Judea', he describes his experience in an extended theatrical metaphor: he writes of the 'floodlights dramatizing the massive weight of the ancient stones', of the evening sky providing a 'gorgeous Oriental nighttime backdrop', and of the square resembling 'an enormous outdoor theater, the stage for some . . . operatic production whose extras one could watch walking casually about, a handful already got up in their religious costumes' (Roth 1986: 84). Having been approached at the Wall by a beggar who abruptly turns on his heels after Zuckerman gives him his spare change, he likens the effect of the mendicant showing him the back of his black coat to 'a curtain dropping when the act is over' (85). Subsequently, Nathan is waylaid by two further strangers: an Orthodox Jew who tries to recruit him to join his prayer group, and an effusive Jewish-American expatriate, Jimmy Ben-Joseph, who claims to be his 'biggest admirer in the world', to have 'studied acting' as an undergraduate in the U.S., and also to be an author himself – of 'the five books of Jimmy' (91–3). As becomes apparent in the next chapter of the novel, Jimmy has stage-managed this encounter and is ingratiating himself with the author as the prologue to a much more audacious performance.

Reviewing these events the following day, Nathan remarks that he was 'left feeling as though I'd had a walk-on role . . . in some local production of Jewish street theater' (101). Later, reflecting with incredulity on the fact that Henry now carries a gun around with him, Nathan recalls Chekhov's aphorism that 'a pistol hanging on the wall in Act One must eventually go off in Act Three' but confesses that he has no idea 'what act we were in, not to mention which play' (108). This is, of course, a sly allusion to the structure of the novel itself (its division into five chapters corresponds to the five-act structure of the classic English play, derived from Horace's prescription in the *Art of Poetry*) and to its disorienting narrative strategies: Zuckerman's struggle to come to terms with the unexpected turn of events echoes the reader's difficulty in getting her/his bearings in the face of unexpected plot reversals. However, it also articulates Nathan's suspicion that Henry's conversion to militant Zionism is more an act of self-liberation from his more conventional roles as husband, father, son, brother, dentist and lover than the result of a religious epiphany. He challenges Henry to explain how he has come to cast himself in this 'part' of a 'tribal epic' and wonders whether this new identity is 'a calculated and devilishly cynical act', a brilliant theatrical coup whereby he gets, selfishly, to slough off all his old responsibilities in the name of selfless dedication to a grand abstract ideal (109). He gets no answers from Henry but is instead regaled by his brother's mentor, Mordecai Lippman. Even though he has been forewarned by his friend Shuki Elchanan about Lippman, Zuckerman is still taken aback by Lippman's display, marvelling at the way that '[e]ven for an audience of one he held nothing back' and wondering 'whether he was deliberately playing it a bit broader at this performance to give me a taste of what had confounded my brother' (116, 130).

In all these instances, theatricality seems synonomous with artificiality and insincerity: Nathan's experiences at the Wailing Wall seem to him surreal; Henry's new sense of vocation appears to Nathan to be more self-delusion than self-discovery; and Mordecai Lippman's behaviour seems to spring as much from showmanship as from ideological conviction. In the closing pages of the novel Nathan claims that he himself is 'nothing more than a theater', with 'an ever-evolving stock of pieces and parts that forms my repertoire' and, furthermore, that in place of an 'irreducible self', at the core of every human being is 'the innate capacity to impersonate' (321, 320). For Debra Shostak, this amounts to a 'radically deconstructive critique of the Western notion of the essential self' that is liberating and empowering (Shostak 2004: 211). 'Freedom exists in the capacity to invent ourselves', Shostak writes, and this freedom manifests itself in *The Counterlife* in a 'kinetic subjectivity' that 'opens up the self to its own power of self-creation' (Shostak 2004: 216). However, it is just as possible to read the prevailing notion of the theatrical self as imprisoning and disempowering. After all, Nathan disabuses Maria of the idea that she might have an autonomous identity – '[t]here is no you, Maria, any more than there's a me . . . we're has-beens at heart, routinely trotting out the old, old act' – suggesting that dispensing with the idea of a stable self does not necessarily offer the infinite possibilities of unbounded self-invention but might just as easily result in the repetitive rehearsal of familiar roles (Roth 1986: 320). Rather than escaping from the narrow confines of a life determined by conventional notions of identity, Nathan and Maria remain trapped in parts that offer no prospect of self-determination. Although Nathan tries to buoy up Maria by assuring her that '[w]e can pretend to be anything we want', in the final words of the novel he concedes that the parameters of their existence are narrow – as narrow as the margins of the page on which their destinies are written. The life that they have, as the creations of another author, is, as Nathan puts it, 'no life', but at the same time 'as close to life as [we] . . . can ever hope to come' (324). Struggle as they might to resist the roles in which they have been cast, Nathan, Maria and Henry are caught in the paradox that any apparent rebellion can only be part of the overall authorial design, a point wittily made in Tom Stoppard's play *Rosencrantz and Guildenstern Are Dead* (1967), when the two eponymous antiheroes contemplate jumping ship en route to England:

> ROS: I could jump over the side. That would put a spoke in their wheel.
> GUIL: Unless they're counting on it.
> ROS: I shall remain on board. That'll put a spoke in their wheel.
> (Stoppard 1968: 79)

If *The Counterlife* is less explicitly concerned with the relationship between an author and his creations than Stoppard's drama or other metatheatre such as Luigi Pirandello's *Six Characters in Search of an Author* (1921), nonetheless it alludes not only to the existential dilemmas experienced by the protagonists of dramas such as these, but also to the responsibilities and dangers of authorial power. On the flight from Israel to London, in the chapter entitled 'Aloft', Nathan finds himself once more the audience for an impromptu performance – this time of religious Jews praying on board. He thinks to himself that 'It was hard to imagine another human drama as intimate and frenzied being enacted so shamelessly in a public conveyance' (141). During the flight he is astonished to find himself seated next to Jimmy Ben-Joseph, the aspiring author and self-styled 'greatest fan' of Nathan's work who had approached him at the Wailing Wall (92). Initially unrecognisable because of a thick beard (which, Nathan suspects, may be a theatrical prop), Jimmy informs Nathan that he intends to hijack the plane to force Israel to revoke its commitment to memorialising the victims of the Holocaust. Although he hands Nathan a leaflet outlining his demands, with the paradoxical heading 'FORGET REMEMBERING', Nathan assumes that he is joking and decides to 'humor him until the performance was over' (167). At first Jimmy tries to persuade Nathan to become his accomplice, threatening him with what he claims is a concealed gun, but then he seems to confirm the accuracy of Nathan's instincts, admitting that he was 'just curious' to see how the situation 'developed': '*You* know. The novelist in me' (169, italics in original). Nathan, relieved but somewhat irritated, tells Jimmy that he was 'made for the stage', and Jimmy responds that it is Nathan who has inspired him to his 'feats of masterful improvisation' (170). Everything is suddenly turned on its head again, as Jimmy produces a real gun, 'Henry's first-act pistol', as well as a hand grenade. Nathan fears that '[t]his then must be the third act in which it is fired' (it is in fact the third chapter in the novel) and that '"Forget Remembering" is the title of the play' (171). However, Jimmy is swiftly disarmed and arrested, together with Nathan, by plainclothes Israeli secret service operatives. When one of these agents begins to interrogate him, Nathan 'half sensed something illusionary, as though perhaps he [the agent] was wigged and completely made-up and . . . it was all a performance' (173). Asked to explain why he didn't intervene when Jimmy spoke of his plans to hijack the plane, Nathan says: 'I thought the whole thing was an act' (175).

This episode seems to me to function as a parable of Roth's own fictional strategies in the novel. Just as Jimmy plays a game of bluff and double-bluff with Zuckerman, so Roth makes a series of fictional gambits, which he subsequently withdraws, reinstates, revises and/or erases. Roth puts on and removes a whole series of masks, each divestment promising, but ultimately withholding, disclosure of the true, the authentic, the original author. Jimmy's 'feats of masterful improvisation' find their analogue in Roth's protean transformations; Jimmy's manipulation of the facts in order to see how things develop is paralleled in Roth's method of narrative speculation and conjecture. Jimmy's thesis – that Israel is endangering its own prospects of survival by 'torturing goyish mankind' with constant reminders of its responsibility for the Holocaust – is swallowed up by his love of hypothesis, his desire to '[s]ee what [Nathan] would do' when confronted with his scheme (171, 166, 169). Similarly, in *The Counterlife*, instead of one master narrative there is a series of co-existing fictional possibilities; instead of a single authoritative voice there is a range of different potential identities so that, to paraphrase the Nathan Zuckerman of *The Anatomy Lesson*, subjectivity itself becomes the subject.

From the outset *The Counterlife* draws attention to the subjective nature of its own storytelling processes. The novel begins with a third-person narrative dealing with the events leading up to Henry's death, but this narrative is abruptly abandoned before his death, to be superseded by another third-person narrative voice that functions as a sort of disclaimer: 'these were not the three thousand words that Carol had been expecting when she'd phoned the evening before the funeral and . . . asked if [Nathan] Zuckerman would deliver a eulogy' (13). Although it begins the novel, then, this passage turns out to be a false start: a text that is defined in terms of what it fails to substitute for – a eulogy for Henry – and that is rapidly replaced by a new narrative. In fact, even before the advent of this new voice, the status of the initial text is uncertain because it is italicised (a device often used in prose fiction to indicate the presence of a text within a text, such as a letter). As the second voice proceeds, it too is repeatedly interrupted by excerpts from Nathan's notebooks – entries dealing with Henry's affair with Maria that are juxtaposed with the eulogy delivered at Henry's funeral by his wife, Carol (the excerpts from the notebook are distinguished from the main text by the use of a smaller font, just as the opening section of the chapter is typographically distinguished by italics). Whereas Carol claims in her speech that Henry died on the operating table because he 'couldn't accept' that the medication for his heart condition had 'put an end to our physical relationship', Nathan's notes suggest that it was extra-marital sex that Henry couldn't live without (25). As Nathan listens to Carol pay tribute to her husband, he is convinced that her words have been carefully rehearsed ('every word had been thought through beforehand and nothing left to chance') but less certain about their sincerity (24). The narrator draws attention to the disparity between Nathan's perspective and Carol's:

> The story Carol had chosen to tell wasn't the one that he [Nathan] had pieced together . . . Hers was the story that was intended to stand as the officially authorized version, and he wondered while she recounted it if she believed it herself. (25)

The juxtaposition of vignettes from Nathan's notebooks recording details of Henry's affair with his Swiss lover Maria, with Carol's portrait of Henry as a loyal, devoted husband, emphasises the divergence between these two versions of Henry's story, a divergence that also manifests itself in an extraordinary passage in which a conversation between Carol and Nathan is reported alongside another conversation that Nathan imagines:

> Zuckerman wondered if he wasn't about to hear her [Carol] say, 'I know about her, Nathan. I've known all along' [. . .]
>
> But . . . all she said was . . . 'It helped me enormously, your being here.'
>
> Consequently he had no reason to reply, 'So that's why you made up that story,' but said nothing more than what was called for . . .
>
> Carol did not then respond, 'Of course that's why I said what I did' . . . Instead she said . . . 'It meant a lot to the children to see you.' . . .
>
> Nathan did not ask, 'And you let him go ahead with the surgery, knowing who it was for?' He said, 'Ruth's a terrific girl.'
>
> Carol replied, 'She's going to be all right' . . . instead of saying, 'If I had stopped him, he would never have forgiven me' . . . instead of, 'If he wanted to risk his life for that stupid, slavish, skinny little slut' . . . instead of, 'It served him right, dying like that after what he put me through.' (47)

In an ingenious variation on the old rhetorical figure of *occupatio*, Roth articulates in some detail a conversation that is never articulated.[14] For a time, this virtual dialogue – all the things that Nathan and Carol do not say, but might have said – might seem to function as a gloss for all that they do say: an authentic, unspoken countertext that subverts the decorum and exposes the inauthenticity of the spoken dialogue, as in Woody Allen's use of subtitles in the sequence in *Annie Hall* (1977) depicting Alvy Singer's courtship of Annie.[15] Yet in the final paragraph, the initial countertext is itself countered by a further series of hypothetical statements, so that the dialogical perspective fragments into a more kaleidoscopic picture. Instead of a primary and secondary layer of signification, we are presented with a series of different possibilities, all of them provisional. Like Jimmy's improvisations on board the El Al flight, this episode seems to me to be a microcosm of the book as a whole. Just as Nathan's and Carol's narratives compete with each other for narrative supremacy, so the different chapters of the novel vie with each other for primacy; Nathan and Carol articulate positions that counter each other but also subvert themselves, and each chapter in the novel not only rewrites the others but also revises itself.

These narrative strategies are by no means unique to Roth: Lorrie Moore's *Anagrams* (1986) and Carol Anshaw's *Aquamarine* (1992) are two examples of novels that are structured in ways that are not dissimilar to *The Counterlife* and, as my discussion of Tim O'Brien's

*The Things They Carried* earlier in this chapter demonstrates, the presentation of different versions of the same event occurs in a number of postmodernist American novels.[16] On a more local level, many novels by Roth's contemporaries proceed more by way of hypothesis than authoritative narration. Thomas Pynchon's *The Crying of Lot 49* (1966) – arguably one of the founding texts of American postmodernist fiction – exemplifies this tendency. The novel's heroine, Oedipa Maas, always seems to be on the verge of an epiphany that will help her make sense of the otherwise inexplicable phenomena that she encounters, but 'revelation' always remains tantalisingly 'just past the threshold of her understanding', and of the reader's (Pynchon 1979: 15). The central mystery of the novel concerns a secretive organisation known as the Trystero, whose existence Oedipa may, or may not, have accidentally – or not so accidentally – discovered:

> Either you [Oedipa] have stumbled indeed . . . on to a network by which x number of Americans are truly communicating . . . Or you are hallucinating it. Or a plot has been mounted against you, so expensive and elaborate . . . that it must have meaning beyond a practical joke. Or you are fantasying some such plot . . . (Pynchon 1979: 118)

Like Pynchon, Roth presents the reader with a series of alternative explanations for his character's predicament without committing himself to any of them. In *The Counterlife* the third-person narrator of 'Basel', reflecting on the twin-track dialogue between Carol and Henry cited above, concludes that '[e]ither what she'd told everyone from the altar was what she truly believed . . . or she was a more interesting woman than he'd ever thought, a subtle and persuasive writer of domestic fiction, who had cunningly reimagined a decent, ordinary, adulterous humanist as a heroic martyr to the connubial bed' (Roth 1986: 48). Similarly, in Pynchon's novel the choices seem clearcut: Oedipa has either established something of importance, or she imagines that she has; either she is being manipulated, or she is paranoid. Indeed, this binary structure is made quite explicit:

> [I]t was now like walking among matrices of a great digital computer, the zeroes and ones twinned above, hanging like balanced mobiles right and left . . . Behind the hieroglyphic streets there would either be a transcendent meaning, or only the earth. In the songs Miles, Dean, Serge and Leonard sang was either some fraction of the earth's numinous beauty . . . or only a power spectrum. Tremaine the Swastika salesman's reprieve from holocaust was either an injustice, or an absence of a wind;

> the bones of the GIs at the bottom of Lake Inverarity were there either for a reason that mattered to the world, or for skin divers and cigarette smokers. Ones and zeroes. So did the couples arrange themselves. (Pynchon 1979: 125)

Characteristically, Pynchon invokes modern technology as a metaphor for what he calls the 'exitlessness' of life in contemporary America (Pynchon 1979: 118). Instead of answering the questions posed by the narrative, Pynchon's narrator restates the problems as a series of antitheses held in suspension.[17] Roth's novel likewise sets up problems it refuses to resolve and the governing metaphor in *The Counterlife* of the theatre also suggests a space which presents the illusion of freedom of movement but which is effectively exitless. However, *The Counterlife* manages to complicate and transcend this oppositional structure. After all, the two versions of Carol's and Henry's dialogue are not, finally, mutually exclusive; Carol's and Nathan's interpretations of Henry's behaviour – and each other's words – co-exist; their texts implicitly contain within them potentially subversive subtexts.

Although the deferral, or refusal, of clarification that permeates *The Crying of Lot 49* is echoed in certain respects in *The Counterlife*, Roth's brand of narrative indeterminacy arguably owes more to the rhetorical strategies of Nathaniel Hawthorne than those of Thomas Pynchon. In Hawthorne's preface to *The Scarlet Letter*, 'The Custom House', he defines the genre in which he is writing as the 'romance', 'a neutral territory . . . where the Actual and Imaginary may meet, and each imbue itself with the nature of the other' (Hawthorne 1986: 66). This seems to me a formulation that describes accurately the dialectical relationship between fact and fiction characteristic of many of Roth's narratives. The affinities between Hawthorne and Roth extend beyond generic hybridity, however, into the rich textures of their prose. *The Scarlet Letter* repeatedly offers alternative, often directly contradictory, accounts of the events it describes. Towards the end of the book, for example, when Hester Prynne returns to her seaside cottage after many years' absence, the narrator describes how a group of children playing by the shore observe her approaching the door of her old home:

> In all those years it had never once been opened; but either she unlocked it, or the decaying wood and iron yielded to her hand, or she glided shadow-like through these impediments – and, at all events, went in. (Hawthorne 1986: 273)

Here Hawthorne's narrator provides two realistic explanations for the ease with which Hester repossesses her property. However, he adds a third possible scenario, which takes the narrative into the realm of the supernatural: Hester is able, like a ghost, to penetrate the physical barrier of the door. This narrative ambiguity is further complicated, most notably in the speculation about what precisely happens at the climax of the book, when the father of Hester's illegitimate child, the Reverend Arthur Dimmesdale, finally appears to confess his adultery by embracing his lover and child on the scaffold in front of his congregants:

> Most of the spectators testified to having seen, on the breast of the unhappy minister, a SCARLET LETTER – the very semblance of that worn by Hester Prynne – imprinted in the flesh. As regarded its origin, there were various explanations, all of which must necessarily have been conjectural. Some affirmed that the Reverend Mr. Dimmesdale . . . [inflicted] a hideous torture on himself. Others contended that . . . Roger Chillingworth . . . had caused it to appear, through the agency of magic and poisonous drugs. Others . . . whispered their belief that the awful symbol was the effect of the ever active tooth of remorse . . . manifesting Heaven's dreadful judgement by the visible presence of the letter. The reader may choose among these theories [. . .]
>
> It is singular, nevertheless, that certain persons, who were spectators of the whole scene, and professed never once to have removed their eyes from the Reverend Mr. Dimmesdale, denied that there was any mark whatever on his breast [. . .] According to these highly respectable witnesses, the minister, conscious that he was dying . . . had desired, by yielding up his breath in the arms of that fallen woman, to express to the world how nugatory is the choicest of man's own righteousness [. . .] Without disputing a truth so momentous, we must be allowed to consider this version of Mr. Dimmesdale's story as only an instance of that stubborn fidelity with which a man's friends . . . will sometimes uphold his character; when proofs . . . establish him a false and sin-stained creature of the dust. (Hawthorne 1986: 270–1)

It is entirely characteristic of Hawthorne that he describes the final action of Dimmesdale's life as one of 'triumphant ignominy' – the oxymoron nicely encapsulating the paradoxical combination of abjection and nobility that defines Dimmesdale. It is also typical of the rhetorical complexity and elusiveness of *The Scarlet Letter* that this long-awaited moment of revelation should be the site of such debate, not just about the nature of that revelation but about whether there was, in fact, any revelation at all. Hawthorne's narrator begins by articulating a series of different possible explanations for the apparent appearance on Dimmesdale's torso of a scarlet letter like the one that the community of Salem forces Hester to wear as a symbol of her adultery. Like the accounts of how Hester gains entrance into her cottage, these explanations vary from the rational (Dimmesdale has harmed himself) to the superstitious (he has been the victim of black magic, or the recipient of divine justice), and again the narrator does not lend his authority to any of them, inviting the reader instead to exercise her or his own judgement and moreover warning that they are all 'conjectural'.

Indeed, the narrator seems to suggest that these theories may all be unfounded, since several 'highly respectable witnesses' testified that there was no sign of an 'A' on the minister's flesh. However, this counternarrative is itself countered by the narrator's assertion that this position can be attributed to the determination of Dimmesdale's allies to defend his reputation. Hence those who are most sceptical of a phenomenon that might seem to derive principally from what the narrator describes elsewhere in the book as the tendency of the 'vulgar, [inhabitants of Salem] who . . . were always contributing a grotesque horror to what interested their imaginations' (Hawthorne 1986: 112) are themselves treated with dry scepticism – in spite, or perhaps because, of their 'highly respectable' status. As well-educated members of the establishment, they might be regarded as reliable witnesses but they also have a vested interest in covering up the truth, since they themselves would be implicated, by association, in Dimmesdale's guilt.

Hawthorne's narrative slipperiness and rhetorical subtlety in *The Scarlet Letter* anticipates Roth's evasive manoeuvres in *The Counterlife*. At the end of 'Basel', the question of which of the two interpretations offered earlier in the chapter for the eulogy delivered by Carol at Henry's funeral is correct – is she a talented actress, putting on a show, or is she deluded and deceived, genuinely believing Henry to be the faithful husband and model family man whom she invokes in her speech? – seems to be resolved once and for all. 'Basel' ends with another entry from Nathan's notebooks, intially forgotten but belatedly rediscovered by the author, in which he had recorded Carol expressing frustration with her sexless marriage in unambiguous terms, imploring Henry to 'Fuck me before I die!' (Roth 1986: 49).

In the light of this 'ending', it is tempting to see the abortive italicised account of Henry's affair with his dental assistant Wendy, and the extracts from Nathan's notebooks dealing with Henry's adultery with

Maria, as subversive countertexts to Carol's 'officially authorized version' of events: the true story as opposed to Carol's useful fiction (25). However, the framing of 'Basel', both internally and in the context of the novel as a whole, militates against such a hierarchical structure of authenticity. After all, if the opening italicised section of the chapter was authored by Nathan (writing about himself, as well as Henry, in the third person), then the narrative that succeeds it might also be Nathan's subjective account, disguised in the form of an objective third-person narrative, in which case his notebook entries have no greater authority than any other part of the narrative. This interpretation is strengthened by Henry's discovery of these notebooks in 'Gloucestershire' (an episode I shall return to shortly), as well as by the fact that Nathan anticipates in 'Basel' one of the narrative twists that takes place later in the novel when he speculates about what might have happened 'if instead of the brother whose obverse existence mine inferred . . . *I* had been the Zuckerman boy in that . . . predicament?' (42, italics in original).

In the first section of 'Gloucestershire', narrated by the Nathan of 'Judea' and 'Aloft', Nathan is indeed confronted by the same dilemma as Henry in 'Basel'. Just as with the beginning of 'Basel', this opening narrative strand is suddenly severed, before the outcome of the operation is known. The ensuing narrative (the second section of the chapter) makes it clear that the brothers' roles in 'Basel' have been reversed: Nathan has died while undergoing an operation intended to alleviate the necessity of taking the drugs that leave him impotent, and Henry finds himself unable to compose a eulogy for the funeral. Instead, as Nathan does in 'Basel', Henry produces a sort of anti-eulogy. Whereas Nathan writes an account of Henry's marital infidelities, Henry condemns his brother's reckless disregard for fidelity to life in his fiction:

> In his mind it never mattered what *actually* happened or what anyone *actually* was – instead everything important distorted, disguised, wrenched ridiculously out of proportion, determined by those endless, calculated illusions cunningly cooked up . . . always this unremittingly dreadful conversion of the facts into something else[.] (232, italics in original)

Whereas Nathan characterises Henry as a man bound by convention, whose real life was insufficiently compelling for the purposes of fiction (in 'Judea' he asks himself if Henry could possibly 'have become . . .

interesting?', before concluding that '[i]f Henry was ever going to turn out to be interesting, I was going to have to do it'), Henry alleges that his brother avoided the risks of engaging with reality altogether, preferring to hide 'behind a life-proof shield of . . . self-protecting words' (120, 156, 232).[18]

Like the second section of 'Basel', the second section of 'Gloucestershire' has an anonymous third-person narrator, but is conveyed very much from the point of view of the surviving brother. At the start of the section we are told that, whenever he read one of Nathan's books, Henry 'would immediately begin to sketch in his head a kind of counterbook to redeem from distortion the lives that were recognizably, to him, Nathan's starting point' and this section of 'Gloucestershire' functions, in a sense, as that counterbook (205). It is Henry's version of events that holds sway here, and Nathan's stories (including the earlier chapter, 'Basel') that are dismissed as wilfully misleading, subjective distortions of reality. Yet Henry's privileged position is only temporary: by the end of the section he has been displaced once again, disappearing from the narrative completely, as the third-person narration of Nathan's funeral and its aftermath gives way to the transcript of an interview of Maria, the English novelist. Just as the final self-subverting narrative turn of 'Basel' calls into question the authorship of the preceding section, so the unannounced, unexplained transition from the description of Henry's revenge on his brother's 'lawless, mocking brain' to the italicised question directed at Maria – *'How did you find out that he was dead?'* – undermines the premises on which the preceding narrative has been operating (239). During the course of this interview, when Maria is cross-examined about her life with Nathan, she notes that Nathan 'intensified and heightened his illness, too, as though it were taking place in a novel . . . Maybe he wanted that operation for copy too, to see what the drama was like . . . Life as an act' (250–1). The word 'copy' here, though used primarily in the journalistic sense of 'material', also serves as a reminder that Nathan's fatal operation in this fourth chapter replicates Henry's in the first. Moreover, the transition in Maria's imagination from one genre (the novel) to another (drama) reiterates the connection between the two forms in *The Counterlife*. Finally, Maria implies that if life for Nathan is an act, then so is his death. This suggestion is reinforced by a mysterious, unnamed mourner at Nathan's funeral (who Henry momentarily imagines 'to *be* Nathan', but who, like Maria's unnamed interviewer, might just as plausibly represent Roth), who offers this review of Nathan's demise: '"No dying, no decay – just death. All very thoughtful. Quite a performance"' (221, 218).[19]

In this light, it appears that even as Henry is apparently giving full rein to his feelings of resentment at Nathan's appropriation of his and everyone else's lives, he may be unwittingly participating in that appropriation. In other words, when Henry complains that everyone in Nathan's fiction is simply a 'dummy up on his knee ventriloquizing his mouthful!', he may himself be one of those dummies (232). That Henry discovers, among the manuscripts in Nathan's apartment, the text of Nathan's eulogy (and that it is delivered at the funeral by Nathan's editor, who presents it as a personal tribute to his late client) seems to confirm that Nathan is continuing to pull the narrative strings even from beyond the grave.

Sure enough, in the final chapter of the novel, 'Christendom', Nathan is resurrected and picks up the narrative where it had left off at the end of the third chapter, 'Aloft'. Although the courtship between Nathan and Maria that is described in the first section of 'Gloucestershire' seems to form part of the implied prehistory of 'Christendom', the subsequent events of that chapter (Nathan's illness and death) have apparently been erased, or have not yet occurred. The fact that 'Christendom' is first mentioned as one of the manuscripts that Henry comes across among Nathan's papers in 'Gloucestershire', and secondly as a published story that is discussed by Maria and her interviewer, suggests that its composition precedes that of 'Gloucestershire', even though it succeeds it in the structure of *The Counterlife*. For most of its course, 'Christendom' proceeds within a realistic framework, but after Nathan and Maria argue bitterly about what he sees as her complicity with the anti-Semitism endemic in genteel English society – which Maria attributes to his obsessive paranoia – the narrative becomes explicitly metafictional.

Returning to the Chiswick house that was to be the idyllic setting for his future life with Maria, Nathan hopes to find his wife asleep in bed, 'her lungs quietly billowing with life's real air', but fears that he may discover 'only a letter beside my pillow' (311). At this point Nathan's prose tails off into an ellipsis and when he resumes the narrative, it is to speculate about what might be in that letter (311). It is not clear whether his fears have been confirmed and he has *actually* found a letter, or whether he has proceeded to *imagine* himself finding a letter. That the word 'imagine' is used imperatively, becoming a refrain in these closing pages of the novel, tends to support the latter reading. At any rate, both Nathan and Maria begin to reflect on their own status as fictional characters. Nathan mourns the loss of Maria not simply out of personal grief but because of the damage it has inflicted on his professional life, lamenting that she is leaving 'not just me but a promising novel of cultural warfare barely written but for the beginning' (312). Maria, for her part, criticises Nathan's portrait of her as insufficiently realistic, on the paradoxical grounds that the more autonomy he appears to grant her, the less authentic she becomes: 'At the point where "Maria" appears to be most her own woman . . . she is least real . . . because she has become again your "character," just a series of fictive propositions' (319). As with Henry's critique, in 'Gloucestershire', of Nathan's representation of him, Maria's dissent is self-cancelling, since the illusion of her autonomy is never greater than at the very moment when she is denouncing that illusion. However, the self-reflexivity of the novel now moves beyond the level of reality at which Nathan is the author of Maria's story – and his own. For while Nathan's reference to a novel that is 'barely written but for the beginning' suggests that he is aware of the existence of 'Christendom' but not of the novel – *The Counterlife* – Maria reproaches him for having failed 'to rise in exuberant rebellion against *your* author and remake your life' (313). This exchange of views represents a watershed of sorts in Roth's career. The debate between Nathan and Maria about the nature of life as it is represented in fiction, and the reality that it is supposed to mimic, looks back to *My Life as a Man* but also forward to the series of 'Roth books' (as Roth now calls them) which he began writing after *The Counterlife*.

Indeed, there are two events in particular in *The Counterlife* that seem to point in the direction which Roth's fiction was to take. When Henry is poring over Nathan's papers in 'Gloucestershire', he is particularly indignant to discover a manuscript in which 'even Nathan, who had never before written about himself *as* himself, appeared as Nathan, as "Zuckerman," though everything in the story was either an outright lie or a ridiculous travesty of the facts' (226). Later, in 'Gloucestershire', Maria concedes to her interviewer that she was similarly discomfited to discover an unpublished manuscript, 'Christendom', in which 'he used our names, he used people who are recognizably themselves and yet radically different', though, unlike Henry, she resists the temptation to dispose of it (244). Both these episodes anticipate the strategy that Roth uses in his next four books, of representing characters bearing his own name and the names of other people in his life. More specifically, the moment in 'Christendom' when Nathan refers to the notes that he habitually makes in which where there is 'no clear demarcation dividing actual happenings eventually consigned to the imagination from imaginings that are treated as having actually occurred', seems closely to prefigure the form and main theme of Roth's next novel, *Deception* (264).

## *The Facts* and *Deception*

> You don't necessarily, as a writer, have to abandon your biography completely to engage in an act of impersonation. It may be more intriguing when you don't. (Roth 2001a: 124)

Ever since the popular reception of *Portnoy's Complaint*, which was widely (mis)read as thinly-veiled autobiography, Roth has exploited the confusion between fiction and non-fiction and placed it at the centre of much of his work. Rather than attempting to clarify the boundaries between his private, professional life and the public persona created by the *succès de scandale* that was *Portnoy's Complaint*, Roth has deliberately blurred them, first by writing a series of novels featuring a protagonist, Nathan Zuckerman, whose experiences as the author of a notorious bestselling novel, *Carnovsky*, seemed expressly to invite the inference that Roth was writing barely disguised autobiography, and then by publishing a further series of books in which he himself (or at least a figure called 'Philip Roth') appears. Although three of these books – *Deception*, *Operation Shylock* and *The Plot Against America* – are generally regarded as fiction and two – *The Facts* and *Patrimony* – as non-fiction, taken together they constitute a sustained interrogation of the relationship between these two labels. I will return to *Patrimony* in Chapter 4 and to *The Plot Against America* in Chapter 5. Here I concentrate on *The Facts* – an autobiography in which Roth's wife is given a fictional name and in which his fictional alter ego, Nathan Zuckerman, is given the last word – and *Deception* – a novel whose protagonist shares Roth's first name and appears to be deceiving his partner, who is also given the same name as Roth's partner of the time, Claire Bloom. Rather than representing these different 'Roths' as more or less authentic versions of the author himself, Roth's treatment of self-representation undermines the dichotomy between what he has called the 'written and unwritten worlds', creating a realm in which, instead of 'clear-cut differences between the two', they seem to converge and overlap (Roth 2001a: xiii).

In *Countertexts, Counterlives*, Debra Shostak strenuously defends Roth against charges of self-obsession and refutes the claim that he writes *romans à clef*, protesting that 'Roth does not write about himself any more than does any other writer of fiction' (Shostak 2004: 8). Yet she also claims that '[f]ew writers dare to name themselves at the center of their inventions, which is why it is so arresting to find a work of fiction that pronounces its author's name within the text' (8, 158). Although I agree that Roth has often been the victim of naïvely and/or viciously reductive biographical readings, I think that both of Shostak's statements are somewhat misleading: Roth undoubtedly writes about himself more than most (if not all) writers of fiction, but incorporation of his own name in his fiction is rather less original than Shostak suggests.

Long before he began what might be seen as a series of generic experiments in which the relationship between fictionalised autobiography and autobiographical fiction is both illuminated and obscured, Roth had confessed his admiration for the audacity of two Eastern European writers – Tadeusz Konwicki and Witold Gombrowicz – who introduce themselves (or rather characters bearing their names) into their fictions in order, as Roth sees it, 'better to implicate' themselves in their narratives, to 'close the gap between the reader and the narrative', 'strengthen[ing] the illusion that the novel is true' by 'impersonating' themselves (Roth 2001a: 125). Yet there is also a tradition of this kind of self-representation in American fiction that, again, can be traced back to Hawthorne's *The Scarlet Letter*,[20] through the new journalism and the 'faction' of some of Roth's contemporaries, such as Norman Mailer, Truman Capote, Tom Wolfe and Hunter S. Thompson, to the work of younger generations of American novelists such as Paul Auster, Bret Easton Ellis and Jonathan Safran Foer. Characteristically evasive about his reliability and candid about his duplicity, Roth's preoccupation with the relationship between his life and art is not simply a self-conscious response to his notoriety as the author of *Portnoy's Complaint*. It is a means of exploring more fundamental, existential questions about the nature of identity, selfhood and subjectivity.

In 1987, after the publication of *The Counterlife*, Philip Roth fell into what he describes in *The Facts* as 'an extreme depression that carried me right to the edge of emotional and mental dissolution' (Roth 1988: 5). It was in direct response to this crisis, so Roth claims, that he wrote *The Facts*: expressing 'exhaustion with masks, disguises, distortions and lies' (6), he resolves to 'demythologize myself and play it straight' (6, 7). Ostensibly, then, *The Facts* represented a radical departure for Roth. Though never as reclusive as Salinger or Pynchon, he had always closely guarded his privacy and always insisted on the distinction between fiction and non-fiction. Yet here he was, not only revealing facts about his own life, but also conceding that he always had been an 'autobiographical writer' (albeit not in the sense that many of his critics had alleged), and acknowledging that certain specific episodes in his fiction (notably from *My Life as a Man*) had been transcribed virtually unaltered from his own life (3).[21]

Although Roth presents *The Facts* as a reaction against his previous work – '*my* counterlife, the antidote and answer to all those fictions' – the allusion to *The Counterlife* suggests the extent to which that novel haunts *The Facts* (6, italics in original). Its sub-title is *A Novelist's Autobiography* and its epigraph a quotation from Nathan Zuckerman in *The Counterlife*: 'And as he spoke I was thinking, *the kind of stories that people turn life into, the kind of lives that people turn stories into*' (Roth 1988: n.p., italics in original). This suggests that *The Facts* is a continuation of Roth's fascination with narrative disguises rather than a shedding of them; more a sequel to than a repudiation of *The Counterlife*. Further evidence is provided by the formal organisation of the book. The main body of the text, comprising Roth's account of his origins as a writer, is framed by two letters: the first, from Roth to his fictional alter-ego, Nathan Zuckerman; the second, a reply from Zuckerman to his creator, Roth. These letters pick up where the pair of letters at the close of *The Counterlife* left off – exploring the processes by which the raw material of experience is transmuted into the fictional artefact – and repeatedly refer to the events of that novel. Moreover, *The Counterlife* provides a constant frame of reference for both Roth and Zuckerman: a yardstick by which to measure *The Facts* itself. In his letter to Zuckerman, Roth confesses that '[t]here is something naïve about a novelist like myself talking about presenting himself "undisguised" and depicting "a life without the fiction"' and points out that 'in autobiography . . . you construct a sequence of stories to bind up the facts with a persuasive *hypothesis* that unravels your history's meaning' (8, italics in original). If Roth hopes, by drawing attention to the subjectivity of his interpretation of the facts of his life, and to the rhetorical nature of *any* authorial self (even an apparently autobiographical one), to disarm Zuckerman, he has another think coming. Far from being impressed by Roth's candour, Zuckerman complains that autobiography is 'the most manipulative of all literary forms', since there is 'always another text, a countertext' to the one presented (172). Zuckerman's letter itself is the countertext here, but although it challenges Roth's version of events, it doesn't replace that version with its own, and like those moments in *The Counterlife* when Henry and Maria try to cast off the roles they have been given, it can only offer the appearance of resistance. Zuckerman can only speak the words that Roth puts in his mouth.

Nonetheless, Zuckerman's critique is telling: it is not enough to acknowledge that the narrative of *The Facts* is shaped by a particular set of premises; it needs to expose the ideological tendency of those premises by articulating alternative theses – as *The Counterlife* had done. *The Facts* fails, according to Zuckerman, because it suppresses the narrative of Josie, Roth's first wife and the prototype for both Lucy Nelson in *When She Was Good* and Maureen Tarnopol in *My Life as a Man*.[22] Unlike *The Counterlife*, in which Nathan's version of events is countered by Henry's, in *The Facts*, where Josie is 'the real antagonist, the true counterself', she is 'relegated . . . to a kind of allegorical role' (179). In this sense, *The Facts* can be read as a (belated) coda to *My Life as a Man*, as well as an epilogue to *The Counterlife*. The epigraph to *My Life as a Man* – 'I could be his Muse, if only he'd let me – *Maureen Johnson Tarnopol, from her diary*' (Roth 1985: n.p., italics in original) hints at a counterlife and a countertext to Tarnopol's 'Useful Fictions' and 'My True Story' that is never fully articulated within the novel. In *The Facts* Roth implicitly acknowledges that he shaped his narrative in response to Josie's – 'my history . . . was recounted in alternating sequence with her own life stories . . . I was . . . a countervoice, an antitheme' – without actually allowing her to voice her 'tales of victimized innocence' (Roth 1988: 93). Whereas in *My Life as a Man* Tarnopol actually reproduces some of the entries from Maureen's diaries, in *The Facts* Josie's words only ever appear as reported speech in Roth's narrative. Zuckerman criticises Roth not simply for denying Josie the agency that he apparently bestows on other characters (paradoxically, such agency can only *be* bestowed and is only therefore an illusion), but for representing her as an archetype rather than an individual. Zuckerman's critique springs not so much from moral indignation as from aesthetic scruples: he objects not to Roth's sexual politics but to the fact that Josie is too 'real' to be represented symbolically. As such, it echoes the debates about the nature of literary realism that inform the method and subject of *My Life as a Man* and

*The Counterlife*. As in these earlier fictions, so in this later work of non-fiction the relationship between these two terms becomes a central concern.

In his prefatory letter to Zuckerman, Roth describes how, in an 'effort to repossess life . . . to retrieve my vitality, to transform myself into *myself*, I began rendering experience untransformed' – which is to say, he began to write *The Facts* (5, italics in original). Yet this apparent explanation is in fact nothing of the sort: rather than offering clarification of his motives, it obscures them beneath a characteristically enigmatic, paradoxical veil. On the one hand, Roth sets up an opposition between that which is 'untransformed' (that is, unadorned experience, life unaltered by art) and that which is transformed (that is, the written self, autobiographical experience as artefact). On the other hand, he disrupts this dichotomy by implying that it his original, unwritten self (the one that has to be transformed into 'myself') that is inauthentic and that only by 'rendering' it (that is, transforming it into a written self) can he restore its authenticity and 'repossess' the 'life' that it contains.

The ambiguities of this passage are deepened, rather than resolved, over the course of the rest of the book. The very existence of Roth's letter to Zuckerman (in which he asks his fictional creation's advice as to whether or not to publish the book that we are reading) and of Zuckerman's reply (in which he advises Roth not to publish) dissolves the distinction between the 'written' and 'unwritten' worlds. Although Zuckerman acknowledges in his letter that he has no real autonomy ('For me to speak of "my" anything would be ridiculous, however much there has been established in me the illusion of an independent existence'), he also suggests, paradoxically, that he exists on the same plane of reality as the Roth of *The Facts* (161). When he alleges that 'you, Roth, are the least completely rendered of all your protagonists', Zuckerman implies that, far from being the unmediated real-life author Philip Roth, the Roth of *The Facts* is simply another of the author's personae, another one of those fictional masks which he claims to have discarded (162).[23] Zuckerman's words carry the further implication that the Roth protagonist is a little more than a pale imitation of Zuckerman, thus inverting the conventional hierarchy of author and character and rendering the author figure an (inferior) alter ego of his fictional creation. Zuckerman is forthright both about Roth's trustworthiness and his own function. At one point he observes that 'having this letter at the end is a self-defensive trick to have it both ways', thereby anticipating, in a typical Rothian manoeuvre, potential objections from those critics who had lamented the self-reflexive, metafictional conceits of Roth's recent Zuckerman fiction (192).[24] Yet even Zuckerman is unclear about whether *The Facts* represents a genuine (if misguided) attempt on Roth's part to recuperate a primary self obscured by countless fictionalised versions laid over it like a palimpsest; whether, as he puts it, 'you've written metamorphoses of yourself so many times, you no longer have any idea what *you* are or ever were'; or whether it is simply the latest gambit in a postmodernist game of 'now-you-see-me-now-you-don't' (162, italics in original). If it is the latter, it is certainly not the endgame, for the book that Roth published immediately after *The Facts* complicated the transaction between the written and unwritten worlds, and between author and character, even further.

If *The Facts* is an autobiography that constantly draws attention to its incestuous intimacy with fiction, then *Deception* is a novel that persistently advertises its proximity to autobiography. Whereas *The Facts* had appeared initially to mark a formal departure from Roth's previous work by presenting the raw material of Roth's life, stripped of its fictional veneer, *Deception* purports to be a series of dialogues from one of Roth's notebooks, all 'expository fat' excised (Roth 1990: 183). That this is the case seems apparent from one of the final scenes of the novel, which dramatises the author's wife's reaction to her discovery of the notebooks, in which she reads about her husband's affair with another woman. In response to her accusation that 'You love her more than you ever loved me!', the author explains that '*she doesn't exist*', adding paradoxically: 'If you didn't exist I'd love you like that too' (175, italics in original).[25] Later he elaborates, claiming that 'I have been imagining myself, outside of my novel, having a love affair with a character inside my novel. If Tolstoy had imagined himself in love with Anna Karenina, had Hardy imagined himself in an affair with Tess –' (176–7).

At first sight, this defence (which is also a form of attack, implying that his lover is a naïve reader) may seem very familiar to readers of Roth's non-fiction. For years, he defended himself against charges of anti-Semitism and self-hatred by invoking great literary precedents to pour scorn on simplistic misreadings of his work. Yet a closer look at this passage in *Deception* (whose very title, of course, serves as a warning about the reliability of any apparently authorial voice) reveals that Roth is not insisting that there is clear water between the worlds of fiction and non-fiction, but deliberately muddying it. Roth claims that he is imagining himself *outside* his novel conducting an affair with a character *inside* that novel, implying, as Zuckerman does in his letter at the end of *The Facts*, that the written and unwritten worlds may not be so much alternative universes, existing in parallel realities, as organisms symbiotically linked, in a dynamic but mutually dependent relationship to each other. This symbiosis manifests itself in the conduits through which fictional experience permeates the ostensibly non-fictional discourse of *The Facts* and through which external reality infiltrates the apparently fictional discourse of *Deception*.

Again and again, the Roth of *The Facts* has recourse to fiction when describing events and people from his life. When he wants to praise his mother's housekeeping, he writes that 'my mother's domestic ingenuity was on a par with Robinson Crusoe's'; when he describes his father's tales of family history, he refers to Herman Roth's fondness for recounting 'the struggles of each of his five brothers . . . with their children, with their Gonerils, their Regans, and their Cordelias' (Roth 1988: 12, 16). Describing his courtship of Josie, he reaches once more for a Shakespearian analogy, together with one taken from French literature: 'The stories I told of my protected childhood might have been Othello's tales about the men with heads beneath their shoulders, so tantalized was she [. . .] I spoke of the artistry practiced within my mother's kitchen with no less enthusiasm than when I enlightened her about the sensuous accuracy of *Madame Bovary*' (92). When Roth explains the seductive power that Josie's tales of her own childhood exerted for him, he again does so in terms that serve at once to erase the borderline between fiction and non-fiction and at the same time to underscore it: 'I felt drawn to a world from which I no longer wished to be sheltered and about which a man in my intended line of work ought really to know something: the menacing realms of benighted American life that so far I had only read of in the novels of Sherwood Anderson and Theodore Dreiser' (94). Paradoxically, Roth prescribes for himself a dose of reality on the grounds that it will provide stimulation for his novelistic imagination and contextualises the 'American life' to which he wishes to expose himself in terms of its representation in American realist fiction.

Most important, however, are the connections he makes between his own fiction and the life that lies behind it. Even when he is emphasising the disjunction between the two, the juxtaposition suggests affinities as well as discrepancies. For example, when he relates the episode that almost resulted in his expulsion from graduate college in Chicago (his landlady discovers that he has been smuggling his girlfriend into his room at night), he reflects that:

> [O]urs was a story about two intelligent, hopeful young people whose college success had given them everything to look forward to but whose infraction of the rules regulating their sexual lives rendered them, before the unlikely powers-that-be, just as powerless as a Roy and a Lucy.' (75)

What is notable here is not just that Roth invokes two of his own fictional characters (Lucy Nelson and Roy Bassart from *When She Was Good*) to register the gravity of the real-life lovers' predicament, but also that he refers to that predicament as a 'story'. Moreover, when he comes to the crisis of *The Facts* (that is, the disintegration of his relationship with Josie and his subsequent struggle to disentangle his life from hers), he attributes his suffering alternately to a failure of literary-critical sophistication on his part and to a triumph of literary imagination on hers. At one moment, he is castigating himself for naively 'swallowing whole her story of relentless victimization' and for 'being so beguiled by the proximity she afforded me to the unknown disorders of gentile family life'; for failing to recognise, that is, the rhetorical nature of her self-presentation. At the next he is acknowledging how compelling and persuasive her dramatisation of her life is, and acclaiming her (albeit with bitter irony) 'a master of fabrication' and a 'specialist par excellence in the aesthetics of extremist fiction' (12, 111, 112). Whereas at the time he had seen Josie as his passport into previously uncharted regions of extra-literary experience, he recognises retrospectively that it is the extravagance of her imagination rather than the facts of her biography that captivated him:

> [H]ow could I be anything *but* mesmerized by this overbrimming talent for brazen self-invention, how could a half-formed, fledgling novelist hope ever to detach himself from this undiscourageable imagination unashamedly concocting the most diabolical ironies? It wasn't only she who wanted to be indissolubly joined to my authorship and my book but I who could not separate myself from hers. (111, italics in original)

The reciprocal dependence that Roth describes is reinforced by the hyperbole of his language ('overbrimming', 'brazen', 'undiscourageable', 'unashamedly', 'diabolical'), whose excesses mirror Josie's penchant for melodrama. However, the most striking aspect of the passage is that in the final sentence Roth actually equates his book with

Josie's life and implicitly grants her the same authorial status as himself, in spite of the fact that her imaginative feats were confined to life (she never published a book, though her surrogate, Maureen Tarnopol in *My Life as a Man*, threatens to).

There is, then, in *The Facts*, an unresolved tension between Roth's tendency to arrogate to himself agency for the arc of his own life's narrative, and his tendency to attribute its trajectory during this period to Josie's narrative authority, even going so far as to claim that his bout of nearly fatal peritonitis was her 'handiwork' (138). Similarly, in *Deception*, Roth vacillates between taking full responsibility for his life and fiction, and evading responsibility for both; between self-incrimination and self-exoneration; between depicting himself as the omnipotent author not just of his own life but of others' as well, and representing himself as merely one item in the mysterious transactions between art and experience.

At one point Philip's English lover in *Deception* complains that:

> 'I don't really know anything about you, you know? Oh, I know a bit about you. From reading your books. But not a lot. It's difficult to know somebody in one room. We might as well be holed up in an attic like the Frank family.'
>
> 'Well, that's what we're stuck with.'
>
> 'I suppose. This is life.'
>
> 'There is no other.' (Roth 1990: 21)

This passage is typical of the complexity of Roth's work during this period: here is the (always contentious) notion that you can know something of an author from his books, rendered as part of a book in which the protagonists complain about the limitations of their lives by comparing those lives to the real lives of a family (the Franks) known to readers only through the publication of a non-fictional book (*The Diary of Anne Frank*), whose authenticity has itself been the subject of much controversy and whose author was reimagined as Amy Bellette in Roth's *The Ghost Writer.*

Towards the end of *Deception* Philip makes an impassioned defence of his right to (re)invent himself in his fiction without being accused of simply recycling his life:

> 'It is *not* myself. It is *far* from myself – it's play, it's a game, it is an *impersonation* of myself! Me *ventriloquizing* myself. Or maybe it's more easily grasped the other way around – everything here is falsified *except* me.' (184, italics in original)

The paradoxical notion that the self-impersonation of fiction is actually a more authentic expression of selfhood than the self who inhabits the real world is articulated in *The Counterlife* more pithily by Nathan Zuckerman, who declares that he has 'decided to give up the artificial fiction of being myself for the genuine, satisfying falseness of being somebody else'. Whereas Zuckerman's epigram in the earlier novel seems to be an expression of the postmodernist idea that, as Nathan puts it, 'we are all the invention of each other . . . all each other's authors', here Roth's artistic credo deconstructs itself, so that what begins as an affirmation of the distinction between fiction and life ends by rejecting such a distinction (Roth 1986: 69, 145). Likewise, in *Deception* this confrontation with his wife, in which he denies absolutely having had a real-life affair, is followed by a dialogue with his lover in which he admits to having lied to his wife about the reality of their affair. Yet contained within this scene are the lover's indignant reactions to Philip's use of her in a novel ('I object greatly to this taking people's lives and putting them into fiction. And then being a famous author who resents critics for saying that he doesn't make things up'), which presumably is not *Deception* itself, since it could not logically include her reaction to its own publication.[26]

At the end of *The Facts* Zuckerman claims that 'unprotected by the cunning playfulness of fictional masquerade . . . you [Roth] are incapable of admitting that you were more responsible for what befell you than you wish to recall' (Roth 1988: 175), and towards the end of *Deception* 'Philip' explains to his wife that in his fiction 'I portray myself as implicated because it is not enough just to be present' (Roth 1990: 177). Excusing himself, accusing himself; Roth's fiction and non-fiction swings on these hinges. For some critics this dual perspective is a case of having your fictional cake and eating it, tricksiness of the most pretentious and self-indulgent kind. For others, it is Roth's way of exploring not simply the aesthetic and ethical dilemmas of a novelist, but also the very nature of personality, what he calls in *Deception* 'the terrible ambiguity of the "I"' (Roth 1990: 94). In his subsequent work of fiction, Roth took this investigation of subjectivity to new extremes, creating an 'I' more ambiguously terrible and terribly ambiguous than in any previous work.

## *Operation Shylock*

> The veil was off, but behind the veil there was another veil. Isn't there always? (Roth 1997: 266)

In his letter to his creator at the end of *The Facts*, Nathan Zuckerman reports his wife, Maria, complaining that 'there must come a point where even *he* [Roth] is bored with his own life's story' (Roth 1988: 188) but as it turned out *The Facts* was not Roth's final word on his biography at all, but rather the springboard for a sequence of autobiographical fictions and fictionalised autobiographies that culminated in the publication of *Operation Shylock* (1993).

The book begins with 'Roth',[27] recovering in New York from a nervous breakdown caused by the side-effects of the sleeping drug Halcion, receiving news from his cousin Apter in Jerusalem that a man who has been (mis)taken for the author has been seen attending the trial of John Demjanjuk, a naturalised American autoworker accused of being the notorious Ukrainian death camp guard, Ivan the Terrible of Treblinka. Four days later 'Roth' hears from his friend, the Israeli novelist and Holocaust survivor Aharon Appelfeld, that Pipik[28] has been using the name 'Philip Roth' to proselytise on behalf of a political project that he calls 'Diasporism'. Posing as a French journalist whom he impulsively – and mischievously – names Pierre Roget, 'Roth' cross-examines Pipik in a telephone conversation that concludes, enigmatically, with Pipik laughing. 'Roth' interprets this laughter as signifying that Pipik has seen through his disguise and 'knows perfectly well who I am' (Roth 1993a: 48). Fearing that this external threat to his identity might precipitate a relapse of the internal existential crisis brought about by his addiction to Halcion, 'Roth' decides, against the advice of his long-time partner of the time (in real life and in this novel), the English actress Claire Bloom, to confront the impostor when he travels to Israel to interview Appelfeld. After an initial meeting with Pipik ends acrimoniously, 'Roth' receives a letter from his imitator urging reconciliation, delivered by Pipik's voluptuous partner, Wanda Jane 'Jinx' Possesski, who tells 'Roth' that she is a member of 'Anti-Semites Anonymous', an organisation founded by Pipik to help anti-Semites recover from their addictive hatred of Jews in the same way as 'Alcoholics Anonymous' helps addicts overcome their dependence on alcohol.

As his initial indignation is gradually superseded by his novelistic taste for intrigue, 'Roth' decides that, rather than taking steps to wrest back control of his own public image, he will turn the tables on his adversary and impersonate his impersonator. In this guise, he accepts a donation intended to fund Pipik's Diasporist movement from an elderly Jew named Smilesburger and then encourages an old friend from college, George Ziad, whom he meets at a market in Jerusalem, in his mistaken belief that 'Roth' and the father of 'Diasporism' are one and the same person. During this part of the novel, 'Roth' attends Demjanjuk's trial in Jerusalem and then, in Ziad's company, the trial of two Arabs by an Israeli military court. After a further encounter with Pipik, and then with Possesski (whom 'Roth' seduces), he is himself arrested and imprisoned by persons unknown. Although he suspects that this is Pipik's revenge, the man behind his abduction turns out to be Smilesburger, a spymaster working for the Israeli secret service, Mossad. At this point in the plot Pipik and Possesski disappear as abruptly and mysteriously as they had appeared and the remainder of the book is taken up with Smilesburger's attempts to persuade 'Roth' to help his organisation identify the Jews whom they believe may be helping to fund the activities of the Palestinian Liberation Organisation and to dissuade him from publishing the final chapter of *Operation Shylock*, which was to have disclosed the details of the mission that 'Roth' undertook.

It will be immediately apparent from this synopsis that *Operation Shylock* is as outrageously fantastical a fiction as anything Roth had published since the surrealist works of the 1970s, 'On the Air', *Our Gang*, *The Breast* and *The Great American Novel*. Indeed, the pyrotechnical style of the prose in this novel – its excesses, its self-indulgent logorrhoea, its addiction to long lists and alliteration – is rather reminiscent of the verbal spritzes of the aptly named Word Smith, the narrator of *The Great American Novel*. Many of the names in the novel – Jinx Possesski, Smilesburger, Supposnik – also seem to place it firmly in the domain of the allegorical and/or the grotesque. Yet Roth, in a series of interviews publicising the book, insisted that it was a factual account of events that took place during his visit to Jerusalem in 1988 to interview Appelfeld.[29] Whereas in *Deception* Philip had complained that 'I write fiction and I'm told it's autobiography' (Roth 1990: 184), on this occasion Roth seemed perversely determined to present a work of fiction as autobiography, within the covers of the book as well as outside it. Critics have interpreted this strategy in directly contradictory ways: H.M. Daleski, for example, claims that 'with so large a part of what takes place [in *Operation Shylock*] immersed in the real, the effect is to make real what is clearly fabulous' (Daleski 2001: 90), while Timothy Parrish argues that '[b]y pretending to write a book that is "really" about himself, Roth actually demonstrates how fictive reality is' (Parrish 2003: 122).

Actually, the novel is more complicated than either of these positions would suggest. Although *Operation Shylock* does indeed appear at times to destabilise the dichotomy between reality and fiction, it also explodes what has become (after Baudrillard) something of a truism of contemporary critical discourse: the notion that in our postmodern world what we take to be reality is, in fact, a simulacrum.[30]

At first sight, *Operation Shylock* seems grounded in the real world. The text itself reproduces parts of Roth's interview with Appelfeld (first published in the *New York Times Book Review* in 1988) and excerpts from the transcript of the trial of John Demjanjuk (who had been extradited by the Israeli authorities from the U.S. to stand trial for war crimes) as evidence of Roth's presence at two historically verifiable events. Moreover, any readers of *The Facts* will know that Roth did indeed suffer some sort of breakdown (though the details are left unclear in the earlier work) just prior to the time when the action of *Operation Shylock* is set. As well as Appelfeld, Demjanjuk, and of course 'Roth', the novel also features characters whose names and roles imply a direct representation of people who exist in the unwritten world, notably Claire Bloom, to whom the novel is dedicated. Yet this realistic framework can hardly disguise the surrealistic nature of a narrative that centres on the mysterious appearance of a man claiming to be Philip Roth, who resembles him not just physically but in every minute detail of dress and mannerism, and who has made it his mission to repatriate all the European Jews of Israel in order to save them from a second Holocaust at the hands of the Arabs.

The mixed generic messages that the book transmits are closely echoed in Bret Easton Ellis's novel, *Lunar Park* (2005). Ellis's career trajectory has followed a pattern similar to that of Roth's early years as a writer. Like Roth, whose first book *Goodbye, Columbus* won the National Book Award, Ellis became a literary celebrity at a very young age: Ellis's first novel, *Less Than Zero* (1985), published while its author was still at college, became a huge critical and commercial success. Roth's second and third books – *Letting Go* and *When She Was Good* – were generally regarded as something of a disappointment; Ellis's – *The Rules of Attraction* (1986) and *The Informers* (1987) – received much less attention, and sold less well, than his first. Both Roth's and Ellis's fourth books – *Portnoy's Complaint* and *American Psycho* (1990), respectively – were publishing sensations that polarised critics and brought their authors fame and notoriety. What Ellis says of *American Psycho* in the opening section of his sixth book, *Lunar Park*

– 'even before its publication the controversy and scandal the novel achieved was enormous'– applies just as accurately to the pre-publication *furor* over *Portnoy's Complaint* (Ellis 2005: 12). Whereas Roth's reaction to becoming a celebrity was to go to ground, however, Ellis was happy to expose himself to the glare of publicity, as he acknowledges wryly in *Lunar Park*:

> I was doing Ray-Bans ads at twenty-two. I was posing for the covers of English magazines on a tennis court, on a throne, on the deck of my condo in a purple robe . . . I did guest spots as myself on *Family Ties* and *The Facts of Life* and *Melrose Place* and *Beverly Hills 90210* and *Central Park West*[.] (Ellis 2005: 10–11)

As in *Operation Shylock*, so in *Lunar Park* the reader is explicitly encouraged to identify the book's author as its protagonist. The narrator of Ellis's novel appears to be himself: he shares the author's name, career and much of his biography (though the Hollywood actress to whom 'Ellis' is married in the novel, and the family unit he forms with her and their son, Robby and her daughter, Sarah, are fictional).[31] The opening words of the novel – '"You do an awfully good impression of yourself"' – emphasise, however, that the Ellis of *Lunar Park* is not the author himself, but rather the author masquerading as himself – doing a guest spot as the protagonist of his own novel, in much the same way as he had done 'guest spots' on the television shows (Ellis 2005: 3). In his previous novel, *Glamorama* (1997), Ellis had satirised the contemporary obsession with celebrity; in *Lunar Park* he turns the spotlight on his own éclat, casting himself in the role of a Frankenstein whose monstrous creations become their author's nemesis.

Like the 'Roth' of *Operation Shylock*, the 'Ellis' of *Lunar Park* encounters a fellow writer – in this case, Jay McInerney – who in the unwritten world is a friend and rival of the real Ellis, and who in the novel functions as one of a number of doubles for 'Ellis', as Appelfeld does for 'Roth'.[32] Like Roth's novel, Ellis's begins very much in a realistic mode, but becomes increasingly grotesque and implausible. Whereas Roth's novel veers towards manic comedy, however, Ellis's modulates into a full-blown Gothic horror story, in which the other doubles of the author (his dead father, the protagonists of two of his earlier novels, Clayton from *Less Than Zero* and Patrick Bateman from *American Psycho*, and his own son) haunt him literally, as well as metaphorically. In this respect, Ellis's novel might seem to owe more to the great nineteenth-century explorations of the *Doppelgänger*, such as James Hogg's *The Private Memoirs and Confessions of a Justified Sinner* (1824), Edgar Allen Poe's 'William Wilson' (1839), Wilkie Collins' *The Woman in White* (1860) and Robert Louis Stevenson's *The Strange Case of Dr Jekyll and Mr Hyde* (1886) than to *Operation Shylock*, but in its playful generic hybridity, self-reflexivity and self-parody it resembles Roth's novel rather closely.

Ellis had flirted with the idea of the double before *Lunar Park*. In *American Psycho* Patrick Bateman finds it hard to distinguish many of his peers from each other and is himself repeatedly mistaken for one of his colleagues (though this is more a running joke about the facelessness of this corporate world than a vehicle for metaphysical terror). In *Glamorama*, Victor's favourite haunt is called 'Doppelganger's' and as the novel proceeds he receives reports of appearances he is supposed to have made at events he has no memory of attending. *Operation Shylock* was by no means Roth's first treatment of the theme of the double either: from 'Eli, the Fanatic' (in which the protagonist exchanges clothes with an ultra-Orthodox Holocaust survivor in a symbolic act of identification with the history from which his own, thoroughly assimilated community had tried to dissociate itself) through to the multiple doubling strategies of *The Counterlife*, it has been a *leitmotiv* in his work from the start. Indeed, there is a moment in Roth's 1974 essay 'Imagining Jews' – when he satirizes the absurd, apocryphal reports of his behaviour that appeared in the press after *Portnoy's Complaint* – that seems to contain the seeds of the novel that was to be published nineteen years later: 'while "Philip Roth" began boldly to put in public appearances where I myself had not yet dared to tread, I took up residence . . . at the Yaddo retreat for writers' (Roth 2001a: 253). In spite of his attempt to escape the attentions of the media, 'news about [his] *Doppelgänger's* activities' continued to circulate.

The ideology espoused by Pipik in *Operation Shylock* had also been partially prefigured in earlier novels: Jimmy Ben-Joseph's madcap scheme to abolish all institutional commemoration of the Holocaust in *The Counterlife*, for example, demands a historical amnesia not dissimilar to Pipik's vision of Jews returning from Israel to their native European homelands. Even the name that Pipik gives to his project – 'Diasporism' – may have been taken from a memoir/philosophical essay by Roth's friend, the artist R.B. Kitaj, entitled *First Diasporist Manifesto* (1989).[33] When Roth claims in the 'Preface' to the novel that he has 'drawn *Operation Shylock* from notebook journals' we seem, again, to be in familiar territory. *Deception* appears to be a series of vignettes culled directly from Roth's notebooks, *The Prague Orgy* is presented in the form of entries 'from Zuckerman's notebooks' (Roth 1989: 509) and 'Basel', the opening chapter of *The Counterlife*, also features extracts from these notebooks, while the contents of *My Life as a Man* are advertised as being 'drawn from the writings of Peter Tarnopol' (Roth 1985: n.p.). In some ways, then, *Operation Shylock* is very much a continuation – even perhaps a summation – of Roth's previous concerns. In other ways, however, it is a significant departure from his previous work. As I have been arguing throughout this chapter, realism and postmodernism co-exist in many of Roth's fictions, but in this novel the tension between the two modes of narration becomes its subject, and at times threatens to pull the novel apart.

Like *The Facts*, *Operation Shylock* is framed by two metatextual paratexts: just as in the novelist's autobiography Roth and Zuckerman adopt opposing positions in a debate about the factual fidelity of that book, so here the Preface that precedes the main narrative, and the 'Note to the Reader' that succeeds it, appear directly to contradict each other on the question of the book's genre. In the 'Preface', Roth takes great pains to establish the autobiographical authenticity of the narrative. He begins by making a declaration familiar from many works of non-fiction – '[f]or legal reasons, I have had to alter a number of facts in this book' – the implication being that, these alterations apart, the book we are about to read will adhere to the facts (Roth 1993a: n.p.). Roth reinforces this impression by asserting in the second paragraph that '[t]he book is as accurate an account as I am able to give of actual occurrences' and in the third paragraph that his reflections on the Demjanjuk trial are recorded 'accurately and candidly' (Roth 1993a: n.p.). In the 'Note to the Reader' that ends the book, however, Roth reproduces the conventional formula designed to avert potential lawsuits: 'This book is a work of fiction . . . Any resemblance to actual events or locales or persons, living or dead, is coincidental' (399).

On the face of it, then, these two bookends make irreconcilable claims: the Preface that the book is a work of non-fiction, the 'Note to the Reader' that it is a novel. A closer reading, however, reveals that both statements are ambiguous and subtly subvert themselves. In the Preface, for example, Roth assures us that where he has deviated from the facts his changes have been 'minor' and have 'little significance to the overall story and its verisimilitude' (Roth 1993a: n.p.). Ostensibly an amplification of the narrative's authenticity, Roth's use of the terms 'story' and 'verisimilitude' actually undermine it. It is, after all, only fiction (albeit realistic fiction) that strives for 'verisimilitude': factual accounts report real events; stories simulate reality. Together with the stridency of tone in the Preface as a whole (a case, perhaps, of protesting too much), and the possibility that Roth's notebook journals, like Nathan Zuckerman's in *The Counterlife*, may not distinguish between 'actual happenings eventually consigned to the imagination' and 'imaginings that are treated as having actually occurred', this apparently inconsequential caveat suggests a subtext that is at odds with the explicit claims set out in the Preface (Roth 1986: 286). Similarly, the final line of the 'Note to the Reader – '[t]his confession is false' (Roth 1993a: n.p.) – throws into doubt the sincerity of the whole disclaimer. Because *Operation Shylock* is subtitled *A Confession*, it is possible to read this line as a retraction of the claims made in the 'Preface' for the confessional nature of the book. But if this is the case then it is simply a tautological restatement of the opening line of the 'Note': 'This book is a work of fiction' (Roth 1993a: n.p.). If, on the other hand, the phrase '[t]his confession' refers not to the novel as whole but only to the contents of the 'Note', then it becomes a disclaimer of the disclaimer, a retraction of the confession that the novel is not a confession. This interpretation is supported by the fact that, within the main narrative, 'Roth' actually debates the pros and cons of inserting 'three formulaic sentences' (beginning 'This book is a work of fiction') which would serve as 'the standard disclaimer' at the front of the book, allowing it to retain 'the appearance of autobiography while acquiring the potentialities of the novel' (361).

There are a number of parallels between Roth's ambiguous use of generic markers in *Operation Shylock* and Bret Easton Ellis's practice in *Lunar Park*. On the back of the dustjacket of the first British edition of Ellis's book a sentence from the novel is reproduced, without further comment: 'Regardless of how horrible the events described here might seem, there's one thing you must remember as you hold this book in your hands: all of it really happened, every word is true' (Ellis 2005: n.p.). In the novel itself, too, 'Ellis' often insists on the factual accuracy of his account, taking pains to explain that although '[n]ames have been changed', the location of the action has been left 'semi-vague' and 'the few "witnesses" who could corroborate these events have disappeared', nonetheless the events that the book describes not only occurred but 'were inevitable' (Ellis 2005: 30). Elsewhere, however, he implicitly acknowledges the fundamental implausibility of his narrative, announcing that 'I am not going to defend what I'm about to describe. I am not going to try to make you believe anything. You can choose to believe me, or you can turn away' (272). He also places dates at the head of successive chapters of the novel to give an impression of documentary precision, but omits the year, so that the narrative action cannot be located in a specific historical period. With similar ambiguity, 'Ellis' declares that '*Lunar Park* follows these events in a fairly straightforward manner, and though this is, ostensibly, a true story, no research was involved in the writing of this book' (Ellis 2005: 29).

These claims, like the paratexts that frame *Operation Shylock*, not only conflict with each other but contain internal contradictions. Even as he urges the reader to 'remember as you hold this book in your hands' that 'every word' of it is 'true', the very terms in which he makes his appeal (the explicit address to the reader and the invocation of the physical object, the book) serve as a reminder of the artifice and the artefact that makes the claims to truth of any book (fiction or non-fiction) problematic. Conversely, when 'Ellis' claims that he will not attempt to persuade the reader of the veracity of his narrative, he loads the terms of the choice that he appears to offer: '[y]ou can choose to believe me, or you can turn away'. A decision not to believe him becomes not a matter of subjective judgement, but rather an indication of cowardice, or betrayal, a result of the reader's own shortcomings rather than the narrative's; a reader who 'turn[s] away' is a reader whose nerve has failed, who prefers to avert her or his glance rather than confront troubling realities. Then again, 'Ellis's' claim that *Lunar Park* is 'a true story' is highly equivocal: why, after all, would any research be required if this were so? And why does 'Ellis' insert the qualifiers 'fairly' and 'ostensibly', which complicate any notion of simple truth? Whereas Roth had, earlier in his career, complained that *Portnoy's Complaint* had been 'a novel in the guise of a confession that was received . . . as a confession in the guise of a novel' (Roth 2001a: 254), and had later written *Operation Shylock*, a novel in the guise of a confession that presents itself as a confession in the guise of a novel, Ellis points out early in *Lunar Park* that his first novel, *Less Than Zero*, 'was mistaken for autobiography' when actually it was 'much less a roman à clef than most first novels' but later claims, paradoxically, that 'I could never be as honest about myself in a piece of non-fiction as I could in any of my novels' (Ellis 2005: 24, 7). He presents material that is clearly invented as though it were factual.[34]

In both Roth's and Ellis's novels contradictory indicators of genre are further complicated by their emphasis on the author-protagonists' mental fragility, the legacy of a dependence on drugs with hallucinatory side-effects. In *Lunar Park*, 'Ellis' is an unapologetic, habitual user of recreational drugs, and it is as products of his addiction that the supernatural elements of the novel – his fictional creations coming to life, his father communicating with him from beyond the grave, his new suburban home gradually transforming itself into a replica of the house in which he had grown up, his daughter's toy pet (a 'Terby') hounding him and finally metamorphosing into a gruesome beast – can be accommodated in a realistic framework. 'Ellis' himself, however, refuses to allow this explanation to go unchallenged. When things begin to spiral out of control (the 'cream-colored 450 SL' car that 'Ellis' keeps seeing turns out not simply to resemble the automobile that his father used to drive, but to carry 'the same exact' licence plates, the furniture in his office keeps mysteriously rearranging itself, the Terby savages a mouse), 'Ellis' explicitly discusses the possibility (repeatedly insinuated by his wife) that he is hallucinating, only then to reject it:

> I was adept at erasing reality. As a writer, it was easy for me to dream up the more viable scenario than the one that had actually played itself out . . . Maybe the marijuana had created those manifestations I had supposedly witnessed . . . As a writer you slant all the evidence in favor of the conclusions you want to produce and you rarely tilt in favor of the truth . . . this is what a writer does: his life is a maelstrom of lying . . . A writer's life is basically one of stasis, and to combat this constraint, an opposite world and another self have to be constructed daily . . . lying often leaked from my writing life . . . into the part of me that was tactile and alive. But . . . I was at a point at which I believed the two had merged and I could not tell one from the other.
>
> Or so I told myself. Because I knew better. I knew what had happened last night.
>
> Last night was the reality. (146–7)

'Ellis' momentarily admits that his drug use might have been responsible for the 'manifestations' that he has 'supposedly witnessed', the qualifying adverb reinforcing the suggestion that he might not be the most reliable of narrators. Yet he presents this interpretation as a convenient evasion of the truth. If he were to present such a version of events, 'Ellis' argues, his book would seem more real, since it would conform to the conventions of realism. Moreover, to do so would be to be true to himself as writer, since his stock in trade is to 'erase reality' and replace it with a 'more viable scenario'. 'Ellis' decides that in this case he wants to reject the tendentious nature of fiction (that 'slant[s] and 'tilt[s]') and offer instead a straightforward account of events. It is the very unlikelihood of the events he describes, he suggests paradoxically, that should convince the reader that they have been left untransformed by the alchemy of fiction. Yet the terms in which he defends his reliability implicitly undermine it. By conceding that lying is his *modus operandi*, he calls into question every assertion he makes, presenting us with a modern version of Xeno's paradox: if a writer is never to be trusted, can his assertion that he can never be trusted, be trusted? Or for that matter his assertion that he has, on this occasion, dispensed with the rhetoric of fiction and adopted the discourse of autobiography? These questions are further complicated by the fact that 'Ellis' acknowledges, in a formulation that closely echoes statements made by Roth, that the writer's antidote to the uneventfulness and inertia of his own working life is to create a series of alternative selves, whose actions in the written world are at once 'opposite' to those of his creator in the unwritten world and shaped by them. Although this passage finishes with 'Ellis' claiming that he is still able to distinguish between these two dimensions, the tendency of the novel as a whole is to suggest that the distinction is purely hypothetical. It is the cross-contamination between these two realms of existence (the 'lying leak[ing]' from one to the other) that is the subject of Ellis's book – and Roth's.

A week after he has spoken to Pipik on the telephone, 'Roth', still suffering from the effects of jetlag, having flown to London to be with Claire Bloom, begins 'to wonder if [his conversation with Pipik] . . . had not perhaps occurred in dreams' and to suspect that 'the imposturing other whose inexplicable antics I had been warned about . . . was a specter created out of my own fear of mentally coming apart . . . a nightmare about the return of a usurping self altogether beyond my control' (Roth 1993a: 29). The suggestion that Pipik might be a symptom of a relapse into mental instability or a figment of 'Roth's' paranoid imagination – a manifestation of schizophrenia or a hallucination inspired by the ironically named sleeping drug, Halcion, to which 'Roth' had become addicted – is, however, no sooner entertained than it is summarily dismissed as wishful thinking: 'I recognized what a pipe dream it was to be telling myself that I had only been dreaming' (30). This might seem a rather paradoxical statement, given that 'Roth's' uncertainty about the reality of Pipik would suggest that his recovery from his breakdown is fragile, if not entirely illusory. It is a scenario arguably more disturbing in its implications than the more prosaic explanation that a conman is appropriating his identity for dubious political purposes. It is also, of course, ironic that 'Roth' seems to discredit definitively the only rational hypothesis for the extraordinary events that follow. Although he does on one further occasion briefly consider the possibility that 'everything I took to be actuality . . . was all a Halcion hallucination', he presents this thought as itself a delusion: the product of a semi-conscious mind, 'half dozing' and capable only of 'groggily thinking' about his situation, rather than analysing it logically (176). And that seems to be that.

Towards the end of the book, however, 'Roth', once more 'strangely uncertain about the book's verisimilitude', finds himself 'half believ[ing] that even if I had not invented *Operation Shylock* outright, a novelist's instincts had grossly overdramatized it' and consequently 'wondering if it might be *best* to present the book not as an autobiographical confession . . . but . . . as fiction' (359–60; 360–1). Even if he publishes it as non-fiction, 'Roth' anticipates '*Operation Shylock*, misleadingly presented as a novel, being understood by an ingenious few as a chronicle of the Halcion hallucination that, momentarily, even I . . . almost supposed it might be' (361). In this passage, 'Roth' again articulates doubts about the veracity of events, but in terms that are themselves so doubtful as to disown the very scepticism they apparently express. By describing his uncertainty about the book's claims to realism as 'strange', 'Roth' implies that his self-distrust is not to be trusted; by discussing the possibility that *Operation Shylock* might '*best*' be published as a novel in order to bypass any potential controversy, 'Roth' invites his readers to infer that such a decision would sacrifice integrity to pragmatism and would be an act of moral cowardice and intellectual fraudulence. Even as he seems to question the authenticity of his own account, 'Roth' hedges his scruples with a series of qualifications – 'I *began* to *half* believe . . .', '*momentarily*, even I . . . *almost supposed* it *might* be' – that paradoxically serve to reinforce, rather than undermine, his credentials as a reliable narrator. It is possible to see this as a case of 'Roth' (and Roth) having his postmodernist cake and eating it: another example of what Nathan Zuckerman in *The Facts* calls Roth's 'self-defensive trick[s]' (Roth 1988: 192). It seems to me, however, that in *Operation Shylock* Roth steps outside the usual generic parameters of his fiction (from realism to postmodernism), and outside its moral continuum (from self-defence to self-accusation), into the realm of self-parody. Moreover, his self-deconstructing strategies are deployed in a larger critique of the premises that underpin contemporary fiction and its critics: *Operation Shylock* is, among other things, a parody of both realism and postmodernism.

Again, there are echoes of Roth's novel in Ellis's. In *Lunar Park*, Ellis deploys the terms 'real' and 'unreal' (and a series of synonyms) in ways that destabilise the meaning of both words. Early in the novel, 'Ellis' describes the way in which his public persona, as viewed through the distorting lens of a celebrity-obsessed culture, began to overwhelm his private sense of self: 'I was on display. Everything I did was written about' (Ellis 2005: 9). As this virtual, written world becomes increasingly dominant, 'Ellis' writes that 'the real world . . . [began] to melt away' (8). It is, he implies, partly as a response to this feeling of self-alienation that he decides, within the pages of *Lunar Park*, to retreat to the suburbs with his family. On the eve of the Halloween party that he is hosting, he announces to Jayne: 'I've decided against wearing masks . . . I want to be real . . . This is what's known as the Official Face' (32). Clearly, this statement works on a number of different levels of signification. Literally, 'Ellis' has decided not to dress up for the Halloween party; metaphorically, he has resolved to discard the inauthentic posturing of his pre-married existence; to embrace his new life and simply, as the popular therapeutic argot has it, 'be himself'. In the context of the novel, however, it also stands as a statement of aesthetic and ethical principles: 'Ellis' is going to play it straight, tell it like it is (was), reject the masks of fictional personae in favour of an apparently autobiographical self. This, of course, highlights another of the novel's paradoxes, the paradox at the heart of the narcissistic, incestuous relationship between contemporary celebrities and the media: 'Ellis' responds to the myths engendered by his over-exposure in the media by exposing himself still further, in the same way that many celebrities decide to 'tell their side of the story', in which they complain of media intrusion into their lives. Unlike many such media figures, however, who promote their autobiographies as their chance to 'set the record straight', to tell their story in their own (or at least in a ghost writer's version of their own) words, 'Ellis' is acutely aware of the ironies involved in such an enterprise. Just as 'Ellis' adds a self-satirical postscript ('This is what's known as the Official Face') to his initial claim that he intends to 'be real', so *Lunar Park* is not a serious attempt at autobiographical realism, but a parody of such an attempt.

Like *Operation Shylock, Lunar Park* ostensibly strives to render the credible incredible, and the incredible credible. Describing his humdrum experiences as a husband and father, 'Ellis' confesses that '[i]t all seemed vaguely unreal to me'; the quiet town in which he has set up home 'seemed dreamed up'; the conversation at a dinner party where marijuana forms part of the menu modulates into 'thick parodies of drug talk' (29, 74, 135). If the quotidian seems queer, the extraordinary is represented as though it were a matter of fact. When 'Ellis' finally discovers that the man committing the copycat murders from *American Psycho* is not the ghost of Patrick Bateman, but a psychopathic fan named Bernard Erlanger (the same man who interviews 'Ellis' earlier in the novel in the guise of a detective named Donald Kimball supposedly investigating the case), he finds it hard to accept this more realistic explanation:

> I still wanted to believe that the killer was fictional. That his name was Patrick Bateman (not Bernard Erlanger, or even Donald Kimball), and for a brief time . . . he had become real, as so many fictional characters ultimately are for their creators – and for their readers as well[.] (301)

Even after Erlanger has been arrested, questions remain unanswered: notably, how is it that he reenacts a murder that never appeared in the final, published version of Ellis's novel, but was part of an earlier version authored by 'Ellis'? Erlanger assures 'Ellis' that he – the author – is not in danger, since the killer only seems interested in murdering the namesakes of characters in *American Psycho,* before posing the metafictional question: 'You're not a fictional character, are you, Mr. Ellis?' (124). When an unidentified caller with intimate knowledge of the author's life cross-examines 'Ellis' over the telephone, 'Ellis' immediately assumes that the voice addressing him is that of Clayton, the protagonist of *Less Than Zero,* come to life. 'Ellis's' attempt to deny the reality of this man ('"You're not even real. You don't exist"') is, as the caller's response implies ('"If you think so, then why are you still on the line?"'), a self-cancelling strategy, since the mere fact of 'Ellis's' engagement in the dialogue presupposes the existence of an interlocutor (230). These ambiguities as to the nature of reality arguably owe less to the prevailing ontological scepticism of postmodernism than to the parody of it that Roth mounts in *Operation Shylock.*

As I have emphasised in the earlier sections of this chapter, the concept of reality is often interrogated in Roth's work, but nowhere else in his *oeuvre* is the word itself as ubiquitous, or as slippery, as in *Operation Shylock*. When 'Roth' first learns of Pipik's existence, he reassures himself by claiming that 'up against reality I had at my own disposal the strongest weapon in anyone's arsenal: my own reality' (Roth 1993a: 36). This statement is, of course, ambiguous: it could mean simply that 'Roth's' (rediscovered) belief in the fact of his own existence enables him to confront unfazed the fact of Pipik's existence. Equally, it could be interpreted as self-contradictory: even as it invokes the (classically realist) belief in an objective, external world (the 'reality' that 'Roth' decides he is 'up against' in the form of Pipik), it has recourse to the (characteristically postmodernist) notion that all existence is subjectively constructed: 'Roth' will oppose the reality of Pipik with his 'own' version of reality. That the two men – and the two versions of reality they represent – cannot peacefully coexist, is one point on which 'Roth' is unequivocal. From the outset, he interprets Pipik as a challenge to his own selfhood but at first he welcomes that challenge, believing that it will, paradoxically, strengthen his self-definition. During the darkest days of his Halcion-induced depression 'Roth' experiences a sense of self-alienation so severe that he is moved to ask '"Where is Philip Roth . . . Where did he go?"'.[35] But with the emergence of Pipik, he feels, for the first time since his breakdown, a renewed vitality, the return of his 'old resolve, vying once again with an adversary a little less chimerical than sickly, crippling unreality' (22, 37).

As the novel proceeds, however, 'Roth' begins to see Pipik not as the solution to the existential anxieties that assailed him under the baneful influence of Halcion, but rather as their embodiment. Instead of using Pipik's reality as a way of negatively defining his own ('I am not he; he is not me'), 'Roth' increasingly represents his 'Jerusalem counterself' as a rival author whose plot he must overwrite with his own (29). This is why, rather than attempting to reclaim his own identity from the man who has tried to usurp it, 'Roth' decides to play him at his own game; instead of disowning the doctrine of Diasporism, he becomes its advocate, out-Pipiking Pipik. By shifting the battleground from the personal to the professional, the question becomes not 'who is the real Philip Roth?' but 'who is the more persuasive author?'. 'Roth' depicts himself as the champion of realism and Pipik as the archexponent of unreality: a postmodernist with a reckless disregard for the integrity of identity and reality. Instead of expressing moral indignation at Pipik's imposture, then, 'Roth' criticises its lack of realism. He decides that Pipik is 'someone trying to be real without any idea of how to go about it, someone who knows neither how to be fictitious – and persuasively pass himself off as someone he is not – nor how to actualize himself in life as he is' (245). He condemns the 'unhistorical imagination that dreamed up the improbabilities and exaggerations of Diasporism' (241).

There are moments when 'Roth' is enraged by Pipik's behaviour. When he learns that Pipik has promised his ('Roth's') cousin Apter that he can live in 'Roth's' 'barn in Connecticut', for example, he imagines 'ripping the tongue out of Pipik's mouth with my own two hands'. Even in this instance, however, the form that this vengeful fantasy takes (depriving Pipik of a voice) and the fact that 'Roth's' initial reaction to this manipulation of his cousin's emotions is to wonder, in a rather more abstract vein, 'Which does Pipik despise more, reality or me?', both tend to situate the private grievance in the context of the public struggle for narrative supremacy (265, 264). Really, such a struggle ought to be short-lived. As 'Roth' puts it, 'it would be only natural, to assume that in a narrative contest (in the realistic mode) with this impostor, the real writer would easily emerge as inventive champion' (247). Again, this formulation underlines the paradoxical nature of realism, since 'Roth' believes that what will enable him to triumph in any competition 'in the realistic mode' are his superior imaginative faculties: a 'real writer' confirms his credentials by demonstrating his capacity to deviate from what is real, his gift for invention. It takes 'Roth' two-thirds of the book to 'think out an effective counterplot in which to subsume the Pipikesque imbecility' and when he finally does write Pipik out of the novel, the mode of the writing remains as unrealistic as ever (246).

This is the central irony of the novel, for while 'Roth' presents himself as an advocate of realism, advising Pipik to '[s]urrender yourself to what is real . . . surrender to reality', he is in fact the real architect of the myriad absurdities of the novel (204). He complains that 'the story of my double was difficult to accept at face value', admits that 'my own behavior [was not] much more plausible to me than anyone else's', and that '[t]he implausibility of so much that is happening even causes [me] . . . to ask [my]self if any of it *is* happening', and finally 'slips silently out of the plot on the grounds of its general implausibility'. In short, he has indicted himself for the very crimes with which he charges Pipik (287, 150, 242, 245).

There is a similar paradox at the heart of *Lunar Park*. From the middle of the novel onwards, 'Ellis', like 'Roth', finds himself struggling for narrative control, first of all with Clayton, the putative phantom from his own *oeuvre*, to whom he refers, ambiguously, as 'the fictional character, the boy who was rewriting my book' (it is not clear whether the book that Clayton is allegedly rewriting is *Less Than Zero* or *Lunar Park* itself), and then with himself. Or rather, with an alternative version of himself, who may or may not be Ellis the author (183). In other words, in the latter stages of the novel, 'Ellis' begins to bifurcate into the self he refers to as 'the writer' and his narrating self. Sometimes the narrating 'Ellis' refers to the two selves as 'we', and they seem to be working in consort; at other times, 'the writer' is presented as an antagonist, whose cryptic utterances, rendered in italics, taunt the narrating 'Ellis' with his superior (fore)knowledge of events ('*You'll find out tonight*', he tells the narrator when 'Ellis' asks him to explain comments that he makes about Robby's computer) and flaunt his authorial omnipotence ('*Look how black the sky is . . . I made it that way*', he instructs 'Ellis' at the end of chapter 20) (222, 216). As 'Ellis's' sense of self continues to disintegrate,[36] and the generic status of the novel begins to fracture, he takes refuge in the notion that its excesses are being dictated by another hand: 'I was gradually becoming comforted by the unreality of the situation . . . I was living in a . . . novel, an idiot's dream that someone else was writing' (190). If this is designed as a disclaimer – a knowing, postmodernist critique of the novel's lack of realism – it is directly contradicted by what 'Ellis' says about his own fictional sequel to *American Psycho* (composed within the pages of *Lunar Park*), in which he constructs a scenario fatal to Patrick Bateman. This story, 'Ellis' observes, 'was static and artificial and precise . . . [not] a dream – which is what a novel should be' (283).

On the one hand, 'Ellis' presents himself as the embattled defender of an old-fashioned notion of realism, repeatedly complaining of the incredulity that he encounters: 'my recollection was deemed unreliable . . . my account of the accident was written off'; Kimball 'didn't trust the story line anymore' (299, 188). On the other hand, he is incredulous when Robert Miller, the paranormal investigator he calls in to exorcise the spirit of his father from his new home, fails to baulk at the improbability of the novel's plot:

> I began explaining what was happening in a calm and linear fashion, but soon I was grabbing at everything I had witnessed . . . and I just kept on

> haphazardly piling on the details . . . He was taking the jagged, nonsensical plotline in stride [.] (255–6)

Like 'Roth', 'Ellis' first accuses his literary rival within the novel of indulging in extravagant fantasy (of writing 'an idiot's dream' whose defining characteristic is its 'unreality'), and then draws attention to the perversities and inconsistencies (the 'nonsensical' nature) of his own storytelling technique. Furthermore, the metafictional terms in which 'Ellis's' credibility as a narrator is challenged echo those in which 'Roth's' authority in *Operation Shylock* is undermined.

The attempts that 'Roth' makes to render 'credible a somewhat extreme, if not outright ridiculous, story' are invariably sabotaged by the other characters in the book, for whom he is as 'out of contact with reality' as he imagines them to be (314, 265). 'Roth's' version of reality is repeatedly threatened. At the beginning of the novel, Claire Bloom responds to 'Roth's' (unwittingly?) ironic plea for calm ('"How about some realism?"') by asking him to '"Promise me you won't do anything ridiculous"' (38). At the end, Smilesburger's verdict on the manuscript version of *Operation Shylock* is: '"This is not a report of what happened, because, very simply, you haven't the slightest idea of what happened. You grasp almost nothing of the objective reality"' (390). When 'Roth' reproaches Pipik for the absurdity of his schemes, Pipik responds, echoing many a critic of Roth's fiction, by accusing 'Roth' of solipsism: 'Reality. So banal, so foolish, so *incoherent* – such a baffling and disappointing nuisance. Not like being in that study in Connecticut, where the only thing that's real is you' (348). Even 'Roth' on one occasion wonders if he is becoming 'one of those writers with no grasp on reality', on another asks 'where the hell *was* my sense of reality?', and further concedes that '[w]hat I was elaborating so thoroughly as a rational explanation of reality was infused with [what] . . . psychiatrists regularly hear from the most far-gone paranoid on the schizophrenic ward' (159, 167, 290).

If the nature of reality in *Operation Shylock* is hotly contested, however, that is not to say that the novel necessarily endorses Vladimir Nabokov's observation that reality is 'one of the few words which mean nothing without quotes' (Nabokov 1971b: 283). At one point 'Roth' explicitly acknowledges – and condemns – the postmodernist piety that reality is contingent and subjective: 'Even the gullible now have contempt for the idea of objectivity; the latest thing they've swallowed whole is that it's impossible to report anything faithfully other than one's own temperature; everything is allegory – so what possible chance would I have to persuade anyone of a reality like this one?' (216). Roth's strategy for resolving this predicament is apparently to insist, as he had done in his 1960 essay 'Writing American Fiction', on the extraordinary improbability of reality itself as an implicit defence of the extravagant hyperbole of his book. As Mark Shechner puts it: '*Operation Shylock* commits its excesses in order to keep pace with a world in which the excessive is the commonplace and the outrageous the ordinary' (Shechner 2003: 135). In other words, if life is stranger than fiction, then fiction has the licence to be very strange while still being true to life. Rather than quoting his younger self (as he might well have done, given the extensive self-citation of the novel), Roth uses the text of his interview with Appelfeld to make this argument. About halfway through *Operation Shylock*, 'Roth' reproduces a portion of his interview with Appelfeld in which he asks the Israeli novelist (with a self-conscious nod to 'Writing American Fiction') whether, given the rich material of contemporary Israeli society, he ever considers writing fiction that deals with this '*news-producing reality*' (217, italics in original). Appelfeld deflects the question politely, but the real reply to this question is contained implicitly in responses he gives elsewhere in the interview. Speaking of his attempts initially to come to terms, and then deal faithfully in his fiction, with his experiences during the Holocaust, Appelfeld observes that wartime reality 'was far beyond the power of imagination . . . everything was so unbelievable that one seemed oneself to be fictional' (56). He extrapolates that '[r]eality . . . is always stronger than the human imagination . . . reality can permit itself to be unbelievable, inexplicable, out of all proportion' (86). The implication here is that the standards for realism in a novel in the realistic mode are too stringent to be able to do justice to the 'unbelievable, inexplicable' forms that reality itself may take, and the concomitant of this position is that the realistic novel may paradoxically become unrealistic precisely because of the constraints that it places upon itself. Seen in this light, *Operation Shylock* becomes, as 'Roth' himself puts it, as 'improbably probable, as life', 'a story whose very *point* was its improbable reality' (360), and whose very audacity testifies to 'the spellbinding reality of his [Pipik's] unreality' (346, 360, 70).

Yet, as the tortuous paradoxes of these statements indicate, this is no more a serious attempt to construct a case for the realism of this novel – to defend it against charges of implausibility – than the copious evidence it assembles of its own absurdity is a serious attempt to question the nature of reality itself, or to prosecute itself for its failure to adhere to the tenets of realism. Rather than reprising the dialectic between self-incrimination and self-exculpation that animates so much of his earlier fiction, *Operation Shylock* seems to me to be parodying it. As Debra Shostak and others (including the author himself) have suggested, Roth's fictions often enter into dialogue with their predecessors, but nowhere is this dialogue advertised so conspicuously as in *Operation Shylock*. As pointed out earlier in this chapter, *The Counterlife* revisits many of the themes of *My Life as a Man*, *The Facts* can be read as a sequel of sorts to both these novels, and *Deception* alludes to many of Roth's previous works. *Operation Shylock*, however, goes further than any of these in its self-referentiality. Timothy Parrish has observed that '*Operation Shylock* implicitly contains within it both everything that Roth ever wrote and every critical attack his work has engendered', but this might be said with equal accuracy of several of Roth's other books (Parrish 2003: 122). What is extraordinary about *Operation Shylock* is the number of *explicit* references to Roth's *oeuvre* and career that punctuate its pages.

In the opening paragraph of the main narrative, 'Roth' refers to 'the four visits [to Israel] I had made while I was working up the Israel sections of *The Counterlife*' and towards the end of the book he explains that it took him some time to decide to 'embark on this non-fictional treatment rather than to plumb the idea in the context, say, of a Zuckerman sequel to *The Counterlife*' (359). When he first meets Pipik, he thinks of him as an amalgamation of all his previous protagonists, a Frankenstein's monster assembled not from assorted physical body parts but from various bits of his literary body of work: 'It's Zuckerman, I thought . . . it's Kepesh, it's Tarnopol and Portnoy – it's all of them in one, broken free of print and mockingly reconstituted as a single facsimile of me' (34). In fact, Pipik resembles more closely supporting characters from previous novels, like Alvin Pepler (in *Zuckerman Unbound*) and Jimmy Ben-Joseph (in *The Counterlife*), whose fanatical enthusiasm for Nathan Zuckerman's work quickly gives way to resentful rivalry and a more sinister sort of fanaticism. Like Pepler and Ben-Joseph, Pipik regales his idol with a series of effusive tributes to his work that also demonstrate his credentials as a knowledgeable reader: '"The books! Those books! I go back to *Letting Go*, my favorite to this day! . . . I go back to 'The Love Vessel' in the old *Dial*! The work you've done! The potshots you've taken! Your women! Ann! Barbara! Claire!"' (71). In singling out for praise Roth's first (and also arguably least well-known) novel, *Letting Go*, as well as an early uncollected short story, 'The Love Vessel' (whose protagonist also visits Israel), Pipik demonstrates that his interest in Roth is anything but casual. Not only has he read all of Roth, but he has also more than a passing acquaintance with his biography (he cites the first names of several of Roth's long-term partners, including Claire Bloom) and an apparently encyclopaedic knowledge of the numerous critical slights that the author has suffered during his career. Expressing indignation at the fact that '*Portnoy's Complaint* [was] not even nominated for a National Book Award!' and that the integrity of *When She Was Good* was impugned, Pipik enumerates a series of grievances, quoting chapter and verse, until 'Roth' finally interrupts him (73). In subsequent conversations, Pipik reveals that he also keeps up with Roth's non-fiction, casually mentioning that 'I read your dialogue with Primo Levi last year in *The Times*' and he also flatters the author by claiming that President Kennedy once mistook him (Pipik) for the novelist and confessed that he was 'a great admirer of *Letting Go*' (181, 194). Pipik's admiration for the author's art, and sympathy for the suffering he has endured for its sake, is echoed by 'Roth's' erstwhile college friend turned Palestinian activist, George Ziad, who 'read[s] aloud to [his] son . . . "The Conversion of the Jews"' (one of the stories in Roth's first book, *Goodbye, Columbus*), 'love[s] *Portnoy's Complaint*' and 'assign[s] it to [his] students at the university' and who credits *Goodbye, Columbus* with exposing the moral bankruptcy of post-war American Jews who happily trade their history in for a slice of apple pie (121). As Ziad puts it, aphoristically: 'Brenda Patimkin dethrones Anne Frank' (132).

It is perhaps hardly surprising that 'Roth' should invoke *The Counterlife* (a novel partly set in Israel that deals with the battle between two counterselves for narrative supremacy and personal authority over their lives) in *Operation Shylock* (a book set mostly in Israel, in which the central conflict is between two men who share the same name and physical features and who attempt to appropriate each other's identity as a paradoxical means of asserting their own autonomy). To put it another way, it would be unrealistic for 'Roth' not to hark back to the earlier book. Pipik's familiarity with the life and career of Roth is also perfectly credible in the context of the plot of *Operation Shylock*. Whether you believe Pipik's own version of events (that his name really is Philip Roth and that he has modelled himself on his namesake because of this coincidence and the further accident of his physical resemblance to him), or 'Roth's' theory (that Pipik is a cynical opportunist), it makes sense that he should know his stuff. Pipik may have used the skills acquired during a career as a private detective to research Roth's past in order to pass himself off as the author, or his knowledge may be the result of amateur enthusiasm: either way, it does not require the reader's suspension of disbelief. George Ziad, too, as a Professor of literature and 'Roth's' contemporary during his time as a graduate student at the University of Chicago, has both professional and personal reasons for his interest in Roth's work. What is rather less plausible are the number of other characters who crop up during the course of the book who also happen to be readers – and fans – of Roth.

Alan Cooper has suggested that 'it would take prior interest in Roth to read *The Facts* or *Deception* with anything like total understanding'. But *Operation Shylock* is more self-reflexive than either of these texts. It is replete with allusions to Roth's *oeuvre* and seems at times to be populated almost exclusively by avid readers of Roth's work (Cooper 1996: 229). When he finds himself surrounded by Israeli soldiers after his Arab taxi driver abandons him on the outskirts of Jerusalem, 'Roth' is addressed by a 'young lieutenant who that very afternoon had read the whole of *The Ghost Writer*'. When he is accosted at his hotel by two high school students eager to question him on the finer points of his story 'Eli, the Fanatic', David Supposnik, an antiquarian book-dealer who may also be a Mossad agent, intervenes, explaining that '[t]he annual teaching of your story is always an experience for the high school students', who are 'mesmerized by Eli's plight' (168, 269). Later Supposnik also alludes to *The Ghost Writer*, reminding 'Roth' of his 'having made Anne Frank into the heroine of a literary work' – and hence also reminding readers of *Operation Shylock* of the interest in the dynamic between fiction and autobiography that the two novels share (279). Even the Israeli spymaster, Smilesburger, during the course of his final meeting with 'Roth' in a café in Manhattan, tells the author that in his retirement he has 'begun to catch up on my reading after many years . . . by reading all of your books'. He offers his verdict on *Patrimony* ('Warmhearted but tough') and finishes by insisting that 'All your writing you owe to [the Jews], including even that book about baseball and the wandering team without a home', an allusion to *The Great American Novel* (387, 380, 388).

Once again, where *Operation Shylock* goes, *Lunar Park* follows. Ellis's novel begins (in a section entitled 'the beginnings') with a series of quotations from his earlier work. The opening line of the novel – '"You do an awfully good impression of yourself"' – is measured against the opening lines of each of his three previous novels in turn, and is itself reproduced at the start of the next chapter ('the party'). The rest of the novel is peppered with references to Ellis's earlier work, particularly *American Psycho*, and the books themselves are ubiquitous – as physical objects as well as textual presences. Clayton, one of 'Ellis's' many doubles and the incarnation of the fictional protagonist of *Less Than Zero*, first appears in *Lunar Park* in the doorway of the author's office, 'holding a copy of [Ellis's] first novel, *Less Than Zero*' and introduces himself by saying 'I'm a big fan, Mr. Ellis' (Ellis 2005: 77). Later in the novel he becomes, as Pipik does for 'Roth', a rival author, who delivers a manuscript entitled 'Minus Numbers' (whose title implies that it will be an alternative version of *Less Than Zero*) (191). The man who introduces himself to 'Ellis' as a detective investigating a series of macabre murders apparently based on those committed by Patrick Bateman in *American Psycho* (but who turns out to be the murderer), arrives at the author's house brandishing a well-worn 'copy of *American Psycho*' and declaring himself 'a fan' (117, 118). Finally, 'Ellis' is continually thinking about, and handling, his own books, whether 'rearranging the endless shelves of foreign editions that lined the walls of my office' or struggling to get on with his latest work (*Teenage Pussy*), or deciding, paradoxically, to revive the character of Patrick Bateman in order to kill him off ('Ellis' hopes that fictionalising his death will enable him to exorcise his ghost) (67).

There is a fine line between representing this sort of narcissism and being guilty of it, but when 'Ellis' complains that 'being America's greatest writer under forty is a lot to live up to' that line becomes clearly visible (48). Similarly, when Alan Cooper writes that it becomes 'insufferable to hear Roth ventriloquize self-praise through a trunkfull of dummies, especially when each of these encomia interrupts the action', he is in my view missing the irony that invariably undercuts the self-praise (Cooper 1996: 265). Although Pipik professes to take Roth's part when reviewing the controversy that has surrounded his career, the fact that he has literally taken his part (i.e. is pretending to *be* him) makes the rehearsal of all these old insults and feuds appear more of an indictment than a defence of the author's reputation. Similarly, the tributes that George Ziad pays to the author are implicitly discredited by 'Roth's' observation that his old friend's speech is a barely coherent stream of 'gush, agitation, volubility, frenzy, imminent apoplexy' (122–3). The serendipity of the Israeli soldier's preferred reading matter is also parodied when, having examined 'Roth's' passport, he announces: 'This is quite a coincidence. I just . . . finished one of your books' (168). As for 'Roth's' conversations with the Mossad operatives, Supposnik and Smilesburger, their apparent approval of his work may simply be a ploy to get the author to agree to help them with 'Operation Shylock'. If this is so, Roth, far from puffing himself up in the way that Cooper suggests, is representing himself as the dupe of the crudest of plots, a sucker for the sucking up of others. Rather than indulging in shameless self-advertising, Roth is satirising the writer as self-promoter: he is parodying his own image as a writer who obsessively reads himself.

Roth had, of course, already dealt with the predicament of the writer as a cultural celebrity and satirized the attendant dangers of solipsism, in *Zuckerman Unbound* and *The Anatomy Lesson*. In *Operation Shylock*, however, the network of self-referencing forms part of a larger, intricate web of metatextuality and intertextuality that the narrative spins. As noted earlier, *Operation Shylock* samples Roth's work, as well as alluding to it, by including passages taken from his conversation with Aharon Appelfeld, but these passages are only one among many secondary texts to be incorporated within the main text of the narrative. *Operation Shylock* is a text in which other texts, and other authors, proliferate. In addition to the exchanges between Roth and Appelfeld, there is the manuscript purporting to be the diaries of Leon Klinghoffer – the Jewish tourist killed by the Palestinian hijackers of the cruise ship the *Achille Lauro* in 1985 – that David Supposnik gives to 'Roth', requesting that he write an introduction for a published version of them. There are Pipik's 'THE TEN TENETS OF ANTI-SEMITES ANONYMOUS' and the transcript of one of the 'workout tapes' that he provides to facilitate the recovery of members of this group, as well as his unfinished autobiography, *His Way* (101, 370). There are the Hebrew lines that 'Roth' copies from the blackboard of the classroom to which he finds himself confined after his abduction by Mossad (lines that 'Roth' in the novel cannot decipher, but which are reproduced and translated into English as one of the epigraphs to the book). There is Smilesburger's cheque for a million dollars, apparently intended for Pipik, but intercepted and then mislaid by 'Roth'. Finally, there are two letters addressed to 'Roth': one authored by Pipik and one by 'Roth' himself, taking on the voice of Jinx Possesski.

Whereas in *The Counterlife* the collision of different narrative voices produces a genuinely dialogic novel, a book where the plurality of voices and variety of subject positions disrupts any sense of a univocal authority, in *Operation Shylock* all texts lead back to the author. All the voices are clearly 'Roth's'. That 'Roth's' hand is behind all the other authors in the book is made explicit in a passage towards the end of the novel in which he admits to having 'no idea what had become of Pipik' and decides to fill in the blanks by 'imagin[ing] a letter from Jinx turning up in my mailbox' (361, 362). In this Pipikian postscript, 'Roth' imagines his namesake 'leaving New Jersey to move to the Berkshires, where he would write a book on Diasporism that would be his legacy to the Jews' (370). In this version of Pipik's life, his obsession with 'Roth' remains unabated, his relocation to Western Massachusetts constituting a perverse homage to 'E.I. Lonoff, whose example of Flaubertian anchoritism confirms the highest literary ideals of writer-worshiping Nathan Zuckerman, the young novice of *The Ghost Writer*' (370). Whereas Zuckerman's sense of vocation is sincere, Pipik profanes the idea of art as sacrament by 'turning into parody . . . the self-obliterating dedication of the selfless Lonoff' (370). As 'Roth' enters further into this fantasy, he decides that the true author of the letter must be Pipik ('[h]e and no one else had written this letter'), before reasserting his authorship: 'So here then is the substance of the letter I ['Roth'] came up with' (364). Yet by the time 'Roth' has finished composing Jinx's account of her life with Pipik (or Pipik's account, presented as his lover's) after their escapades in Jersusalem, he has become so involved in his own fabrication that he feels moved to write a reply to Jinx, in which he offers to 'ghost-write' for the now-deceased Pipik 'a treatise on Diasporism that he would have been proud of' (376). 'Roth' then informs us that '[t]his letter remained unanswered', but of course it could only have been answered by himself (376). Jinx's final silence echoes that of *Operation Shylock* itself (from which the final chapter – that gives the novel its name – is supposedly excised) and of Pipik in the letter that 'Roth' writes in her name: 'Roth' has her report that after his death she discovers that the pages on which Pipik had supposedly been writing his autobiography, as well as the audiotapes 'on which he'd claimed to have been recording his Diasporism book', are blank (373). It also confirms what is implicit throughout the book: that the characters of *Operation Shylock* are merely what Henry Zuckerman in *The Counterlife* refers to as the author's 'dumm[ies]' (236). When 'Roth' receives Pipik's letter, he notices 'how skillfully he had worked to make his handwriting resemble my own', when in fact it is 'Roth' himself who appropriates all the texts in the novel and makes them 'his own' (101). As soon as he receives Pipik's second communication – 'THE TEN TENETS OF ANTI-SEMITES ANONYMOUS' – he begins rewriting them; as he reads the forged Klinghoffer diaries, his voice subsumes the diarist's, so that he translates the '[u]neventful monotony' of Klinghoffer's prose into a paradoxical testimony to '[t]he incredible drama of being a Jew' (329). Even the Hebrew words on the classroom blackboard become part of 'Roth's' authorial discourse, as he copies them into his notebook and then reproduces them in the form of an epigraph to the novel.

Edmund Smyth has argued that postmodernist novels in which the author appears paradoxically involve 'both the abandonment of the authorial mode and a reinsertion of the author constructed as a discursive entity' (Smyth 1991: 13 ). This is true, I think, of *Operation Shylock*, in which 'Roth' can complain that 'I am not writing this thing . . . I don't even exist', while at the same time exerting such complete control over the narrative that even his fellow novelist, Aharon Appelfeld, 'feel[s] that I'm reading to you out of a story you wrote' (155, 31).

On the one hand, then, *Operation Shylock* is a novel about what one of its chapter titles describes as 'The Uncontrollability of Real Things' and the powerlessness of the novelist who gets caught up in a reality not of his making; a novel in which the novelist's agency disappears and he 'couldn't have felt more like everyone else's puppet' (329). On the other hand, it is a novel that constantly draws attention to the ways in which its characters are themselves puppets being manipulated by the author. 'Roth's' claim that Jinx Possesski exuded a 'radiant realness' and was 'pantingly alive' notwithstanding, the characterisation in this novel is anything but realistic: you can always see the puppets' strings; you can always hear 'Roth's' voice behind the masks of the characters (101, 104). No other Roth novel has so many long set-piece speeches – so many performances, so many turns, so many rants, riffs, tirades and diatribes – and whether the speaker is 'Roth' himself, Pipik, Possesski, Ziad, Supposnik or Smilesburger, the tone is always quintessentially Rothian. It is a novel of extremes, excesses, and paradoxes: it contains some of his strongest writing but is finally one of his least satisfying books; it is his most postmodernist novel and also the novel in which he disowns postmodernism; both a defence of traditional realism and a parody of the classic realist novel; both a self-indulgent, self-obsessed book and a book that parodies its own self-indulgence and self-obsession.

In an interview with *The Paris Review* Roth claimed that '[t]here is nothing "modernist," "postmodernist," or the least bit avant-garde' about the narrative strategies of *The Counterlife*, but that they reflect the way in which we all construct 'fictitious versions of our lives all the time, contradictory but mutually entangling stories that . . . constitute our hold on reality and are the closest thing we have to the truth' (Roth 2001a: 161). Yet the qualifications with which he hedges the terms 'reality' and 'truth' imply a scepticism on Roth's part about epistemology and ontology that is consistent with, indeed one of the defining characteristics of, postmodernist thought in all its various forms. Roth has always been ambivalent about both realism and postmodernism, preferring 'to establish a kind of passageway from the imaginary that comes to seem real to the real that comes to seem imaginary, a continuum between the credible incredible and the incredible credible', rather than working exclusively, or comfortably, in the mainstream of either tradition (Roth 2001a: 80). In *Reading Myself and Others* he describes his early floundering attempts to write what would eventually become *Portnoy's Complaint*, 'oscillating between the extremes of unmanageable fable or fantasy and familiar surface realism' before finally finding a way of marrying the two, 'joining . . . precise social observation with extravagant and dreamlike fantasy', in the manner of Lenny Bruce (Roth 2001a: 33, 18). Similarly, writing of the composition of *The Breast*, he notes that the greatest 'difficulty in writing this kind of story is deciding what sort of claim to make on the reader's credulity: whether to invite him to accept the fantastic situation as taking place in the recognizable world (and so to respond to the imagined actuality from that vantage point, with that kind of concern) or whether to ignore the matter of belief and move into other imaginative realms entirely – the worlds of dream, hallucination, allegory, nonsense, play, literary self-consciousness, sadism, and so on' (Roth 2001a: 57). Although he has tended either to dismiss literary criticism as irrelevant ('structuralism . . . really hasn't played any part in my life') or to represent himself as antagonistic to it ('[t]he fashion now is to praise books you don't believe in . . . But I *want* belief, and I work to try to get it'), it is clear that the kind of thinking generally referred to in the academy as 'theory' has influenced him, directly or indirectly (Roth 2001a: 103, 111). Whereas the interest in Freudian psychoanalysis in works such as *Portnoy's Complaint* and *The Breast* is signalled explicitly, the emphasis in *My Life as a Man, The Counterlife, The Facts, Deception* and *Operation Shylock*, on the self as contingent, mutable, provisional, perennially improvised – as a performance and/or rhetorical construction – cannot be so readily associated with one particular figure or school. Nonetheless it has coincided with work by many theorists across a range of disciplines (sociology, philosophy, psychology, anthropology, linguistics, gender studies) that challenges and deconstructs the idea of a unified, sovereign, stable, core Cartesian self. Indeed, the idea of the self as fractured and fragmented – the product of language and/or of social structures rather than the expression of an essential identity – is one of the central tenets of postmodernism and has become a new orthodoxy. Whether or not we label the works that I have discussed in this chapter postmodernist is finally a matter of taste, or fashion; what remains plain is that for a period of two decades or so, from the mid-1970s to the mid-1990s (a period that saw the heyday of postmodernism), Roth engaged in a series of generic experiments that seem quite distinct from the work that preceded and succeeded them and that not only reshaped his own career but also extended the possibilities of contemporary American fiction.

If Roth's period of generic experimentation rehabilitated him in the view of some postmodernist critics, it arguably alienated him from many of his earlier readers, generating modest sales. Moreover, the mixed reception of *Operation Shylock* – and John Updike's reservations in particular – came, as Claire Bloom puts it, 'as a great blow to Philip's morale' (Bloom 1996: 212). These things may or may not have preyed on his mind, but at any rate after *Operation Shylock* Roth returned to the realist novel. If the form of *Sabbath's Theater* was relatively conventional, its content was as radical as anything Roth had ever published.

## Notes

1 For example, she quotes Halkin's claim that Roth cares 'less about bestowing independent destinies on his fictional protagonists and more about maintaining them in a dialectical relationship to their creator' (Halkin 1994 quoted in Shostak 2004: 9). She also summarises in some detail Patrick O'Donnell's Lacanian reading of *My Life as a Man*, in which he argues that Peter Tarnopol, the ostensible author of the three sections of the novel, is 'more a process than a character' (O'Donnell 1988 quoted in Shostak 2004: 171).

2 Again, Shostak agrees with Halkin, who has 'no sense of outside influences' in Roth's fiction, suggesting that 'had postmodernism not existed, he [Roth] would have been quite capable of inventing aspects of it himself' (Halkin 1994 quoted in Shostak 2004: 188).

3 Although there is no clear consensus on the meaning of the word, definitions of postmodernism tend to be couched in these terms. Edmund Smyth, for example, observes '[t]hat the self can no longer be considered a unified and stable entity has become axiomatic in the light of poststructuralism' and lists '[f]ragmentation, discontinuity, indeterminacy, plurality, metafictionality, heterogeneity, intertextuality, decentring, dislocation, ludism', as well as '[p]arody, pastiche, quotation and self-quotation' as postmodernism's defining features (Smyth 1991: 10, 9, 10). For Morris Dickstein, postmodernism 'conveys the sense that all texts are provisional, that we live in a world already crowded with texts, that originality is a romantic illusion, and techniques like collage, pastiche and pseudocommentary are better than realism for conveying a sense of belatedness and repletion' (Dickstein 2001: 74). Elaine Safer points out that '[p]ostmodern novelists usually mix genres – history, fiction, non-fiction, film – and they delight in exploring the contrarieties and confusion of twentieth century [sic] society. They are encyclopedic in scope, utilizing details from élite and from popular culture. And they show an anti-rationalist and an antirealist emphasis, as they look to the word . . . to determine a metareality. Meaning, if it exists at all, exists only in the words and the structure we impose on language' (Safer 2003a: 102).

Many critics have also emphasised the paradoxical nature of post-modernism: Linda Hutcheon observes that the 'negativized rhetoric' that pervades postmodernist discourse – 'discontinuity, disruption, dislocation, decentring, indeterminacy and antitotalization' – 'incorporate[s] that which [it] aim[s] to contest – as does . . . the term postmodernism itself' (Hutcheon 1988: 3). Alexander, likewise, suggests that 'the postmodern novelist . . . renders the poststructuralist reading redundant: the text which refuses to stabilize its own meaning cannot be further destabilized' (Alexander 1990: 15).

4 Of course these terms that are used to define realism are themselves the product, and reflect the premises, of postmodernist discourse.

5 See Brauner 2005.

6 See Brauner 1995: 79–88.

7 I am indebted to Christine MacLeod for a number of observations that inform my discussion of *The Things They Carried.*

8 In recent years, Roth has begun grouping his books under different headings – 'Zuckerman books', 'Roth books', 'Kepesh books', 'Miscellany', and 'Other books' – in the preliminary pages. In this taxonomy, *My Life as a Man* is listed under 'Other books' rather than under 'Zuckerman

books', but that does not invalidate this reading, particularly given the characteristically disingenuous nature of this arrangement, which imposes, retrospectively, a pattern that is potentially misleading.

9 See Roth 1985: 58, 122, 268–70, 272–3.

10 Milly Theale is a wealthy American heiress in Henry James's novel *The Wings of the Dove* (1902), Hans Castorp is the protagonist of Thomas Mann's *The Magic Mountain* (1927) and Arthur Dimmesdale is the minister who secretly fathers Hester Prynne's child in Nathaniel Hawthorne's *The Scarlet Letter* (1850). *The Scarlet Letter* is one of the 'core' texts that Tarnopol teaches his senior literature students and the novel contains several other allusions to it, for example when Tarnopol observes that his analyst Spielvogel 'reminded me of . . . Dr. Roger Chillingworth' while he himself 'sat facing him as full of shameful secrets as the Reverend Arthur Dimmesdale' (Roth 1985: 233, 203). *The Scarlet Letter* seems to me to be one of the syringes that feeds most consistently into Roth's fiction, from the prologue to *The Great American Novel* in which Smitty devotes two pages to debunking Hawthorne's claim to that title (Roth 1981: 36–8) through to *The Human Stain*, in which the relationship between public stigma and private shame closely echoes the theme of Hawthorne's romance, and in which Hawthorne himself is mentioned explicitly on several occasions. Mark Shechner notes in passing that '*The Human Stain* is . . . a *Scarlet Letter* [sic] about race' (Shechner 2003: 188), but for a detailed discussion of these allusions see Duban 2002. As I shall suggest later in this chapter, *The Scarlet Letter* also anticipates some of the rhetorical strategies deployed by Roth in *The Counterlife*.

11 See Roth 1988: 107–8; 149–50.

12 In 'Salad Days', Nathan Zuckerman has an older brother and a father who owns a shoe shop; in 'Courting Disaster' he has an older sister and a father who is a bookkeeper.

13 Both these suggestions are implicit in the novel's structure, in which the brothers are sometimes placed in antagonistic opposition to each other, and at other times are made to resemble each other so closely in terms of both character and situation as to seem almost identical. Characteristically, the novel reflects explicitly on their relationship in terms that reinforce this dualism. In 'Basel', Nathan Zuckerman wonders how he would respond 'if instead of the brother whose obverse existence mine inferred – and who himself untwinnishly inferred me – I had been the Zuckerman boy in that agony?', a question that is of course answered in 'Gloucestershire', when he is faced with the same dilemma that Henry faces in 'Basel' (Roth 1986: 42). In 'Judea' Nathan tells Carol that he and Henry 'know each other . . . as a kind of deformation of themselves' and later concedes that, while he is thinking that Henry has found in the Judean landscape 'a correlative for the sense of himself he would now prefer to

effect', Henry 'could have been thinking much the same of me' (80, 113). He also emphasises that, in spite of their considerable differences, their self-image is inextricably bound up with each other: 'These boys are . . . about as unlike as brothers come, but each has taken the other's measure and been measured against the other for so long that it's unthinkable that either could ever learn to remain unconcerned by the judgment his counterpart embodies' (137). In 'Christendom', Maria, exasperated by what she sees as Nathan's persecution complex, exclaims that 'You are your brother!' (304).

14 Roth's familiarity with the strategy of classical oratory is clear from Nathan's letter to Roth at the end of *The Facts*, in which he relays to his author, Maria's recommendation that 'there should, at least, be some of what Cicero calls *occupatio*' to compensate for all the omissions in the autobiography (Roth 1988: 190).

15 Alvy (played by Allen) and Annie (played by Diane Keaton) have just played tennis together, after which she drives him (hair-raisingly) back to her apartment, where they talk about photography on Annie's terrace, Alvy's spoken words undermined by a series of subtitles revealing his actual thoughts. I am indebted to Jonathan Ellis for helping me locate this scene.

16 Moore is an admirer of Roth's, as she confesses in her review of *The Human Stain* for the *New York Review of Books* (see Moore 2000: 7). I owe my acquaintance with Carol Anshaw's novel to Alison Kelly, who discusses *Aquamarine* alongside *Anagrams* in her doctoral thesis on Moore.

17 Again, I would like to acknowledge a debt here to Christine MacLeod in my reading of this passage.

18 It may be no coincidence that, in this novel that so self-consciously dissects the conventions of realism and postmodernism, Henry's metaphor recalls the title of Tony Tanner's classic study of post-war American fiction, *City of Words* (1971).

19 Given Henry's identification of the bearded mourner with Nathan, it may be significant that in his letter to Roth at the end of *The Facts* Nathan refers to his decision to grow a beard 'to mark myself symbolically as a middle-aged man in the grip of a great transformation', though Maria interprets it as a deliberate attempt to accentuate his Jewish difference (Roth 1986: 182).

20 In the opening section of 'The Custom House', Hawthorne presents his readers with an ostensibly autobiographical account of his stewardship of this institution in Salem in which he combines the disclosure of historically authentic details with the narration of purely fictional events (most notably his discovery of the scarlet letter itself). He justifies the inclusion of this 'sketch' by claiming that 'we may prate of the circumstances that lie around us, and even of oneself, but still keep the inmost Me behind its veil' (Hawthorne 1986: 35, 36). Whether or not he intended a pun on 'lie',

Hawthorne's sophisticated – and sophistical – methods of self-fashioning in this prefatory section of *The Scarlet Letter* seem to me to prefigure the strategies employed by Roth and other contemporary American novelists, serving as another reminder that many of the qualities commonly identified as postmodernist actually have a much longer literary pedigree.

21 Most striking is Roth's admission that '[t]he description in *My Life as a Man* . . . of how Peter Tarnopol is tricked by Maureen Johnson into believing her pregnant parallels almost exactly how I was deceived by Josie in February 1959' (Roth 1988: 107).

22 In real life, Roth's wife's name was Margaret. Characteristically, Roth draws attention to his decision not to give Josie her 'real' name by having Nathan Zuckerman question his motives: 'It's only right that she have her real name in there, just as you have yours' (Roth 1988: 180).

23 This accusation echoes statements that Roth himself had made in interviews with Alain Finkielkraut ('I am nothing like so sharply delineated as a character in a book') and Hermione Lee ('I am like somebody who is vividly trying to transform himself out of himself and into his vividly transforming heroes') (Roth 2001a: 110, 148).

24 By the time of the publication of *The Facts*, Roth was indeed already an able practitioner of the 'self-defensive trick to have it both ways', or, as I have put it elsewhere, 'getting in your retaliation first'. *The Great American Novel*, for example, concludes with an epilogue in which the narrator, Smitty, reproduces a number of (supposed) letters from publishers rejecting the novel on the grounds that it is 'sick', 'facile', 'far-fetched', '[t]oo long' and 'old-hat' and, as I have argued earlier in this chapter, *My Life as a Man* incorporates into its narrative several critiques of itself (Roth 1981: 378). For a detailed discussion of Roth's deployment of this strategy in *Portnoy's Complaint*, see Brauner 2005.

25 The author is implicitly identified as Roth when one of his interlocutors calls him 'Philip' and another lists a number of Roth's previous novels and female protagonists while indicting him in a mock-trial on charges of misogyny.

26 Some critics have seen it as a reference to the affair depicted in *The Counterlife* between Maria Freshfield and Nathan Zuckerman, which seems to have been based in part on the real-life relationship between Roth and the late English novelist Janet Hobhouse.

27 In order to avoid confusion, I refer to the narrator of *Operation Shylock* as 'Roth', thereby distinguishing him both from the real-life author and from his namesake in the novel itself, Pipik.

28 Although 'Roth' does not name him Pipik until much later in the narrative, the title of the book's opening chapter, 'Pipik Appears', gives him the mocking nickname (Yiddish for bellybutton) from the beginning.

29 See, for example, Roth 1993b.

30 See, for example, Baudrillard 1983.
31 In order to avoid confusion, I refer to the narrator of *Lunar Park* as 'Ellis', thereby distinguishing him from the real-life author.
32 In *Lunar Park*, 'Ellis' points out that he and McInerney had been closely associated with each other from the start of their respective literary careers and he recounts how one of his new neighbours, Mitchell Allen, at a summer barbecue, had 'pretended to mistake me for Jay McInerney' (Ellis 2005: 130).
33 In the book, whose epigraph is taken from *The Counterlife*, Kitaj expresses the 'fear' that 'if most Jews were concentrated in the Holy Land . . . it would be easier than ever to finish them off . . . with a bomb or two' (Kitaj 1989: 23).
34 Such material is not confined to details about 'Ellis's' private life, or to the supernatural elements of the novel, but extends also to the invention of a political landscape in which the worst fears of contemporary America have been realised. Hence, 'Ellis' explains that his wife, Jayne, decided that their family had to live 'at least two hours away from any large city, since that's where suicide bombers were blowing themselves up in crowded Burger Kings and Starbuckses and Wal-Marts and in subways at rush hours' (Ellis 2005: 27).
35 This is an echo of the moment of desperation in which Peter Tarnopol, reviewing his latest futile attempts to redeem his life through fiction, asks: 'Where was I when this was written?' (Roth 1985: 104).
36 This disintegration manifests itself not just in the appearance of Clayton and the writer, but in 'Ellis's' repeated self-externalisation, his sensation that he is looking at another body that is also himself ('I kept thinking I had been in that car with Aimee Light. I thought the guy in the passenger seat was myself'); 'I saw myself lying on that chaise longue, looking back up at myself') and also in his conviction that his identity has merged with that of others, whether fictional characters like Clayton ('Clayton and I were always the same person') or Patrick Bateman ('I found myself in Patrick Bateman's shoes'), or members of his own family ('I was now my father. Robby was now me') (Ellis 2005: 112, 148, 295, 122, 160).

# 4

# Old men behaving badly: morality, mortality and masculinity in *Sabbath's Theater*

> For a *pure* sense of being tumultuously alive, you can't beat the nasty side of existence. (Roth 1995: 247, italics in original)
>
> To take what's thought to be the disgraceful side of men – and by no means to apologize for it . . . But the circus, the circus of being a man – it's a circus, and the ringleader is the phallus. (Roth quoted in Shostak 2004: 21)
>
> [H]e didn't have a life, except at the cemetery. (Roth 1995: 51)

In an 'interview with [him]self' on *The Great American Novel* in 1973 (reprinted in *Reading Myself and Others*), Philip Roth recalls how he came upon a letter from Herman Melville to Nathaniel Hawthorne, in which Melville describes his elation upon completing *Moby Dick*: 'I have written a wicked book, and feel spotless as a lamb' (Melville quoted in Roth 2001a: 76). Roth 'pinned it up along with the other inspirational matter on [his] bulletin board', while at the same time acknowledging to himself that 'no matter how hard [he] tried, he could never really hope to be wicked' (76). This tension – between the desire to be morally transgressive, and a powerful sense of moral rectitude – is one which Roth repeatedly invokes when reading himself. In 'Writing and the Powers That Be', an interview with the Italian critic Walter Mauro, Roth characterises himself during his teenage years as a 'a good, responsible, well-behaved boy' and claims to have 'never written anything . . . intentionally destructive', and in his 'self-interview' he asks himself to '*explain why you are trying to come on like a bad boy – although in the manner of a very good boy indeed?*' (3, 8, 67, italics in original). Explaining the genesis of *Portnoy's Complaint*, Roth reveals that the novel partly grew out of two abandoned projects entitled *The Nice Jewish Boy* and *The Jewboy*: 'Not until I found . . . the voice that could speak in behalf of both the "Jewboy" (with all that word signifies . . . about aggression, appetite and marginality) and the "nice Jewish boy" (and what that epithet implies about repression, respectability, and social acceptance) was I able to complete a fiction that was expressive, instead of symptomatic, of the character's dilemma' (30, 29, 31). In 'Imagining Jews', Roth suggests that part of the appeal of *Portnoy's Complaint* lies in the fact that it represents 'a Jew . . . admit[ting] . . . that . . . his secret desire was really . . . to . . . be bad' (Roth 2001a: 259).

In *The Facts*, a much older Roth, recalling the timidity of his earliest undergraduate stories, observes that he had been unconsciously engaged in a project of 'proving that I was a nice boy' and that these fictions were consequently infected by a 'prissy tenderness' (Roth 1988: 60, 64). According to Roth's own account, it was only when he discovered, in a satirical attack on the anodyne platitudes of the college newspaper, his 'talent for comic destruction' that he began to find his voice as a writer (66). In a letter to his creator at the end of *The Facts*, Nathan Zuckerman suggests that the 'whole point' about Roth's fictional imagination is that it is 'always in transit between the good boy and the bad boy' (Roth 1988: 167).

Many of Roth's critics, following his lead, have commented on this moral dichotomy, particularly in relation to Roth's most notorious novel, *Portnoy's Complaint*. In a feature on Roth published on the eve of the publication of *Portnoy's Complaint*, Albert Goldman traced the origins of the novel to the childhood larks of Roth and his peers. On their way to Hebrew School, writes Goldman, 'those highly regimented Jewish kids could . . . afford to be bad. Being bad and being funny were much the same thing in Roth's mind' (Goldman 1969: 62). Many years later Alan Cooper reflected that 'Roth wants to explore what it is like to want to be bad – that is, acquisitive and carnal – when one is essentially good – that is, restrained by moral upbringing and cultural values' (Cooper 1996: 47). Cooper goes on to argue that this aspect of Roth's fiction is an expression of a culturally specific perspective: 'Many a literary hero has fallen in the heroic quest to be good . . . It is a peculiarly Jewish burden, as Roth sees it, to have to aspire to be bad' (49). More recently, Al Alvarez observed that, even at the height of his notoriety, after the publication of *Portnoy's Complaint*, Roth 'couldn't help being a good boy however much he yearned to be bad' (Alvarez

2004: 20). In an article entitled 'Purity and Danger: On Philip Roth', Ross Posnock pursues this argument further, suggesting that '[t]he unending struggle of the nice Jewish boy . . . to be a bad man comprises Roth's consuming subject in a number of novels' (Posnock 2001: 86). The thing that 'annoys or threatens' Alexander Portnoy, Roth's most notorious bad boy, more than anything else, Posnock suggests, is what Roth's protagonist terms the 'anti-humanity that calls itself nice' (85). In his efforts to disown the inheritance of the nice Jewish boy, Portnoy's antics scandalised many readers when *Portnoy's Complaint* was first published in 1969. Yet Portnoy, even at his most provocatively amoral, is a model of decorum compared to the septuagenarian anti-hero of *Sabbath's Theater* (1995).[1]

Whereas Alexander Portnoy's determination to 'be bad – and enjoy it!' smacks of adolescent rebellion, and his moral transgressions are invariably accompanied by guilt and self-reproach (only a nice Jewish boy would be so intoxicated – and at the same time horrified – by his own shamelessness), Sabbath's compulsive taboo-breaking is the expression of a credo of antagonism, his immorality an article of (bad) faith. If there was something slightly desperate, even hysterical, about Portnoy's sexual hijinks, Sabbath's concupiscence is atavistic, the expression of a primitive comic priapism; at once a defiance and an affirmation of mortality. In this chapter, I will discuss in some detail this relationship between morality, mortality and masculinity in *Sabbath's Theater*, as well as pointing out some resemblances between Roth's novel and 'The Guest' (1966), a short story by one of Roth's Jewish-American contemporaries, Stanley Elkin, and *No More Mister Nice Guy* (1998), a novel by the Anglo-Jewish writer, Howard Jacobson.

As Roth's novel opens, Mickey Sabbath is an old man whose powers are on the wane. Having enjoyed a brief moment of notoriety as a young street artist in the sixties (when he is prosecuted for obscenity after complaints about the sexual content of one of his shows), Sabbath, now in his sixties, is a 'forgotten puppeteer', unable to practise his art because of the arthritis that has deformed his fingers (Roth 1995: 3). His two alternative careers – as an avant-garde theatre director and a teacher of puppetry at a liberal arts college – both collapse suddenly, the first as a consequence of the sudden disappearance of the star of the company (Sabbath's first wife Nikki Kantarakis), and the second as a result of the confiscation by the college authorities of an audiotape of Sabbath engaging in explicit 'phone sex with one of his young female students. The 'uncensored[2] transcription' of this conversation, which is printed on the bottom half of twenty pages in the middle of the novel, demonstrates as graphically as anything else, the difference between Portnoy's decadence and Sabbath's depravity, between the *chutzpah* of the thirty-six-year-old author of *Portnoy's Complaint* and the radical audacity of the sixty-two-year-old author of *Sabbath's Theater* (215).

Although *Portnoy's Complaint* was banned from a number of public libraries in the U.S., and quickly earned a reputation as a 'dirty' book, there is actually little to offend the prudish or titillate the prurient in its pages. If its candid treatment of adolescent male masturbation is genuinely daring, readers of James Joyce and D.H. Lawrence, Henry Miller and Norman Mailer, would not have found anything novel, let alone revolutionary, in the novel's sex scenes. When, in *The Anatomy Lesson*, Nathan Zuckerman reinvents himself as Milton Appel, a famous literary critic turned pornographer, the joke is not simply on Irving Howe (on whom Appel seems to have been partly based), but on Roth himself, a serious novelist who, in the aftermath of the *succès de scandale* of *Portnoy's Complaint*, briefly occupied a place in the American popular imagination alongside Hugh Hefner and Larry Flynt as one of the pioneers of mainstream pornography.[3]

If this was a grotesque distortion of the truth – if, as I have been suggesting, there is nothing pornographic about *Portnoy's Complaint* – it must conversely be acknowledged that parts of the 'transcription' of the conversation between Mickey Sabbath and Kathy Goolsbee in *Sabbath's Theater* would not be out of place between the covers of *Playboy* or *Hustler*. Times have moved on, of course, since the publication of *Portnoy's Complaint*, and Frank Kermode's contention that in *Sabbath's Theater* Roth 'can startle hardened readers, make them pause to remark that they cannot remember having seen such language in print before' may say more about his own sense of what a 'hardened' (a deliberate pun?) reader might have encountered than it does about the experience of a wider literate audience (Kermode 2001b: 258).[4] Yet, in the context of the novel, this dialogue *is* unsettling, disturbing, even startling, on a number of levels. Because it is so unapologetically, brazenly pornographic, replete with the most hackneyed of clichés ('I want your cock. I'll get it really, really hard./ Want me to stick it in you?/I want you to stick it into me hard'), because it has no obvious redeeming literary qualities, and because this flat, banal piece of writing is inserted abruptly into the middle of a novel that displays Roth's rhetorical brilliance in almost every paragraph, it interrupts and disrupts the narrative conspicuously (221). This subversive power is amplified by the typographical device that Roth deploys in this section of the novel: rather than incorporating the Sabbath/Goolsbee conversation into the main body of the narrative, he prints the two texts concurrently, the third-person narrative voice continuing on the top half of each page, while the transcript runs along the bottom half, sectioned off in the manner of footnotes. This poses a number of dilemmas, aesthetic and ethical, for the reader. Do you continue with the main narrative and double back to read the conversation later (implicitly prioritising the authoritative narrative voice and resisting the temptation to read the more salacious material below the dividing line)? Do you read the conversation first (implicating yourself as a voyeuristic witness of the intercourse between Goolsbee and Sabbath – and in a pornographic transaction between reader and author – and relegating the narrative voice to a subsidiary role)? Or do you try to read the two texts in tandem (maximising the possibilities for confusion but averting the need for backtracking and avoiding the choice of which text to follow first)? Irrespective of the choice you make, the juxtaposition of the two texts has further implications for the way you read the novel as a whole.

The text that unravels at the top of the page (which I shall refer to as 'text 1' for the sake of clarity and convenience) consists of snatches of another conversation between Sabbath and Goolsbee – this time in his car – interpolated into Sabbath's interior monologue. Whereas in the telephone dialogue (henceforth 'text 2') the old man and the young girl speak the same language, each adhering to their roles as defined by the narrow conventions of pornographic discourse, over the course of the car journey their voices diverge. Or rather, Goolsbee's frantic attempts to reprise their earlier pornographic encounter ('"I want to suck you"'; '"I want to suck you hard"'; '"I want to suck you right here"') are juxtaposed with Sabbath's reflections on the predicament he finds himself in, and the narrator's mediation and contextualisation of those thoughts (216, 217, 223, 237). To give an accurate sense of the complex interplay of these different levels of discourse, it is worth quoting at some length:

> Across the road a couple of pickup trucks were parked in the dirt lot of the roadside nursery whose greenhouses constituted the first reassuring sign of the white man's intrusion into these wooded hills (once the heartland of the Madamaskas, to whose tribes the local falls were said – by those opposed to the profane installation of a parking lot and picnic tables – to have been sacred. It was in the numbingly cold pool of one of the remotest tributaries of those sacred falls, the brook that spilled down

the rocky streambed beside the Grotto, that he and Drenka would gambol naked in the summer. See plate 4. Detail from the Madamaska vase of dancing nymph and bearded figure brandishing phallus. On bank of brook, note the wine-jar, a he-goat, and a basket of figs. From the collection of the Metropolitan Museum. XX century A.D.)

'Get out. Disappear.'

'I want to suck you hard.'

A worker in coveralls was loading mulch onto one of the trucks – otherwise there wasn't anyone in sight. Mist was rising beyond the woods to the west, the seasonal mist that to the Madamaskas undoubtedly meant something about their reigning divinities or departed souls – their mothers, their fathers, their Morties, their Nikkis – but to Sabbath recalled nothing more than the opening of 'Ode to Autumn'. He was not an Indian, and the mist was the ghost of no one he knew. This local scandal, remember, was taking place in the fall of 1989, two years before the death of his senile mother and four before her reappearance jolted him into understanding that not everything alive is a living substance. This was back when the Great Disgrace was still to come, and for obvious reasons he could not locate its origins in the sensuous stimulus that was the innocuously experimental daughter of the Pennsylvania baker with the foreboding surname [Goolsbee]. You besmirch yourself in increments of excrement – everyone knows that much about the inevitabilities (or used to) – but not even Sabbath understood how he could lose his job at a liberal arts college for teaching a twenty-year-old how to talk dirty twenty-five years after Pauline Réage, fifty-five years after Henry Miller, sixty years after D.H. Lawrence, eighty years after James Joyce, two hundred years after John Wilmot, second Earl of Rochester – not to mention four hundred after Rabelais, two thousand after Ovid, and twenty-two hundred after Aristophanes. By 1989 you had to be a loaf of Papa Goolsbee's pumpernickel not to be able to talk dirty. If only you could run a '29 penis on relentless mischief, oppositional exuberance, and eight hundred different kinds of disgust, then he wouldn't have needed those tapes. But the advantage a young girl has over an old man is that she is wet at the drop of a hat, while to engorge him it is necessary at times to drop a ton of bricks. Aging sets problems that are no joke. The prick does not come with a lifetime guarantee. (216–19)

This passage offers both a striking counterpoint to the sexualised language of the conversation that appears beneath it and a justification of it. On the one hand, the insistent references to high culture display an erudition that is entirely alien to the genre of pornography (from the pastiche of classical pottery, with its sylvan scene that recasts Sabbath and his lover, Drenka Balich, as an amorous nymph and satyr, to the invocation of Keats, to the long list of risqué canonical writers who have made art of obscenity). On the other hand, the image of the priapic Pan-like figure depicted on the imaginary Madamaska vase, the roll call of literary pornographers, and even the allusion to Keats' poem, with its decadent imagery of sensual surfeit, ensure that the air in text 1, though rarefied, is hardly purified.[5] What finally subverts and redeems the pornography of text 2, however, is the irreverence and mordant irony of text 1.

If pornography is not usually infused with the scent of high culture, it cannot abide the heady aroma of comedy or the stench of mortality. In pornography there is no performance anxiety, no phallic flaccidity, no penile pratfalls, no flagging or ebbing of manhood or manliness. In the passage above, comedy and intimations of mortality abound. When Sabbath casts himself and Drenka as two pastoral lovers, sporting and disporting themselves with the innocence of Adam and Eve, 'gambol[ing] naked', he is parodying the genre, as is made clear from the mock attribution at the end of the first paragraph above ('From the collection of the Metropolitan Museum. XX century A.D.'). Towards the end of the second paragraph, when the subject of his penis rears its head again, Sabbath employs a metaphor drawn from contemporary life to satirise his own phallocentricity, comparing his penis to a vintage car. If the earlier image seems to connote potency, the later makes it clear that, these days, Sabbath's penis does not always rise to the occasion with the alacrity of a Greek god's ('The prick does not come with a lifetime guarantee'). What both images have in common is their representation of the penis as a comical character with a life of its own: the he-goat is depicted 'brandishing a phallus' as though it were not simply a part of himself, but an external tool, or weapon, and the conceit of 'a '29 penis' that runs on heavy fuel extends to Sabbath's member an existence independent of him. This is also true of the moment, late in the novel, when Sabbath exposes himself to Michelle Cowan, the wife of his old friend Norman: 'He chose then to undo his own robe rather than hers . . . to introduce her to his hard-on. They should meet' (336).

Sabbath's presentation of his penis as an unruly, unreliable but undaunted vehicle of pleasure is celebratory and self-aggrandising – he is blowing his own trumpet, as it were – but at the same time rueful and self-satirical. Writing of the ubiquitous satyrs of ancient Greek pottery to whom Sabbath compares himself, Howard Jacobson observes that:

> No living creature is safe from them: not women, not men, not deer, donkeys, not the goblet of the amphora itself. One pokes his phallus into a wine jug . . . another performs a feat of spectacular phallic juggling . . . They masturbate without shame . . . Their agility, no less than their libidinousness, is of an order not available to mere mortal man. (Jacobson 1997: 46–7)

Part of this description certainly applies to Sabbath: he is forever poking his penis into places it shouldn't be (from the mouth of his lover's niece to the anus of Norman Cowan's maid) and he masturbates as frequently as and more indiscriminately even than the legendary onanist Portnoy (at Drenka's grave, over a photograph of Norman Cowan's daughter and to the accompaniment of hundreds of taped conversations with young female students from Athena College). If Sabbath's libido is limitless, however, his body is all too painfully circumscribed by its mortality. At one point in *Sabbath's Theater* the narrator reminds us that '[in] the fingers uncovered, or even suggestively clad, there is always a reference to the penis' and, indeed, the youthful puppeteer relies on the dexterity of his digits not simply for the success of his street performances (the climax of which involves using one finger to undress a member of the audience while another finger distracts her with a theatrical performance), but implicitly for advertising the agility of his manhood (122). The commonplace of the finger as surrogate for the penis is also reprised in the Goolsbee/Sabbath exchange at the bottom of the page when Sabbath tells her to 'Fuck it [her 'cunt'] with your finger' (221). This being the case, it is difficult not to see the arthritis that cripples Sabbath's fingers as a symbolic castration. It is not just the physically debilitating effects of aging that afflict Sabbath, however. According to Howard Jacobson, in comedy 'the phallus [functions] as [a] site of comic forgetfulness, irresponsibility, freedom', but for Sabbath in this passage – and in the novel as a whole – phallic clowning does not banish, but rather evokes, tormenting memories: of lost loved ones, of forsaken responsibilities, of the cost of taking liberties (Jacobson 1997: 44).

The epigraph to *Sabbath's Theater* – 'Every third thought shall be my grave', from Shakespeare's *The Tempest*[6] – applies to Mickey Sabbath metaphorically, and at times literally: Roth devotes an extended episode late in the novel to Sabbath's attempts to buy a cemetery plot for his burial. In the long passage quoted above, although the 'seasonal mist' is 'the ghost of no one he knew', it is associated with the 'departed souls' of the native Indians' nearest and dearest: 'their mothers and fathers, their Morties, their Nikkis' (217–18). The movement here from generic losses – mothers and fathers – to Sabbath's personal bereavements (Morties and Nikkis referring, respectively, to Sabbath's brother, Mort, killed in action during the Second World War and to his first wife, Nikki, whose sudden disappearance Sabbath experiences as a death) belies Sabbath's apparent detachment. Although the narrator reminds us that these events precede the death of Sabbath's mother, whose ghost returns to reproach him, it is clear that Sabbath is death-haunted long before his encounters with his mother's spirit. Mortality hovers over this passage, not just in the form of the spectral mist, but in the first name of Sabbath's cousin, Morty (a pun on 'mort', French for dead/death), in the 'foreboding surname' of Sabbath's student, Goolsbee (containing a pun on 'ghoul'); and of course in Sabbath's memory of cavorting with Drenka, whose death from cancer (later in terms of chronology, but earlier in terms of the novel's narrative structure) precipitates a new morbidity in Sabbath (218).

Moreover, as we learn a few pages later (still in the section with the two partitioned texts), Sabbath's second wife, Roseanna, has tried to commit suicide on this very stretch of road, less than twenty-four hours previously, after listening to the contents of the taped conversation between Goolsbee and Sabbath (which is being broadcast by 'an ad hoc committee calling itself the [Society of] Women Against Sexual Abuse, Belittlement, Battering, and Telephone Harassment' – ironic acronym 'SABBATH' – in order to expose Sabbath's guilt) (214). Blaming Goolsbee for this (he believes – though he has no evidence – that she has deliberately allowed her recording of their conversation to fall into the hands of this committee, and the Dean of the college) – and suspecting her of trying to entrap him with repeated offers of sex on the car journey described above – Sabbath plots revenge, 'planning to take Kathy to the top of Battle Mountain and strangle her' (229). In the event, he settles for scaring her by claiming that he murdered his first wife, Nikki (a claim he will later repeat to Norman Cowan).

Before she bolts, however, Goolsbee announces: 'I love your mind. I love how you expose your mind when you talk' (244). Sabbath replies: 'My mind? Well, this is quite a revelation. *I* thought you loved my ancient penis . . . You have extracted mental favors from me without my even knowing and against my will! I have been belittled by you! My *dick* has been belittled by you' (244, italics in original). Sabbath once again characterises his penis as an autonomous creature in the spirit of self-irony. He knows full well that Goolsbee is attracted to him in spite, rather than because, of his physical condition, as the hyperbole of the epithet 'ancient' makes clear. There is also a vein of embittered sarcasm here: a heavy-handed satire on the self-righteous appropriation of the rights of victimhood by Sabbath's feminist antagonists. The method of this satire is to invert the conventional moral scheme in which men exploit women physically, so that Sabbath accuses Goolsbee of exploiting his mental attributes. This comic inversion implicitly returns us to the text of the telephone sex and takes us to the heart of the novel.

It is striking that one of the most frequently used words (recurring fifteen times in all) in the transcription of the Goolsbee/Sabbath conversation is 'good' and it concludes, after Sabbath has brought himself to orgasm, with the following exchange (in which Sabbath speaks first):

> Oh, sweetheart.
> You're an animal.
> An animal? You think so?
> Yeah.
> A human animal?
> Yeah.
> And you? What are you?
> A bad girl.
> That's a good thing to be. It's better than the opposite. You think you have to be a good girl?
> Well, it's what people expect.
> Well, you be realistic and let them be unrealistic. (234)

Roth's interest in society's expectations of 'good girls', and in their expectations of their menfolk, goes back a long way.[7] But the focus here is on Sabbath's Nietzschean attempt to recalibrate conventional indices of morality. On the subject of realism, Sabbath is ambivalent: we are told that he is 'ferociously a realist' yet he seems to have no trouble believing in his mother's ghostly presence and is well aware that in art realism is simply another mode of artifice, observing epigrammatically: 'That was realism for you. More meaning than was necessary in the nature of things' (16, 353). Elsewhere, he denounces Michelle Cowan's decision to stay married to Norman as the '"realism"' of 'putting up with it' (346). In this particular context, however, Sabbath is advancing the term 'realistic' as an antidote to the poisonous idealism of those with rigid notions of morality. To be 'unrealistic' about human sexuality, in Sabbath's view, is not simply to exhibit a tenuous grasp of reality, but to create a climate of intemperate morality that is, paradoxically, immoral.

While visiting his second wife, Roseanna, who is convalescing at a local sanitarium after her suicide attempt, Sabbath encounters one of her fellow inmates, Donald, who tells him that '[w]hoever imagines himself to be pure is wicked . . . There *is* no human purity! It does not exist! It cannot exist!' (274).[8] This sums up Sabbath's own position nicely. For Sabbath, to be fully human is not to transcend one's animal instincts but to acknowledge them; to be 'bad' is paradoxically better than to be 'good', because to be bad is to embrace one's (fallen) human condition. It is no coincidence that text 1 contains so many allusions to lost innocence – from the 'white man's intrusion into [the] wooded hills' of Madamaska, the sacred ground of its native American inhabitants, to the invocation of the Garden of Eden myth in Sabbath's description of his naked revels with Drenka, to Keats's memorable description (in 'Ode to Autumn') of the last moments before the transition from the fresh to the stale, the ripe to the rotten, to the sobbing figure of Goolsbee herself, the 'good girl' whom Sabbath 'get[s] . . . to think that she is a "bad girl"', according to SABBATH (215). Of course, SABBATH, in their crusading zeal, have oversimplified matters: Sabbath does not try to convince Goolsbee that 'it is her fault', but rather challenges the very basis on which moral labels such as 'good' and 'bad' are applied (215). For Sabbath, Goolsbee was 'his most trusted accomplice in the fight for the lost human cause' (235). It is to this cause – what we might call an amoral crusade, or the paradoxically moral imperative to insist on the essentially amoral nature of humanity – that Sabbath dedicates himself throughout the novel with a quasi-religious fervour.

In Sabbath's lexicon 'good' is always 'bad', 'bad' 'good'. When we are told[9] that Drenka was brought up by 'nice, dreary people', or that it was their 'relentlessly genial good manners that made the Balich men so impenetrably dull', it is clear that the words 'nice' and 'good' are virtual synonyms for 'dreary' and 'dull' (18). Similarly, when Sabbath expresses his admiration for Christa (one of his lovers) because she was '[u]nbesmirched by selflessness' (54), the implication is that – contrary to conventional morality – selflessness is not a desirable quality, but rather something that sullies one's good name (which is to say, something that threatens to purify one's impure humanity). Sabbath is constantly defining himself in opposition to the ethical norms of society, both linguistically ('[w]hat he loathed the way good people loathe [the word] *fuck* was [the word] *sharing*') and behaviourally (he is 'indifferent to the untransgressive run of normalized pursuits') (85, 126, italics in original). During his days as a puppeteer he takes pains to explain that 'puppets were not for children; puppets did not say, "I am innocent and good." They said the opposite' (96). In keeping with this philosophy, the atmosphere at his shows is 'insinuatingly anti-moral, vaguely menacing, and at the same time, rascally fun' (97). It is this approach to his art that leads to Sabbath's arrest on charges of indecently assaulting a young student (she allows him to undo her brassiere with his lewd finger-puppet), an episode that prefigures his run-in with the college authorities over the Goolsbee tape. If the 'insinuatingly anti-moral' tone of Sabbath's art, which he understands as both his puppetry and his taped seductions of his college students ('there was in these tapes a kind of *art* in the way that he was able to unshackle his girls from their habit of innocence'), can also be interpreted, more benignly, as 'rascally fun', the same cannot be said of his conduct as a houseguest at his old friend Norman Cowan's (213, 97, italics in original). It is this episode, even more than his treatment of Goolsbee, or of his second wife, Roseanna, that seems to place Sabbath beyond the pale, morally.

As a young man Sabbath had been taken up by two up-and-coming lawyers, 'sons of prosperous fathers and Jersey City friends since childhood': Norman Cowan and Lincoln Gelman (142). These two young men 'had extended to Sabbath that respect edged with reverence which was associated in Sabbath's mind less with the way you deal with an entertainer [. . .] than with the manner in which you approach an elderly clergyman', yet mingled with their humility is a certain pride, their idealism tempered by opportunism:

> There was something exciting for these two privileged Jewish boys in having, as they liked to say then, 'discovered Mick Sabbath.' It kindled their youthful enthusiasm to learn that Sabbath was the son of a poor butter-and-egg man from a tiny working-class Jersey shore town [. . .] There was an excitement about the way he affronted people without caring. He was not just a newcomer with a potentially huge theatrical talent but a young adventurer robustly colliding with life, already in his twenties a real-lifer, urged on to excess by a temperament more elemental than either of their own. Back in the fifties there was something thrillingly alien about 'Mick.' (142)

What this passage (which I shall return to later) illustrates, is the ambivalence of the relationship between Sabbath and his two sponsors.

There is an uneasy mixture of awe and condescension in the way that Cowan and Gelman relate to Sabbath. They address him familiarly as 'Mick' (the narrator's speech marks suggesting that this intimacy is more assumed than actual) and yet are seduced by all that is unfamiliar ('thrillingly alien') about him. They romanticise and at the same time belittle his working-class origins, exploiting the kudos that their association with him brings them, basking in his reflected glory.

When Gelman dies, Norman Cowan invites Sabbath (whom he hasn't seen for twenty-nine years) to the funeral and to visit him in New York. When Sabbath arrives, he is disappointed to see that '*nothing* about him [Norman] seemed changed' (139). Norman, however, is dismayed to see how much Sabbath *has* changed:

> Sabbath had washed his hands, face, and beard in the bathroom, and still, he realized, he unnerved Norman no less than if he had been a tramp whom Norman had foolishly invited to spend the night. Perhaps over the years Norman had come to inflate Sabbath's departure to a high artistic drama – a search for independence in the sticks, for spiritual purity and tranquil meditation; if Norman thought of him at all, he would, as a spontaneously good-hearted person, have tried to remember what he admired about him. And why did that annoy Sabbath? He was irritated not nearly so much by the perfect kitchen and the perfect living room and the perfect everything in all the rooms that opened off the book-lined corridor as by the charity. (140)

Once again, a word that is customarily a term of approbation – 'perfect' – assumes negative connotations. What provokes Sabbath even more than Norman's 'perfect' home – the external manifestation of Norman's financial success, though not of his marriage, which turns out be far from perfect – is his good-heartedness. For Sabbath, Norman's benevolence is proof of his inauthenticity, part of the project of assimilation in which so many of his Jewish generation in America enthusiastically engaged:

> He'd [Norman] made himself into that impressive American thing, a nice guy. It all but says he's one on his shirt. A nice rich guy with some depth, and dynamite on the phone at the office. What more can America ask of its Jews? (342)

By (re)inventing himself as a 'nice guy' – an unexceptional, unexceptionable, responsible citizen – Norman has become a 'normal' (the proximity of the two words is not coincidental) American, comfortable with his own material comforts. Sabbath, on the other hand, had dedicated himself at an early age 'to marshaling the antipathy of just about everyone as though he were, in fact, battling for his rights' and had 'never lost the simple pleasure . . . of making people uncomfortable, comfortable people especially' (26, 141). The rhetorical question with which Sabbath concludes his reflections on Norman's wholesome image implies that Norman has become a blandly neutral figure – the archetypal American 'nice guy' – as a way of neutralising his (threatening Jewish) difference, neutering himself. The fact that Norman is taking anti-depressants that render him impotent takes on symbolic resonance in this context.

At one point, Sabbath contemptuously observes that Norman is:

> Another sentimental Jew. You could fry the sentimental Jews in their own grease. Something was always *moving* them. Sabbath could never really stand either of these morally earnest, supercoddled successes, Cowan *or* Gelman. (145, italics in original)

Sabbath is offended as much by the adherence of his erstwhile companions to conventional social mores – by their earnest morality – as he is by their conspicuous professional achievements. As ever, his response is to be (and to go on the) offensive; to flaunt his own immorality. Just as Sabbath's sexual appetites put Portnoy's in the shade, so here he manages casually to throw off a remark (about frying Jews) whose bad taste easily exceeds any of Portnoy's infamous diatribes against his Jewish heritage. With its apparent allusion to the fate of Jewish victims of the Holocaust (I'm reminded of Bob Dylan's lines from 'With God On Our Side': 'Though they murdered six million, in the ovens they fried/The Germans now too have God on their side'), Roth at moments such as these seems to risk irrevocably alienating readers from Sabbath.[10] Sabbath's apparent anti-Semitism is not simply gratuitously insulting; it also directly contradicts earlier remarks about Norman's assimilation: is Norman too Jewish or not Jewish enough?

Generally, Sabbath seems to associate Jewishness not with sentimentality, but with something like its opposite: an unapologetic, egoistic realism, if not outright cynicism. This is apparent in a conversation late on in the novel between Sabbath and his uncle Fish (who speaks first):

> 'I got my neighbor next door I see. He's a goy. A Gentile.'
> 'Is he a nice fellow?'
> 'Yeah, yeah, he's nice.'

> 'That's good. As it should be. They're taught to love their neighbors. You're probably lucky it's not a Jew.' (388)

Once again, Sabbath's use of the words 'good' and 'nice' is imbued with irony. At the same time he is at least partially sincere when he tells his uncle that he is 'probably lucky' that his neighbour is not a Jew: Gentiles may be bland, Sabbath implies, but that is what you want in a neighbour. A Jew might be less constrained by the social niceties – less genteel than a Gentile – and give his uncle trouble. This suggestion that Jews are combative by nature echoes Sabbath's remarks earlier in the novel during an argument with Roseanna, who rebukes him for shouting at her in an irrational way. Sabbath responds by claiming that '"It's only when I'm shouting that I *begin* to think straight! It's my rationality that *makes* me shout! Shouting is how a Jew *thinks things through!*"' (95, italics in original). So how should one reconcile Sabbath's use of Jewishness here to connote hard-headed belligerence with his comment about Jewish sentimentality? The answer, I think, is to do with class (which, according to the nation's myths, is absent from, but in reality is pervasive in, American society).

What Sabbath really resents about Cowan and Gelman is not so much their privileged background *per se*, as the ways in which this background influences their view of him. Although they are well-meaning and generous to Sabbath (they foot the legal bills for his trial for obscenity and help him set up his theatre project), there is something fundamentally patronising in their patronage. Their pride in having 'discovered Mick Sabbath' has less to do with their sponsorship of a 'potentially huge theatrical talent' than the vicarious thrill they derive from identifying themselves with (but at the same time maintaining a safe distance from) his working-class *chutzpah* and effrontery. As Sabbath himself puts it, laconically: 'a lot of well-bred people need their real-lifer' (331). When he refers to Cowan and Gelman as two 'sentimental Jews', Sabbath is implicitly drawing up a (class) line between working-class Jewish realists (of whom he counts himself one) and middle-class Jews, who are insulated from the harsh realities of life, 'supercoddled' idealists who condescend to their less fortunate brethren to appease their guilt at their own sense of privilege.

When Sabbath is reunited with Norman, he encounters the same condescension (as he sees it) masquerading as hospitality. Norman gives Sabbath his daughter's room to stay in, makes an appointment for him to see his psychiatrist, brings him some warm milk to help him sleep and even gives him five hundred dollars, attached to a note 'beginning GOOD MORNING. In caps' (161).[11] Sabbath repays him by masturbating to a picture of Norman's daughter and ransacking her belongings, sodomising his maid, attempting to seduce his wife, and finally running off with some nude photographs of her in an envelope (also containing a thousand dollars), which he discovers hidden away in her bottom drawer.

These events partly echo those of 'The Guest', a short story by Stanley Elkin, published in his collection *Criers and Kibbitzers, Kibbitzers and Criers* in 1966. In Elkin's story Bertie, an aging itinerant loafer, turns up uninvited at the home of a younger middle-class couple, Richard and Norma Preminger, in search of a place to stay. The Premingers are not intimate acquaintances of Bertie, only friends of friends, and his feelings about them are at best ambivalent ('The girl [Norma] had danced with him . . . and one night – he imagined he must have been particularly pathetic, engagingly pathetic – she had kissed him', while Richard had 'patronized him'). Nonetheless, Bertie convinces them that, as he reflects to himself melodramatically, he 'had to rest or he would die' (Elkin 1990b: 92).

Bertie arrives on their doorstep just as the Premingers are preparing to depart for a vacation in New England. After an awkward conversation, Norma suggests that Bertie stay in their apartment while she and her husband are away, and Richard agrees:

> 'Sure . . . there's no reason you *couldn't* stay here. As a matter of fact you'd be doing us a favor. I forgot to cancel the newspaper, the milk. You'd keep the burglars off. They don't bother a place if it looks lived in.' He put twenty dollars on the coffee table. 'There might be something you need,' he explained. (97, italics in original)

Unable to believe his luck – '[a]t last he had a real patron' (97) – Bertie seeks reassurance from Richard and the following exchange takes place:

> 'Certainly it's all right,' Preminger said. 'What harm could you do?'
> 'I'm harmless,' Bertie said. (97)

As it turns out, however, Bertie is anything but harmless. Left alone in the apartment, he quickly begins to violate the Premingers' trust, and their possessions. He 'scoop[s] up as many of Preminger's [vinyl] recordings as he could carry . . . pile[s] them on indiscriminately . . . t[ears] the playing arm [of their turntable] viciously away', then 'browse[s] through' their books 'with his fly unzipped' in search of erotic stimulation, before 'g[etting] into drag and walk[ing] around the apartment in Norma's high heels' (100). 'Twice a day he masturbate[s] in the Premingers' bed', and he takes drugs, under the influence of which he 'pack[s] all of Norma's underwear' into a suitcase, dismantles her steam iron and defaces her paintings, taking 'some tubes of white paint and with a brush work[ing] over the figures, painting back into the flesh all their original whiteness' (110, 118). Finally, when the apartment is broken into, he allows the burglars to do their worst, even directing them towards Norma's (now ruined) paintings.

Bertie's abuse of the Premingers' hospitality, like Sabbath's of the Cowans', seems at first inexplicable: gratuitously and inexcusably malicious. Embedded in Elkin's story, as in Roth's novel, however, are the motivations for Bertie's apparently motiveless malignity. Both Sabbath and Bertie cynically exploit the liberal guilt of their hosts by exaggerating their own dependency. Bertie relies on 'all the pathos of the figure he knew he deliberately cut' (Elkin 1990b: 102). Sabbath, even while apparently in the midst of a nervous breakdown, reflects that '[i]f he was . . . only simulating, then this was the greatest performance of his life' and later is 'fairly sure that he was half faking the whole collapse' (Roth 1995: 149, 185). The ambiguities here notwithstanding (the first sentence is couched in the conditional tense, and the second is full of qualifications), there is an insistent emphasis on Sabbath as 'a lover and master of guile' (Roth 1995: 147, my italics). Even when Sabbath faints we are told that '[t]here was craft in Sabbath's passing out' (Roth 1995: 349), just as Bertie, though genuinely pathetic, also self-consciously accentuates his pitiable condition. At the same time they resent the smug superiority implied by their hosts' generosity, the conceit of their condescension, and they have a deep-rooted desire to punish them for this complacency. Sabbath describes himself, paradoxically, to Norman as a '[f]ailure at failing' (Roth 1995: 152). Bertie, similarly, thinks of himself as a man who 'had no forte. *That* was his forte' and regards telling his friends of his failings as 'a sort of responsibility' (Elkin 1990b: 95, 122). Yet they both recognise that there is in their very abjectness a paradoxical power; the power, as Sabbath puts it, 'of being no one with anything much to lose' (Roth 1995: 151). When Bertie finds himself alone in the Premingers' plush apartment, he quips '[h]ow the fallen are mighty!' (Elkin 1990b: 97); Sabbath compares himself both to a 'holy man' and to the devil himself: 'You'd think I'd burst forth in a boiling blaze, incandescent from

Pandemonium' (Roth 1995: 141, 309). Just as Sabbath chafes at the 'perfect' veneer of the Cowans' household, so Bertie is irritated by '[a]ll that licit love, that regularity' that is symbolised by the 'bland bad taste' of the Premingers' 'big . . . well-furnished' home. (Elkin 1990b: 111). If Sabbath is allergic to Norman's normality, Bertie is similarly affected by the Premingers (in fact, he warns one of his imaginary interlocutors[12] not 'to overlook the significance of that name "Norma". Norma/Normal, you see?') (Elkin 1990b: 108). Just as Sabbath thinks of himself as fundamentally of a different class to the Cowans, so Bertie marvels at having penetrated the 'capitol' of 'the squares', his term for the conformist middle class, of whom he sees the Premingers as typical (Elkin 1990b: 111). Both old men cast themselves in the role of scourge of middle-class respectability.

As the burglars leave the Premingers' apartment, they wonder whether they ought to 'do something about the clown' – Bertie – but in the end they decide, as the Premingers had, that he is harmless (Elkin 1990b: 125). With apparent perversity, Bertie is not relieved at his lucky escape, but rather indignant:

> They had no right to patronise him like that. If he was a clown it was because he had chosen to be. It was a way of life. Why couldn't they respect it? [. . .] For a moment it was impossible for him to distinguish between the thieves and the Premingers. (126)

It is at this moment that he resolves not to beg forgiveness of the Premingers (if he does, he believes that '[l]ike the thieves they would make allowances for him'), but rather to compound his crimes against them by stealing some costume jewelry that the thieves had left behind (Elkin 1990b: 126). He does so not in the expectation of getting away with it, but, on the contrary, in anticipation of being apprehended:

> How they [the squares] hounded you if you took something from them! He would be back, no question, and then they would send him to jail, but first there would be the confrontation, maybe even in the apartment itself: Bertie in handcuffs, and the Premingers staring at him, not understanding and angry at last, and something in their eyes like fear. (Elkin 1990b: 126)

It is this fear that Sabbath and Bertie want to inspire in their would-be benefactors. While they are tolerated, pitied, forgiven, they are humiliated, emasculated; but when they respond to the kindness, the niceness, the goodness of their hosts not with the gratitude that convention demands but with insult heaped on injury, they are then able to reclaim their dignity and their manhood. It is no coincidence that practically the first thing that Bertie and Sabbath do in the homes where they have been given refuge is to masturbate. It is through this performance of potency that they can assert the manhood that is implicitly threatened by the material success of their male hosts, make their mark in enemy territory. Indeed, this tribal and sexual rivalry extends to their friends' wives: Sabbath tries to seduce Michelle Cowan, Bertie recalls the time when Norma Preminger kissed him. When Sabbath observes, incredulously, that '[t]his generous, lovely, *bolbotish* success [Norman Cowan] continues to kowtow to a putz [i.e. Sabbath himself]', there is literal as well as metaphorical meaning to his words: Cowan's anti-depressants have made him impotent, so that he bows before the 'putz' (penis) that is Sabbath('s). For both Sabbath and Bertie, behaving badly is their way of reassuring themselves of their continuing vitality and virility, in spite of their advancing years; by implication the niceness of their male rivals signifies enervation and impotence.[13]

This dialectic is spelled out even more explicitly in Howard Jacobson's novel, *No More Mister Nice Guy* (1998). Jacobson's novel relates the picaresque adventures of fifty-year-old Frank Ritz, a cynical television critic exiled from his home by his wife, Mel, so that she can have some respite from the 'ceaseless racket of [his] masculinist universe' (Jacobson 1999: 3). Like Sabbath, Ritz 'considered himself to be a Rabelaisian man. He drank, he fornicated, he pigged out, he belched, he farted . . . He was a force of nature . . . the functions disporting themselves' (131). Though ten years younger than Sabbath, Ritz is similarly morbidly obsessed with his own mortality. Early in the novel he instructs an electrician to provide him with enough sockets in his study to last him until the fifteenth year of the new millennium ('[b]y which time he will be dead', he thinks), and towards the end he adopts as his mantra one of St. Benedict's sayings: 'Day by day remind yourself . . . that you are going to die' (2, 250). The novel is liberally sprinkled with epigrammatic reflections on the sense of waste and regret of men whose best years are behind them. For example: 'By the time you are Frank's age life is a teeming saga of things you never did anything about'; 'He's not a boy anymore; he's looking down both barrels of fifty. What does he have left except the capacity to enter imaginatively into another's distress, and a sense of the ridiculous?' (77, 13).

Like Sabbath, Ritz regards his age not as an excuse for bowing out of the sexual arena, but rather for raising his standard as often as he can while he still can. Sabbath vows 'never [to] . . . voluntarily depart this stupendous madness for fucking' and is always on the lookout for 'a chance for the old juicy way of life to make one big, last stand against the inescapable rectitude . . . of death', his battle-cry 'God willing, more cunt!' (Roth 1995: 329, 324, 247) ringing out. Ritz, for whom 'the only truly passionate pursuit in his life has been fucking', attempts to 'hang out against age, against the suck of respectability', on the grounds that '[i]f . . . a man of his age isn't for fucking, then what the fuck is a man of his age for?' (Jacobson 1999: 140, 200, 140). While Sabbath 'devote[s] [him]self to fucking the way a monk devotes himself to God', styling himself 'The Monk of Fucking' (Roth 1995: 60), Ritz actually becomes 'a fucking monk', living a chaste life in a Benedictine monastery for a while, only to discover that, paradoxically, 'renunciation [can] turn on you, tempting you with visions far more voluptuous than any you have to deal with in the ordinary sublunary world of regulation sin' (Jacobson 1999: 253, 240). Whereas Sabbath, with characteristic perversity, is indignant when his lover Drenka asks him to 'forswear fucking others', believing this to be a betrayal of their own paradoxical 'sacrament of infidelity' (Roth 1995: 3, 31), Ritz recognises that sexuality is the natural domain of the oxymoron: 'This is what fucking's for. The reconciliation of opposites' (Jacobson 1999: 256).

This may explain the curious ambiguity of these old men's masculinity. For it is one of the paradoxes of 'The Guest', *No More Mister Nice Guy* and *Sabbath's Theater*, that the intensely masculinist protagonists' sexuality and gender identity is subject to sudden inversion. In Elkin's story there is merely a hint of androgyny and transvestism when Bertie dresses up in Norma Preminger's clothes. The protagonists of Jacobson's and Roth's novels undergo more radical feminisation. Although Frank Ritz attempts to reduce male sexuality to a simple mathematical equation – 'M.A.N. = F.U.C.K.' – who, how, and why men fuck in Jacobson's novel is a far from simple matter (Jacobson 1999: 140). Reminiscing about a former lover, Ritz muses that '[b]eauty in a woman either has to have some boy in it or some baby' and later he asks himself '[w]hat is so desirable about the French comedian Fernandel?' and concludes that 'it's [that] she looks like a man' (23, 123). He also has a recurring dream in which he performs fellatio on his erstwhile best friend and sexual rival, Kurt, and in his final sexual encounter of the novel – with Clarice, a former lover of his and also of his wife – she makes him 'wear her pants . . . put lipstick on his mouth' and, it is implied, penetrates him with 'something' that '[d]raw[s] blood' (244).

In *Sabbath's Theater* Sabbath is drawn towards Drenka in part because 'this woman was someone who thought like a man' and as part of their sexual play 'he would suck on her [Drenka's] big toe, pretending it was her cock' (Roth 1995: 9, 226). He also 'intermittently kept imagining his be-denimed wife [Roseanna] as one of Hal's pretty young homosexual friends' and explains his decision to pick up Christa, who becomes his lover and also Drenka's, by observing that '[i]t was impossible to leave standing all alone on the side of the road with her thumb lifted a young blond girl in a tuxedo who looked like a young blond boy in a tuxedo' (83, 53). Most extraordinary of all, is the episode in which Sabbath discovers that he is not the only one of Drenka's former lovers to pay homage to her by masturbating at her graveside. Having frightened off his rival (a credit-card magnate named Lewis) by hurling a stone at him, Sabbath retrieves the flowers that Lewis has left, but then realises that the bouquet is covered with the man's jism:

> Then he did something strange, strange even for a strange man like him, who believed himself inured to the limitless contradictions that enshroud us in life . . . [he began] licking from his fingers Lewis's sperm and, beneath the full moon, chanting aloud, 'I am Drenka! I am Drenka!' (78)

Several critics have attempted to defend Sabbath (and Roth) against charges of misogyny in this novel, not always convincingly. Alan Cooper's argument – that 'Mickey Sabbath is not a misogynist. If he constantly hurts weak women, it is in a continual search for strong ones' (Cooper 1996: 287) – seems to me to bury where it intends to praise, while Robert Greenberg's allegorical interpretation of Sabbath's relations with the opposite sex – 'Sabbath's wayward impulse to manipulate and debase women provides a metaphorical representation of Philip Roth's relation to his postmodern novels' smacks somewhat of special pleading (Greenberg 2003: 98). Debra Shostak argues that in *Sabbath's Theater* Roth 'offers a profound critique of the mythology of masculine power' but also claims that Sabbath 'represents a textbook case of what Arthur Brittan has called "masculinism"', the ideology based on the premise that '"A man is only a man in so far as he is capable of using his penis as an instrument of power"' (Shostak 2004:

22, 51). Both these statements are accurate, but somewhat reductive: they tell only part of the truth about the novel's sexual politics and they do not do justice to the complexity of the novel as a whole. That Sabbath is misogynistic is incontestable, but to label him as a misogynist is to miss everything that is interesting and peculiar about Sabbath's sexuality. For, as the passage above illustrates, if Sabbath often objectifies women, he is also capable of positioning himself as the female subject: when he tastes Lewis's sperm he does not simply identify *with* Drenka, he identifies himself *as* Drenka.

This episode could be seen as evidence of a hitherto repressed homoeroticism on Sabbath's part – another manifestation of his polymorphous perversity, an expression of his compulsive desire to break all taboos, from necrophilia (at one point Sabbath asks himself 'Could he have fucked her [Drenka] after she was dead?' and replies 'Why not?'), to sodomy, to three-way sex; another bid to ensure that, as the narrator of the novel punningly puts it, describing Sabbath's first sex session with Drenka, 'Little was left undone' (138, 23). As Sabbath points out to Kathy Goolsbee, with mock ingenuousness, when it comes to sexual activity 'There are lots of things to do, aren't there?' (229). Given Sabbath's sexual adventurousness and his fixation on the phallus, it is perhaps hardly surprising that his desires should blur the boundaries of sexuality and of gender identity. It is arguably not such a big step from listening to Drenka describing her sexual exploits with other men (as Sabbath likes to do), to imagining himself *as* her. What better way of establishing full possession of the other than imaginatively to become that other?

Yet there is another aspect to Sabbath's momentary abnegation of masculinity, another explanation for this metaphysical transformation into his own lover. As with his attitude to Jewishness, Sabbath is capable of the most flagrant self-contradictions. Like Walt Whitman, who was famously insouciant on the subject in 'Song of Myself' (1855) – 'Do I contradict myself?/Very well then I contradict myself' (Whitman 1996: 123) – Sabbath is 'a great fan of human inconsistency', and this applies as much to his sexuality as to his ethnicity (Roth 1995: 65). Like Whitman's poetic persona, Sabbath 'contains multitudes' (Whitman 1996: 123), while at the same time he is 'reduced the way a sauce is reduced, boiled down by his burners, the better to concentrate his essence and be defiantly himself' (Roth 1995: 126). It is this paradox that makes Sabbath himself so much more than a textbook case of masculinism, or 'one of those marionettes with a long wooden dick', as he describes himself in a characteristic moment of self-satire, and *Sabbath's Theater* so much more than a 'critique of the mythology of masculine power' (Roth 1995: 132).

In *Seriously Funny* (1997), his study of the nature of comedy, Howard Jacobson points out that:

> Clowns and jesters everywhere are parti-coloured, striped, part black part white, neither half a true mirror-image of the other. It is of the essence of comedy to kaleidoscope extremes, to jam together opposites so that they are simultaneously true; in this it defeats the laws of an inexorable linear logic of cause and effect, beginning and end, action and consequence. (Jacobson 1997: 240)

Furthermore, he claims that the sign of a great comic writer is that 'contrariety is able to have its way with him' (240–1). This is clearly what Jacobson aspires to in *No More Mister Nice Guy*: Frank Ritz's contradictions are all in the service of Jacobson's comic vision. Yet the contrarieties of Jacobson's novel are as nothing compared to those to which Roth gives free rein in *Sabbath's Theater*. Roth's novel abounds in paradoxes, whether in the form of casual observations such as 'Sabbath's sixty-four years of life had long ago released him from the falsity of sense' and 'Anyone with any brains knows he is leading a stupid life', or in the form of a more sustained analysis of human inconsistency, such as Sabbath's interpretation of Michelle Cowan's laughter as signifying 'that she was sick of staying, sick of plotting leaving, sick of unsatisfied dreams, sick of satisfied dreams, sick of adapting, sick of not adapting' (Roth 1995: 138, 204, 306). Sabbath is a paradox, a man 'trapped in a process of self-division'. He sees 'all the antipathies in collision, the villainous and the innocent, the genuine and the fraudulent, the loathsome and the laughable'; he is a caricature of himself and entirely himself, embracing the truth and blind to the truth, self-haunted but 'barely what you would call a self' (201). Above all, Sabbath is a stern moralist who dedicates himself to a life of immorality; a man intolerant of other people's tolerance, impatient with other people's patience, a misanthrope whose hatred of the world attaches him to it with bonds as strong as love, as the final lines containing the final paradox of the novel make clear: 'He could not fucking die. How could he leave? How could he go? Everything he hated was here' (451).

All Sabbath's immoral acts are committed in the service of a (perverse) morality. Norman Cowan calls him an 'inverted saint whose message is desecration', but Sabbath is actually as much a satirist as a nihilist (347). Frank Kelleter claims that Sabbath 'is victim as much as he is victimizer', and that his 'hatred for bourgeois propriety and his lust for desecration clearly arise from a feeling of being threatened', but in fact Sabbath is emphatically neither victim nor victimiser (Kelleter 2003: 172, 173). Rather, he is a comic apologist for his own 'shit-filled life' (where 'shit' signifies authentic degradation) and a comic scourge of the 'genteel shit' (where 'shit' signifies bullshit, hypocritical pretence) on which polite society is built (247, 343). Although Sabbath claims not to 'have a pitch', much of his outrageous behaviour seems deliberately designed to expose the limitations of middle-class liberalism, to excoriate bourgeois complacency (347). From this perspective his rudeness becomes a 'forthrightness' that exposes 'the solace of conventional lies' and his affair with Drenka a 'counter-marriage in which the adulterers attack their feelings of captivity', a didactic project in which Sabbath, 'a teacher of estrangement from the ordinary', enlightens Drenka, 'assist[ing] her in becoming estranged from her orderly life and in discovering the indecency to supplement the deficiencies of her regular diet' (20, 27, 9). Sabbath is, finally, an advocate of immorality and mortality – the two essential conditions of humanity. His conduct – even, or perhaps especially, when most scandalous – is not arbitrary or anarchic, but rather part of what he calls 'the fight for the lost human cause', a concerted campaign against the 'terrible lies' of those who misrepresent as 'sinister villainy' what is 'the ordinary grubbing about in reality of ordinary people' (235, 236). Seen in this light, Sabbath's verdict on himself serves, paradoxically, as both a (premature) epitaph and a manifesto: 'I may not have been a matinee idol, but say what you will about me, it's been a real human life!' (247).

For many critics, myself among them, *Sabbath's Theater* stands as Roth's masterpiece, the novel by which all his others must be judged. From J.M. Coetzee's sober tribute, implied in his review of *The Plot Against America* – '[b]y the standard set by *Sabbath's Theater, The Plot Against America* is not a major work' (Coetzee 2004: 6) – to Harold Bloom's characteristically absolute judgement that the novel 'has earned [Roth] a permanent place in American literature by a comic genius that need never be doubted again', there is a widely-shared sense that in this portrait of the artist as an old man behaving badly Roth found the perfect marriage of form and content (Bloom 2003: 6). In Roth's earlier fiction, comedy tended to arise out of what he called his protagonists' 'superseriousness', their 'comic predicament result[ing] from the repeated attempt to escape [their] comic predicament' (Roth 2001a: 159). However, in Sabbath Roth created a figure who, like the greatest of old profane, immoral men in literature, Falstaff, is 'not only witty in [him]self, but the cause that wit is in other men' (*2 Henry IV*: I ii 9–10).

If Sabbath was Roth's ultimate portrait of a(n) (old) man behaving badly, his next novel, *American Pastoral*, featured a protagonist whose main vice seemed, paradoxically, to be his lack of vices. If Roth's challenge with *Sabbath's Theater* had been to render a monster sympathetic, in *American Pastoral* he set about explaining how an apparent paragon of virtue might become a monster. Indeed, all three of the novels that followed *Sabbath's Theater* – *I Married A Communist* and *The Human Stain* comprising the rest of the trilogy – can be seen as a continuation of Roth's analysis of the inherent dangers of moral idealism.

## Notes

1 A number of reviewers have noted the resemblance between Portnoy and Sabbath, though none comment on the structural similarity of the two novels' titles: they are the only books in Roth's large *oeuvre* to use the name of its protagonist in the possessive mood, followed by a noun.

2 Actually, the transcript is censored (by the 'Women Against Sexual Abuse, Belittlement, Battering, and Telephone Harassment' committee), though ironically not in order to erase any of the obscene content of the tape, but rather to ensure that Goolsbee's identity remains obscure. Hence, every time Sabbath uses her name, the transcript inserts '*bleep*' for 'Kathy'.

3 Roth himself provides a good illustration of the extent of his public notoriety at this time when he quotes Jacqueline Susann, the author in the 1970s of a number of bestselling novels in what came to be known as the 'bonkbuster' genre, telling viewers of the 'Johnny Carson Show' that she would like to meet Roth but 'wouldn't want to shake [his] hand' (Roth 2001a: 252).

4 Many readers of contemporary American fiction would, for example, have been familiar with Nicholson Baker's novel *Vox* (1992), which consists entirely of a sexually explicit dialogue conducted over the telephone.

5 Roth had alluded to Keats' 'Ode to Autumn' before in the context of sexuality. In *Portnoy's Complaint*, recounting a blissful weekend in Vermont with Mary Jane Reed, Portnoy wonders whether it was 'tenderness for one another that we experienced, or just the fall doing its

work, swelling the gourd (John Keats) and lathering the tourist trade into ecstasies of nostalgia for the good and simple life?' (Roth 1969: 171).

6 There are further analogies that might be made between Sabbath and Prospero: both old men manipulate the other characters in their lives as though they were puppets in a theatre (Prospero even stages a formal masque) before eventually renouncing their art.

7 Not just to *When She Was Good* (1963), which tells the story of a young woman, Lucy Nelson, who is constantly disappointed by the failure of the men in her life (notably her father and husband) to meet her own rigorous standards of morality, but even farther back, to the early short story 'The Good Girl', in which Laurie Bowen, having evaded the attempts of her boyfriend to snatch a goodnight kiss 'with scornful virtue', is then horrified to discover her father in an embrace with her mother's best friend (Roth 1960: 99).

8 This idea was one that Roth developed in much greater detail in the three novels published after *Sabbath's Theater* (see the following chapter).

9 Although such statements are ostensibly made not by Sabbath himself, but by the narrator of the novel, more often than not the third-person narration functions as indirect interior monologue, so that the distinction between the third-person and first-person perspectives collapses.

10 The song appears on the album 'The Times They Are A-Changin'' (1967).

11 Again, there is an echo here of *Portnoy's Complaint* (see Brauner 2005: 49–50).

12 Like Sabbath, Bertie is a performer of sorts, a mimic who, for much of Elkin's story, ventriloquises the voices of a range of characters – Klaff, Gimpel, Graham MacNamee – and consequently has what Elkin calls 'the fool's ancient protection, his old immunity against consequence' (Elkin 1990: 125).

13 Bertie's age is never specified, but there are many hints that he is an old man (considerably older than the Premingers). Like Sabbath (who thinks about how he might '[c]heck into a motel, borrow the night clerk's razor to shave, and slit [his own] throat from ear to ear', he has clearly contemplated suicide (Roth 1995: 109). At one point in Elkin's story he takes out a 'bottle of carbon tetrachloride' which, we are told, 'was what he would use to kill himself when he had finally made the decision'. The narrator also observes that Bertie is living out the rest of his life 'conscious . . . that he was forever encountering experiences which would never come his way again' (Elkin 1990b: 103, 107).

# 5

# History and the anti-pastoral: Utopian dreams and rituals of purification in the 'American Trilogy'

> And then the loss of the daughter [. . .] blasting to smithereens his particular form of utopian thinking, the plague America infiltrating the Swede's castle and there infecting everyone . . . transport[ing] him out of the longed-for American pastoral and into [. . .] the counterpastoral – into the indigenous American berserk. (Roth 1997: 85–6)

> 'Ira called his utopian dream Communism, Eve called hers Sylphid. The parent's utopia of the perfect child, the actress's utopia of let's pretend, the Jew's utopia of not being Jewish, to name only the grandest of her projects to deodorize life and make it palatable.' (Roth 1998: 179)

> The musicians had laid bare the youngest, most innocent of our ideas of life, the indestructible yearning for the way things aren't and can never be. (Roth 2000: 207)

Philip Roth's fiction has always been characterised by the tension between the individual capacity for self-determination and the deterministic forces of history; between seductive dreams of harmony, idealism and purity and the troubling realities of discord, disillusionment, corruption; between the desire to exert control, impose order, explain, and the impulse to break free from all constraints; to revel in anarchy, chaos and disorder; to celebrate the indeterminate, the unknowable, the inexplicable. Nowhere are these tensions more clearly articulated than in what has become known as his 'American Trilogy' of novels: *American Pastoral* (1997), *I Married A Communist* (1998) and *The Human Stain* (2000).[1] Embedded in the rich, dense, allusive language of these novels is a dialectic between what Roth in *The Counterlife* calls 'the pastoral . . . womb-dream of life in the beautiful state of innocent prehistory' (Roth 1986: 323) and what, in *American*

*Pastoral*, he describes as 'the fury, the violence, and the desperation of the counter-pastoral' (Roth 1997: 86). I prefer the term 'anti-pastoral', partly because I used it before the appearance of Roth's novel to define a certain trend in post-war Jewish fiction,[2] and partly because I believe it describes more precisely what is not simply a reaction or response to the pastoral genre but its ideological antithesis. In Roth's fiction the pastoral and the anti-pastoral represent not simply alternative modes of fiction, but two irreconcilable worldviews. For Roth, the pastoral signifies an ahistorical, Utopian dream world in which man lives in harmony with nature, his fellow man (and woman), and himself.[3] In the world of the anti-pastoral, man is subject to historical forces, forces that bring him into conflict with nature, with his fellow man (and woman), and with himself. It is the unbridgeable gulf between these two realms that tears apart the protagonists of *American Pastoral*, *I Married a Communist* and *The Human Stain* – Seymour Levov, Ira Ringold and Coleman Silk – who try to straddle them.

A number of critics and reviewers have commented on the similarities between the plots of *American Pastoral* and *The Human Stain*.[4] Both novels tell the (fictionalised) stories of men endowed with extraordinary talents as schoolboys: Coleman 'Silky' Silk is an outstanding boxer who might have turned pro and also a brilliant student, the class valedictorian; Seymour 'the Swede' Levov is a prodigious athlete, hero-worshipped by his peers and exalted by his local Jewish community. Ira Ringold in *I Married A Communist* is rather less precocious but nonetheless becomes, in the guise of 'Iron Rinn', a nationally renowned actor who 'was heard on network radio every Thursday night on *The Free and the Brave* – a popular weekly dramatization of inspiring episodes out of American history – impersonating people like Nathan Hale and Orville Wright and Wild Bill Hickok and Jack London' (Roth 1998: 18). Silk, Levov and Ringold are tragic figures in the classical sense: great men who fall from grace, partly because of their own hubris and partly because they are caught up in historical forces beyond their control.[5] Their self-mythologising nicknames demonstrate a shared conviction that they are masters of their own destinies, with the power to make of their lives – and themselves – what they will, but the allegorical elements of their first names suggest, on the contrary, that their fate is predetermined: Coleman can be read as 'coal man', a reference to the racial identity that he tries to efface; Seymour as 'see more', an ironic reference to Levov's lack of insight and foresight; and Ira is the latin for anger, which

Ringold struggles unsuccessfully to control throughout the novel and which eventually undoes him.[6]

Although these protagonists leave their lowly origins far behind, remaking themselves and making good in the great American tradition of self-reliance, their pre-eminence proves precarious, their successes short-lived. Seymour's life is destroyed by his daughter's participation in the militant campaign of the 1960s against American involvement in Vietnam; Ira's is destroyed by his wife's exposure of his Communist affiliations during the McCarthyite witch hunt of the 1950s; and Coleman's by the same Zeitgeist – what Nathan Zuckerman calls the 'persecuting spirit' of a 'morally stupid censorious community' – that blighted Bill Clinton's second term as President in the 1990s (Roth 2000: 2, 311). In fact, all three are victims of what might be seen as different manifestations of American Puritanism, or, to put it another way, different versions of the pastoral dream of a Utopian world that has always been at the heart of America's mythology of itself.[7] For all their obvious differences and apparent political incompatibilities, the sixties radicalism which sweeps up Meredith Levov and sweeps away her father's dreams of domestic bliss, the anti-Communist hysteria of the fifties that allows Eve Frame to engineer Ira's public disgrace, and the febrile political correctness of the nineties that sees Coleman hounded into early retirement, are all arguably motivated by a similar moralistic impulse, all species of what Roth calls (after Sophocles) 'purifying rituals'.[8] All three movements seek to eradicate what they see as a form of contamination (American imperialism; Communism; racial and sexual prejudice) in the quest for an ideal state/State of purity (an America purged of all military ambition, political dissent, or inequality). Yet Seymour, Ira and Coleman are equally agents of their own downfall, for they all invest heavily in their own pastoral visions, cleansing themselves of inconvenient impurities in their histories in an attempt to realise their Utopian dreams.[9]

In *American Pastoral*, Seymour Levov, a third-generation urban Newark Jew, plays the role of an all-American WASP pillar of the rural community of Old Rimrock; in *I Married A Communist* Ira Ringold jettisons his working-class Jewish past in order to enjoy the high life of a showbusiness star. In *The Human Stain* Coleman Silk, the grandson of African-American slaves, reinvents himself as 'one of those crimped-haired Jews of a light yellowish skin pigmentation who possess something of the ambiguous aura of the pale blacks who are sometimes taken for white' and becomes a Professor of Classics and

Dean of Athena College (Roth 2000: 15–16). In all three cases, their attempts to recreate themselves are represented ambivalently: on the one hand as heroic feats of liberation, epitomising the quintessentially American ideal of the self-made man and the immigrant dream of successful assimilation; on the other hand as futile fantasies of escape, illustrating the limitations of American social mobility and the impossibility of transcending historical circumstances. In this chapter I explore different aspects of this paradox as it plays itself out in each of the three novels, dealing with them in the chronological order of their historical settings rather than their publication dates.

## *I Married A Communist*

Ira Ringold's idealism makes and breaks him. To the young Nathan Zuckerman, whom Ira adopts as a surrogate son and political disciple, Ira emanates 'an aura of heroic purity' (Roth 1998: 54). Convinced that he is 'an instrument of history', Ira leaves behind his lowly origins as the son of working-class Jewish immigrants and a shady past of juvenile delinquency that includes the murder of an Italian boy who hurled anti-Semitic abuse at him, to become an eminent radio actor known as 'Iron Rinn' (180). When he marries Eve Frame, a glamorous, sophisticated former silent film star, his 'heroic reinvention of himself' seems complete (301). Ira's brother, Murray, who tells Ira's story to Nathan Zuckerman (a former high school English pupil of Murray's), explicitly figures Ira's biography as a project of self-invention and self-determination, 'a great big act of control over [. . .] his life' (60). Murray recalls Ira's euphoria when he first introduces Eve to her future brother- and sister-in-law, observing that he seemed to be '[t]he master of life, exulting in his own existence' (58). However, Ira's act of control turns out to be an act not just in the sense of 'deed' but in the sense of 'simulation'; his belief in his mastery of his own fate is brutally exposed as a 'naïve dream' (60). Ironically, his marriage to Eve, which begins as a romantic idyll – the consummation of his journey from street brawler to aristocratic thespian – proves ultimately to be an expression of self-betrayal rather than self-fulfillment.

Like Ira, Eve has a history, an identity, that she has worked hard to shed. Unlike Ira, however, whose transformation is also a reformation of sorts (the former murderer, womaniser and alcoholic becomes a respected actor and a responsible family man), Eve's attempt to disown her origins is not part of a project of self-improvement but rather the product of self-hatred. Born Chava Fromkin, the daughter of 'a poor immigrant [. . .] uneducated Polish Jew' who settled in Brooklyn, Eve invents for herself a Freudian family romance, a pastoral myth of origin purified of all traces of Jewishness, in which she is the scion of an old Massachusetts 'seafaring family' with a patent lawyer for a father and a mother who ran 'a very nice tearoom' (306, 308). However, this generically genteel, gentile version of her past is implicitly challenged by the constant attentions of 'the Jewish ladies who loved her, who recognized her, who came up and asked for her autograph' (52). The word 'recognized' here is ambiguous: it certainly means that her Jewish fans identify her because of her fame as an actress, but it also contains the suggestion that they identify *with* her on the grounds of their shared ethnicity; that they are aware – and proud – of the very markers of which she is so ashamed (Murray Ringold observes that Eve's face 'was subtly quite Jewish, all the physiognomic nuances Rebecca-like, right out of Scott's *Ivanhoe*') (152). Moreover, Eve is 'embarrassed that her daughter look[s] like a Jew' and passes on to Sylphid the disease of self-contempt (152). The two most shocking moments in the novel are expressions of this internalized anti-Semitism, projected outwards – the first when Sylphid calls her mother a 'kike bitch' and the second when Eve denounces her sister-in-law, Doris Ringold, as a 'hideous, twisted little Jew' (111, 253). As Murray Ringold points out, Eve's attempt to rid herself and her daughter of all signs of Jewishness – to 'wash away the Jewish stain', as Jimmy Ben-Joseph in *The Counterlife* put it (Roth 1986: 170) – is a Utopian fantasy, a dream of personal purification that echoes Ira's dream of political purification through Communism. It is an attempt to, as Murray puts it synaesthesically, 'deodorize life and make it palatable' (Roth 1998: 179). Like all Utopias, however, Ira's and Eve's are also dystopias – both practically unattainable and morally undesirable. Just as Communism (notably in Stalinist Russia and Maoist China during the period in which *I Married A Communist* is set) ruthlessly purged all dissidents in the name of preserving the purity of the revolution, so Eve outlaws all dissent in the service of her grand project of ethnic self-cleansing.

Ironically, Eve's skills as an actress are compromised by her insistence on maintaining this pretence in her private life. While her professional success relies on understatement and nuance – 'as a stage actress she was all moderation and tact, nothing exaggerated' – off stage she is forever contriving scenes of vulgar melodrama (58). Able brilliantly to impersonate reality in her art, in her life, as Doris Ringold notes, playing wittily on her sister-in-law's name, '[r]eality doesn't seem to make a dent in Miss Frame' (250). In spite of his own reputation as a down-to-earth man of the people, Ira Ringold is seduced by Eve's pastoral escapism. Her penchant for 'render[ing] inconvenient facts inconsequential' seems a particularly attractive strategy when faced with the threat of being placed on the blacklist of suspected Communists and so Ira 'began to try to save his political hide by letting all that unreality of hers flow freely over him' (255, 248). Johnny O'Day, Ira's erstwhile mentor, says of his former *protégé* that 'all Ira ever cared about was everybody thinking what a hero he was. Always impersonating and never the real thing' (288). Although his verdict may be jaundiced somewhat by his own dogmatic political creed (Murray observes sardonically that his Utopian ideology makes O'Day 'purer than the rest of us'), it has a certain validity (289). Just as Eve tries to pass as non-Jewish, so Ira denies his Communist affiliations: both are ultimately exposed.

The 'unreality' of Eve's and Ira's position is contrasted in the novel with the uncompromising realism and integrity of Murray Ringold. Ira belies his name of 'Iron Rinn', running scared of HUAC and its agents and literally retreating from reality, hiding out in a 'two-room shack on the Jersey side of the Delaware Water Gap', selling coloured mineral fragments from the local disused zinc mine to tourists, but Murray stands by his political principles in the face of intimidation and eventual dismissal from his job as a high school teacher (71). Moreover, Murray warns Zuckerman of the dangers of his former pupil's pastoral hermitage, which, Zuckerman confides to the reader, is 'an upgraded replica' of Ira's own 'beloved retreat', 'tucked away on a dirt road as his was' and lacking only that 'dark, drooping ramshackle look that proclaimed, "Hermit here – back off"' (71). Whereas Zuckerman romanticises his isolation, representing his seclusion in quasi-spiritual terms by invoking Rousseau and Thoreau, as well as the legend, ubiquitous in 'Eastern philosophical thought', of the 'ageing man [who] leaves and goes into the woods', Murray instructs him to '[b]eware the utopia of isolation [. . .] the utopia of the shack in the woods, the oasis defence against rage and grief' (315). Zuckerman has become disillusioned with, and estranged from, a series of father figures (his real father Doc Zuckerman, his college tutor Leo Glucksman, the Irish Communist revolutionary Johnny O'Day, Ira) throughout the course of the novel.[10] Murray is the most enduring of these gurus. It is he who initiates Zuckerman the schoolboy into the mysteries of literature and it is he who has to warn Zuckerman the old man of the dangers of forsaking life for literature, of subscribing to another version of the pastoral myth with which Ira deluded himself and eluded his history. Murray also provides – in the form of his narrative, framed by Zuckerman's own – an anti-pastoral version of Ira Ringold's story that counters Zuckerman's pastoral version.

Zuckerman insists on seeing Ira as a representative American figure, whose fate is inextricably bound up with his historical circumstances. He claims that 'I had never before known anyone whose life was so intimately circumscribed by so much American history' and argues that '[t]o imagine Ira outside of his moment was impossible' (189). For Zuckerman, Ira is a 'historical casualty'; he is 'impaled on [his] moment', a moment at which:

> History had been scaled down and personalized, America had been scaled down and personalized: for me, that was the enchantment . . . of the times. You flood into history and history floods into you. You flood into America and America floods into you. And all by virtue of being alive in New Jersey and twelve years old and sitting by the radio in 1945. (318, 322, 39)

The implication is that Zuckerman's treatment of Ira is the product of his Whitmanesque enthusiasm for the America of his childhood, a quasi-transcendentalist belief in an organic connection between the individual and the national destiny, and self-confessed susceptibility to 'the enchantment . . . of the times', rather than an objective portrait of the man himself. In the young Zuckerman's imagination Ira becomes identified with those 'heroic Americans who fought against tyranny and injustice, champions of liberty for America and for all mankind' whom he reads about in novels that fuel his natural inclination towards 'idealism' (25).

The reality of Ira's story, as his brother Murray sees it, is rather less romantic. Ira's defeat does not take place 'on the great American battlefield he would himself have chosen for his destruction', but on the more mundane battleground of married life (3). Ira is, in Murray's view, a victim of domestic rather than national politics, for 'despite ideology, politics, and history, a genuine catastrophe is always personal bathos at the core' (3). This version of Ira's life is, of course, just as coloured by its narrator's values as Zuckerman's. Murray's Aristotelian analysis of his brother's 'catastrophe' reflects his pedagogical background, as does his invocation of the legend of Beauty and the

Beast in his description of the dynamic of Ira's marriage to Eve: 'She [Eve] needs the brute to redeem her purity, while what the brute [Ira] needs is to be tamed' (299). Murray also implicitly acknowledges that Ira's narrative has a certain historical resonance, though he characteristically domesticates that resonance, when he tells Nathan that 'betrayal' is 'at the heart of history' (299, 185). In spite of his own occasional weakness for philosophical abstraction, however, Murray's voice in general provides a counterweight in the novel to Zuckerman's tendency to idealise Ira, and to Ira's tendency to mythologise himself. Indeed, Murray identifies Ira's conviction of his own historical significance as the root cause of his propensity for self-destruction.

Early on in his life, Ira's ire gets the better of him and he commits a murder. Having initially beaten up a neighbourhood hoodlum who had been goading him, the young Ira, enraged by the Italian boy's anti-Semitic jibes, turns around and kills him. Later that evening, when he confesses – or rather boasts – of his actions to his brother ('Strollo just took his last strollo'), Murray turns on him:

> 'You just made the biggest mistake you've ever made [. . .] You *got* your victory . . . But to make the victory *total*, to go back and then *murder* him – for *what?* Because he said something anti-Semitic? . . . The whole weight of Jewish history falls on Ira Ringold's shoulders? Bullshit!' (300, italics in original)

If Murray's hypothesis is correct – that Ira feels justified in killing his attacker because he casts himself (with characteristic delusions of grandeur) in the role of avenger of the history of anti-Semitic persecution – then Ira's decision to marry a woman who is both a victim and an agent of anti-Semitism takes on an added resonance. It becomes, paradoxically, an attempt to redeem himself (by offering love to Eve and Sylphid, in spite of their anti-Semitism) and at the same time to punish himself (by marrying an anti-Semite who will come to despise him). The exposé of Ira's Communist affiliations in Eve Frame's book (ghostwritten by the gossip columnists Katrina Van Tassel and her husband Bryden Grant) is primarily the product of Eve's desire to avenge herself for Ira's adultery with Sylphid's friend Pamela and his masseuse Helgi Pnär, and Grant's determination to pay back Ira for publicly insulting him at a society party. Nonetheless, these personal motives are inextricably linked with political ideology. As Murray reminds Zuckerman, 'Cold War paranoia had latent anti-Semitism as one of its sources' (274). It is because of the political climate in 1952 (the year in which Eve's book – also called *I Married A Communist* – is published), a period in American history when the activities of McCarthy and his accomplices 'looked like a democratic pogrom full of terror', that Eve is able 'to transform a personal prejudice into a political weapon by confirming for Gentile America that . . . the Communist under every rock was, nine times out of ten, a Jew to boot', and that Bryden Grant is able to use a 'national obsession to settle a score' (266, 274, 9).

Ever since *My Life as a Man*, Roth has been interested in the relationship between personal and political history, but *I Married A Communist* is his most explicit consideration of the relationship between private lives and public policy.[11] The most significant passage in the novel in this context is the exchange between Murray Ringold's daughter, Lorraine, and Bryden Grant, after Murray's refusal to testify before a HUAC hearing. Grant, one of the members of the Committee and the man personally responsible for summoning Murray for questioning (as part of his personal vendetta against Ira), approaches Murray and offers to help him if only he will agree to testify and 'clear [his] name' (11). At this juncture Lorraine intervenes:

> 'Clear his name? *He* doesn't have to clear his name – it's not dirty,' she told Grant . . . 'Your father has a history,' Grant said. 'History?' Lorraine said. 'What history? What's his history?' (11, italics in original)

By challenging Grant's use of the term 'history', Lorraine Ringold highlights the ambiguity of that term, an ambiguity that *I Married A Communist* repeatedly emphasises. In the sense that Grant uses it, 'history' signifies a shameful past, a stain on one's character that can only be erased by a public ritual of purification – in this case a confession of guilt before HUAC. When Grant tells Lorraine that her father 'has a history', he intends his assertion to function as an accusation of guilt against Murray and, by association, his family (Murray remarks that 'the Ringolds were the Rosenbergs to the Grants'), but when Lorraine throws the word back at him, it becomes instead an indictment of Grant himself (7). For it is clear that Grant, 'the incarnation of pampered privilege', knows nothing of the (poor Jewish immigrant) family history of the Ringolds (8). Grant's attempt to expropriate Murray's personal history and incorporate it into his own historical narrative of a righteous crusade against Communism is exposed by Lorraine as an ignorant distortion of 'history' in the further sense of an accurate record of events. Lorraine counters Grant's

Utopian narrative of sin (Communism) redeemed through purification (confession of guilt followed by renewal of allegiance to American values) with an alternative interpretation of history as a realistic chronicle. These opposing versions of history are central to *I Married A Communist* and to the other novels in Roth's 'American Trilogy'. The ideological conflict between pastoral Utopianism – epitomised by Eve Frame's determination 'to empty life of its incongruities, of its meaningless, messy contingencies, and to impose on it instead the simplification that coheres' – and anti-pastoral humanism – exemplified by Murray Ringold's conviction that 'purity is petrafaction', 'the big lie of righteousness' that deprives human beings of their humanity – is a *leitmotiv* that also runs through *American Pastoral* and *The Human Stain*. In the remainder of this chapter I will explore some of the ways in which this tension manifests itself in these two novels (305, 318).

## *American Pastoral*

The narrative trajectory of *I Married A Communist* – a life and career that rises on an edifice whose foundations are then undermined by the exposure of its faulty materials – echoes *American Pastoral* and anticipates *The Human Stain*. All three novels might be read as parables about ethnic and racial identity and the seductive pastoral dream of 'passing' in American society. In *I Married A Communist*, Murray Ringold suggests that Eve Frame's attempt to renounce her Jewish origins to become a member of upper-class New York society is a deformed version of the American ideal of self-making:

> 'You're an American who doesn't want to be your parents' child . . . You don't want anybody to know you were born Jewish? . . . Fine. You've come to the right country. But you don't have to hate Jews into the bargain. You don't have to punch your way out of something by punching somebody else in the face.' (Roth 1998: 157)

Eve's crime, according to Murray, is not her denial of her ethnicity but her hatred of it. Yet to pass oneself off as a WASP in American society entails displaying the prejudices that the WASP establishment harbours against ethnic and religious minorities. Hence, when Coleman Silk in *The Human Stain* antagonises the promoter of his fourth (and last) professional boxing bout, Solly Tabak, by stopping his black opponent in the first round rather than, as Solly had instructed him to do, prolonging the fight to 'give the people their money's worth', he explains his actions by aping the racist discourse of white America, proclaiming: 'I don't carry no nigger' (Roth 2000: 117). The pugilistic metaphor that Murray Ringold uses to frame Eve's struggle to break free of her Jewish ethnicity manifests itself literally here: Coleman beats (and beats up) an opponent who represents his own racial background. Moreover, by reminding us at this moment that Coleman is a 'classics major from NYU and valedictorian son of the . . . grammarian . . . Clarence Silk', Nathan Zuckerman, the narrator of the novel, implies that Coleman's deployment of an ungrammatical idiom ('I don't carry no') constitutes as much of a betrayal of his origins as his studiedly casual reference to his opponent as a 'nigger'. In pronouncing this word Coleman also unwittingly betrays himself, just as he does later in life when he uses another pejorative term for African Americans – 'spooks' – to allude to two absent students who turn out to be black and when he calls his white lawyer, Nelson Primus, 'lily-white', clearly intending it as an insult. It is precisely because Coleman is carrying the identity of a 'nigger' with him – that is to say, the consciousness of belonging to an ethno-racial group historically perceived as subhuman by many white Americans – that he makes these injudicious remarks.

Although Coleman's use of the word 'spooks' is apparently innocent (he is unaware that the absentees are black, since they have never turned up for class), and 'lily-white' slips out in a moment of rage, these incidents, together with his deliberately provocative use of 'nigger', provide evidence that Coleman is unconsciously inviting retribution upon himself. Like his successor as Dean of Athena College, Delphine Roux, of whom Zuckerman observes that she is '[a]fraid of being exposed, dying to be seen', and Bill Clinton, to whom Coleman is implicitly compared throughout the novel, and whose desperate attempts to cover up his affair with Monica Lewinsky were sabotaged by a cavalier disregard for subterfuge in his conduct of the affair itself, Coleman paradoxically craves the revelation of his secret even while apparently going to great lengths to preserve it (85). In other words, when Coleman tells Solly that he 'don't carry no nigger' he may be attempting to render himself immune to the kind of prejudice that he experiences when addressed as a 'nigger' in a Woolworths store on his first day at Howard University. He adopts the position of the white racist oppressors in order to avoid being their victim but he is also exposing his own vulnerability to such taunts. Likewise, when he uses the words 'spooks' and 'lily-white', his repressed consciousness of his blackness returns (as it does also when he misreads the word 'neck' in a poem by his college girlfriend, Steena Palsson, as 'negro'), colouring his language in ways that colour himself (112).

Whereas Eve Frame's attempt to pass is condemned unequivocally, Coleman's is represented more ambivalently. Zuckerman, for example, refers to Coleman as 'the greatest of the great *pioneers* of the I', albeit in a passage that can be read as a paraphrase of Coleman's own thoughts (2000: 108, italics in original). At his funeral one of Coleman's colleagues (ignorant of his true origins but wishing to defend – belatedly – Coleman's refusal to apologize for his use of the term 'spooks') eulogizes him as 'an American individualist' in the tradition of Hawthorne, Melville and Thoreau, who 'refused to leave unexamined the orthodoxies of the customary and of the established truth' (310–11). Yet Zuckerman also emphasizes the treachery with which Coleman lives up to his middle name of Brutus, by ruthlessly casting off those closest to him. His cold-blooded resolution to disown his mother is particularly damning. Moreover, his mother's response when he tells her that he intends to marry Iris Gittelman (a secular Jew who ironically would most likely have married Coleman even if he had chosen to disclose his true identity to her) suggests that his new identity, far from liberating him from his origins, is likely to chain him to them: 'You're white as snow and you think like a slave' (139). Once again, Zuckerman's comment on the paradoxical nature of Delphine Roux – '[s]he seemed to have subverted herself in the altogether admirable effort to *make* herself' – seems to apply equally well to her antagonist Coleman (272, italics in original). Arguably, in trying to eradicate the 'stain' of his blackness by passing as Jewish, Coleman sacrifices not simply his own history (which comes back to haunt him in the form of his verbal indiscretion), but his humanity.

Like Coleman, who rises from humble beginnings to become a classics professor and Dean of the Faculty at Athena College, Seymour Levov in *American Pastoral* is a self-made man in both the economic sense of the term (although he inherits his father's glove-making business he expands it considerably and displays a real flair for business) and in the existential sense (he creates a new identity for himself). Once again, the narrator Nathan Zuckerman is ambivalent about this project of self-(re)invention. On the one hand, he admires Seymour's determination to shape his own destiny, paying tribute to his 'desire to go the limit in America with your rights, forming yourself as an ideal person who gets rid of the traditional Jewish habits and attitudes, who frees himself of the pre-America insecurities and the old, constraining obsessions so as to live unapologetically as an equal among equals' (Roth 1997: 85). On the other hand, he describes Seymour as both 'an *instrument* of history' and its 'plaything' (5, 87, italics in original). The diction of the first passage – particularly the words 'rights', 'ideal', 'free' and 'equal' – echoes that of the U.S. constitution, but the terms 'instrument' and 'plaything' undermine Seymour's own declaration of independence, depriving him of any individual agency.

Zuckerman is acutely aware of the self-deception and self-loathing that inevitably accompanies the project of assimilation to which Seymour dedicates himself, and that is signified implicitly by the nickname – 'the Swede' – that Seymour is given as a schoolboy because of his (ethnically atypical) blond hair and blue eyes. Describing the origin of the nickname, Zuckerman observes that:

> [A]s long as Weequahic remained the old Jewish Weequahic . . . Doc Ward was known as the guy who'd christened Swede Levov . . . a name that made him mythic in a way that Seymour never would have done . . . He carried it with him like an invisible American passport, all the while wandering deeper and deeper into an American's life, forthrightly evolving into a large, smooth, optimistic American such as his conspicuously raw forebears . . . couldn't have dreamed of as one of their own. (207–8)

Roth's language reveals the ironies involved in Seymour's transformation: he is 'christened' the Swede because the name involves an implicit change not simply of ethnic identity (from Jewish to Swedish) but of religious identity (from Jewish to Christian). The phrase 'wandering deeper and deeper into an American's life' suggests that Seymour never fully inhabits this life himself – never makes it his own – and, furthermore, that his attempts to do so involve a loss of direction and identity, an uncertain and treacherous journey into terrain in which he finds himself out of his depth, in too deep. The word 'evolving' might imply that Seymour attains a level of existence superior to that of his ancestors, but the sacrifice this entails is great: he severs his connections to his roots so completely that he becomes unrecognizable even to his own family. The contrast between the 'raw' Jewish immigrants and the 'smooth' American Seymour is itself ambiguous: smoothness may denote sophistication and refinement but it also connotes complacency and insincerity. Finally, the fact that

Seymour's place in local mythology is secure only 'as long as Weequahic remained the old Jewish Weequahic' reinforces the impression created earlier in the novel that Seymour's credentials as an all-American hero are convincing only while he remains in a community whose idea of Gentile identity is itself based more on legend than reality:

> [T]hrough the Swede, the neighborhood entered into a fantasy about itself and about the world [. . .] *almost* like Gentiles (*as they imagined* Gentiles), our families could forget the way things actually work and make an athletic performance the repository of all their hopes. (3–4, my italics)

It is precisely because Seymour's sporting prowess conforms to a Jewish stereotype of WASP values (and because it refutes the anti-Semitic stereotype of the Jew as physically frail and cowardly) that he is feted as a local hero in whom the Jewish community invests its aspirations for the future. In other words, Seymour paradoxically fulfils the fantasies of his community by deviating definitively from its conception of itself, not only by excelling at all the traditional American sports (baseball, basketball, football), but by marrying Dawn Dwyer, an Irish-American former Miss New Jersey and contender for Miss America, and moving out of the (predominantly Jewish) urban neighbourhood of Weequahic to live in the (predominantly WASP) rural village of Old Rimrock.

For Seymour's brother, Jerry, this constitutes both a calculated betrayal of Seymour's origins and a naïve retreat from the reality of life itself. When Seymour rings up Jerry in despair, having discovered his daughter, Meredith – ironically abbreviated to Merry – living in appalling poverty in a slum district of Newark, instead of sympathy what he gets is a lengthy diatribe, in which Jerry derides his brother's choice of life as an infantile fantasy: '"Out there with Miss America, dumbing down and dulling out. Out there playing at being Wasps . . . you thought all that façade was going to come without cost. Genteel and innocent. *But that costs, too, Seymour*"' (280, italics in original). As is often the case in Roth's fiction, gentility is associated with Gentiles, and living in the countryside with a self-deluding desire for an idealized bucolic existence: a pastoral Utopia. For Jerry, the disaster that befalls Seymour and his family when Merry blows up the local post office in protest at American policy in Vietnam is retribution for Seymour's attempt to escape from his ethnic identity as a Jew and from the exigencies of American history:

> 'You wanted Miss America? Well, you've got her, with a vengeance – she's your daughter! You wanted to be a real American hotshot with a beautiful Gentile babe on your arm? You longed to belong like everybody else to the United States of America? Well, you do now . . . The reality of this place is right up in your kisser now. With the help of your daughter you're as deep in the shit as a man can get, the real American crazy shit. America amok! America amuck!' (277)

The near-pun ('amok . . . amuck'), reinforced by the metaphor that Jerry uses to dramatize the discrepancy between the serene 'façade' of Seymour's life 'out there' (as he contemptuously puts it) and the brutal 'reality' of American life ('you're as deep in the shit as a man can get'), is resonant, both in the context of Seymour's recent reunion with Merry and in the larger context of Roth's pastoral/anti-pastoral dialectic.

When Seymour meets Merry for the first time since her sudden disappearance after the bombing of the Old Rimrock post office, he is dismayed to discover that she was indeed responsible both for that terrorist act (in which a local doctor had been killed) and for two further bombings (in which three other people died). Worse even than this, however, is the revelation of Merry's latest reinvention of herself as an extremist of a different sort: a devout Jain who has renounced 'vices . . . sexual pleasures . . . all attachments' and who wears a veil in front of her face lest she unwittingly harm any microbial organisms with her breath (239). When Seymour rends this veil from her and pries open her mouth in an attempt to force her to speak to him without the literal and symbolic barrier, he smells a 'human being who grubs about for pleasure in its own shit . . . a human mess stinking of human waste' (265). Levov's words here are carefully chosen by Roth: the phrases 'human mess' and 'human waste' signify fecal excretion but also refer to Merry's psychological state and to the squandering of her potential as a human being, and it is this second, metaphorical level of meaning that tragically escapes Seymour. Physically repelled by the overpowering stench of his daughter (she will not bathe or brush her teeth in case she contaminates the water), Seymour is even more repelled, morally, by her beliefs, in particular by the fact that she is degrading herself in this way '[f]or purity – in the name of purity' (240).

Again, ironies abound. Firstly, in her previous incarnation as his precociously bright, loving daughter, Merry had been plagued by a severe stutter; now her speech is fluent but she will not utter a word. After Seymour tears the veil from her face she remains silent. Secondly, her withdrawal from the realm of ordinary human interaction in order to achieve a state of 'purity' is a distorted echo of Seymour's own flight from the reality of contemporary American life in an attempt to create a timeless pastoral idyll. Finally, the shit that so disgusts him is, in a paradoxical sense, the anti-pastoral antidote to the pastoral virus that has poisoned his life, a symbol of the 'messy contingencies' that Eve Frame in *I Married a Communist* tries to clean up as part of her attempt to 'deodorize life and make it palatable' (Roth 1998: 179).

There is a lot of shit in Roth's novels.[12] Not, I think, because of any Swiftian scatological obsession, but because of what it symbolizes for him: namely, human life in all its visceral, indecorous, noisome messiness (hence the fact that the word 'human' resounds through Seymour's description of his daughter, exposing the paradox of the dehumanizing pronoun 'it' that he uses to refer to her). In *Patrimony*, his memoir of his father, Herman Roth, there is an extraordinary passage in which Philip Roth describes having to clean up the mess after Herman loses control of his bowels and defecates all over the bathroom. Surveying the scene, Roth observes: 'It's like writing a book . . . I have no idea where to begin' (Roth 1991: 173). The analogy is, of course, humorous, yet as the episode proceeds it becomes clear that the emotions aroused in Roth by the task – a heady mixture of horror and exhilaration – are indeed not unlike those aroused in the novelist confronted by the sight of the blank sheet of paper (or screen). Having completed the job as best he can (there's so much shit, spread even into the corners and crevices of the room, that he cannot erase all sign of his father's accident), Roth reflects:

> I felt awful about his heroic, hapless struggle to cleanse himself before I had got up to the bathroom . . . and yet now that it was over . . . I thought I couldn't have asked for anything more for myself before he died – this, too, was right and as it should be. You clean up your father's shit because it has to be cleaned up, but in the aftermath of cleaning it up, everything that's there to feel is felt as it never was before. It wasn't the first time that I'd understood this either: once you sidestep disgust and ignore nausea and plunge past those phobias that are fortified like taboos, there's an awful lot of life to cherish. (175)

The details of Roth's diction are noteworthy. He writes of his father's struggle to 'cleanse' himself (rather than 'clean', as one might expect) because it connotes moral or spiritual purity as well as physical hygiene. For Roth's father, incontinence creates not simply a physical stain, but also a metaphysical one: a stain on his character. Like Seymour Levov (whose father, Lou, closely resembles the Herman Roth of *Patrimony*),

Herman equates incontinence with immorality. Yet Herman's son sees it rather differently. He goes on to claim, in terms that indicate the centrality of this scene to the book: 'So *that* was the patrimony. And not because cleaning it up was symbolic of something else but because it wasn't, because it was nothing less or more than the lived reality that it was' (176). This last disclaimer notwithstanding, it seems clear from this passage that his father's incontinence does indeed symbolize something, and if we want to know what, we need only recall the fictional father of *Portnoy's Complaint*, whose chronic constipation his son Alex reads in symbolic terms: 'all catharses were in vain for that man: his *kishkas* [bowels] were gripped by the iron hand of outrage and frustration' (Roth 1969: 9). If Jack Portnoy's hapless retention of shit signifies emotional blockage, repression and impotence then Herman Roth's explosive diarrhoea (which erupts after days of constipation) represents a tremendous release, an uninhibited expression of vitality: 'I shit, therefore I am'.

With regard to Merry Levov, what Seymour fails to realise is that the smell of shit that clings to his daughter is not a sign of her decay but rather a sign of her *impurity*, of her failure to achieve a state of perfect purity (which can only mean death) and therefore of her continuing humanity. In spite of her minimal intake of nourishment (she is emaciated), Merry is still alive and potentially redeemable. If Seymour, like the Roth of *Patrimony*, could have sidestepped his disgust and ignored his nausea he might have been able to reclaim some connection with his daughter, to rediscover his paternity in the way that Roth rediscovers his patrimony. Instead he vomits over her and flees in terror.

Yet Seymour's visceral reaction to Merry's physical state does not seem sufficient cause to explain his sudden flight from her. Why does Seymour run away from Merry, having longed for their reunion over so many years? Why, later, does he not, as his brother Jerry suggests, simply 'go in there and get her' (Roth 1997: 281). Doesn't Jerry in fact have a point when he tells his brother '"If you were a father who loved his daughter [. . .] you would never have left her in that room!"' (278)? One possible explanation may be inferred from Seymour's encounters with Rita Cohen, the girl who tells Seymour that she is acting on Merry's behalf during her time as a fugitive, but of whom Merry denies all knowledge. Rita first appears in the novel in the guise of a student doing a thesis on the leather industry in Newark, visiting Seymour's glove factory to assemble material for her research. As Seymour takes

Rita, whose 'bland baby face' and slight frame lend her a prepubescent appearance, on a tour of the Newark Maid factory, he is reminded of the young Merry's girlish joy during her visits to the factory, 'flitting from floor to floor, so proud and proprietary, flaunting her familiarity with all the employees' (117, 122). From the outset, then, Rita is implicitly identified with Merry in Seymour's imagination and the slightly flirtatious tone that creeps into his conversation with Rita (he 'take[s] hold of her hand' to measure it for a glove fitting and begins to address her as 'honey') seems prompted by his memories of Merry's skittish behaviour, a skittishness reinforced by the strong alliteration ('flitting . . . flaunting . . . familiarity') in the passage above (124, 129).

When, later in the novel, Rita summons Seymour to a rendezvous in a room at the New York Hilton, she taunts him by exposing her genitalia and parroting some of the phrases he had used while measuring her for a glove fitting during her visit to the factory ('"I'm guessing you're a four [. . .] In a ladies' size that's as small as they come. Anything smaller is a child's"') in a manner that renders them obscene: 'I'm guessing that it's a four size. In a ladies' size that's as small as cunts come. Anything smaller is a child's' (124, 145). By transposing Seymour's words from the apparently innocent context of the glove fitting into the context of a sexual seduction, Rita highlights not only the latent sexual content of their earlier conversation (the word 'come' takes on a suggestive ambiguity) but also the dangerous slipperiness of the categories of 'lady' and 'child'. Furthermore, Rita makes explicit the paedophilic and incestuous desires that were implicit in Seymour's unconscious identification of her with Merry as a young girl by imitating Merry's stuttering speech and addressing Seymour as though he were her father, saying repeatedly '"Let's f-f-f-fuck, D-d-d-dad"' and telling him that that her vagina '"tastes like your d-d-d-daughter"' (143, 147). Confronted with this determined assault on his sense of propriety, Seymour initially tries to focus on Rita's eyes – 'a child's eyes, he discovered, a *good* child's eyes that had nothing in common with what she was up to' – before finally 'bolt[ing] . . . from something that he could no longer name', just as he later bolts from Merry's presence (145, 147). Although Seymour tries to find evidence in Rita Cohen's eyes that she is (or at least once was) a 'good child', the juxtaposition of this phrase with Rita's provocative insistence on being a bad girl – 'I'm twenty-two years old. I do everything' – only serves to complicate the neat moral distinctions that these labels promise (143). Seymour's futile struggle to maintain an idea of childhood innocence in the face of adult corruption has as much to do with Merry as it does with Rita herself. For years after Merry's disappearance, Seymour clings to the belief that Merry could not have been responsible for the bombing because she was herself a good girl. His encounter with Rita Cohen forces him to recognise that good girls can commit unspeakable acts.

The question remains: what causes Seymour to flee from the hotel room, even though Rita has promised to take him to Merry if he stays and accedes to her demands. What is the fear so dreadful that he cannot name it? Before he flees from Merry later in the novel, she tells him that she has been raped twice. It is this revelation, more than anything else – more, even, than the confirmation that she is behind the Old Rimrock bombing and a number of other terrorist acts that claimed a total of four lives – to which Seymour cannot reconcile himself:

> The rape was in his bloodstream and he would never get it out. The odor of it was in his bloodstream, the look of it, the legs and the arms and the hair and the clothing . . . The stupendousness of the rape blotted out everything. (270)

Seymour compulsively imagines and reimagines the rapes of his daughter in graphic sensory detail, at the same time flailing wildly at his ignorance of the true circumstances of these rapes.[13] Finally, he attempts to purify the image of Merry's violated body by overlaying it with a memory of her 'uncorrupted' childhood body (270). Even while invoking images of Merry in a state of presexual innocence, however, Seymour cannot help defining that state in terms of the promise of sexuality that it contains. So he admires her 'cleft' as a 'beautifully beveled joining that will petal outward, evolving in the cycle of time into a woman's origami-folded cunt' and is charmed by the 'lovely dormancy of the invisible bosom before the swell begins' (271). Similarly, when he recalls the 'abandon of her body flying into his arms, granting him a father's permission to touch', the question of whether his feelings towards his daughter are purely paternal is implicitly raised. Should a father have licence to 'touch' his daughter in ways that other adults don't? Although he insists that integral to 'the absoluteness of their intimacy' is 'the knowledge that he is not going too far', the very fact that it occurs to him at all that he might go 'too far' suggests that Seymour is uneasy about the nature of this intimacy.

This uneasiness manifests itself most dramatically in an incident related earlier in the novel. After a day on the beach together, Seymour and the eleven-year-old Merry are driving back home when, 'dopily sun-drunk, lolling against his bare shoulder, she had turned up her face and, half innocently, half audaciously, precociously playing the grown-up girl, said, "Daddy, kiss me the way you k-k-kiss umumumother"' (89). Looking at his daughter, Seymour notices that 'one of the shoulder straps of her swimsuit had dropped over her arm, and there was her nipple' (90). Seymour then does two things that haunt him for the rest of the novel: he mocks Merry by stammering his response – '"N-n-no"' – and then, when her attempt to apologise for her inappropriate request is arrested by a particularly acute fit of dysfluency, he 'kisse[s] her stammering mouth with the passion that she had been asking for' (91). Is this rash moment – as Seymour at times suspects – the origin of Merry's subsequent rebellion and increasing alienation from her parents? It is entirely characteristic of a novel that is full of questions that are posed but never answered that the true significance of this scene is never established.[14] What is clear, however, is the symbolic force of this episode: when he kisses Merry as a lover rather than a father, Seymour 'overstep[s] a boundary fundamental to civilized life', to borrow a phrase that Zuckerman uses in another context but which seems to me to allude to Seymour's transgression here, as well as to Merry's acts of terrorism (423).[15] In the context of the novel's own Miltonic moral structure, this kiss, as much as – maybe more than – the bomb that Merry detonates at the Old Rimrock post office, constitutes the fall.

It is precisely because so much of Seymour's pastoral dream is invested in his relationship with his daughter that the sexualisation of this relationship – first in the form of the kiss, and then in his encounters with Merry's surrogate, Rita Cohen – has such a devastating effect on Seymour. Even before she is born, Merry is an integral part of Seymour's vision of his future. As a sixteen-year-old high school kid, Seymour, on his way to a baseball game, spies the old stone house which is to become his future home:

> A little girl was on a swing suspended from a low branch of one of those big trees, swinging herself high into the air, just as happy, he imagined, as a kid can be. It was the first house built of stone he'd ever seen, and to a city boy it was an architectural marvel. (189)

Enchanted by this idyllic pastoral image, Seymour begins 'dreaming about that house' and the life that he will lead in it, and the image of the little girl insinuates itself into his dreams: 'he would imagine himself going home after work to that house back of the trees and seeing his little daughter there, his little daughter high up in the air on the swing he'd built for her' (190). The fantasy figure of the doting daughter soon takes on a name – '"Merry" because of the joy she took in the swing he'd built her' – and in time the dream becomes a reality. Seymour acquires the house, marries his dream girl – a contender for Miss America, no less – and has a daughter whom he duly names Meredith, 'Merry' for short (191).

In this light, Merry's failure to live up to her name can be seen as a self-conscious rebellion against her father's complacent preconceptions about her life. Just as Coleman Silk in *The Human Stain*, realising that 'it was [. . .] his father who had been making up Coleman's story for him' (Roth 2000: 107), decides to define himself in opposition to this master narrative, so Merry instinctively resists playing a part that has already been written for her by a man who believed that he 'foresaw, in perfect detail, the outcome of his story' and that of his daughter, 'who was to have been the perfected image of himself' (Roth 1997: 192, 85–6). The dramatic irony of this passage, which echoes that of an earlier episode when Dawn 'wonder[s] aloud if anything so wonderfully unforeseen as that week in Atlantic City [venue of the Miss America pageant] would ever happen to her again', is that Seymour's 'presumptuous innocence' makes him peculiarly vulnerable to the blows delivered by what Zuckerman calls 'the strong arm of the unforeseen' (192, 36).

If *American Pastoral* can be read as a tragedy in the Aristotelian tradition, with Seymour's repressed incestuous desires for his own daughter leading to the *hamartia* (fatal error of judgement) of the kiss, which in turn leads to his and his family's destruction, it is also a social-historical novel that explores the tension between the idealism of Seymour's generation of Americans and the cynicism of Merry's. In this context, Rita Cohen's symbolic function in the novel is to confront Seymour not just with his sexual feelings for Merry but, as she herself puts it, '[t]o introduce you to reality' (143). When she visits the glove factory, Rita tells Seymour that '[n]othing is further from your understanding than the nature of reality' (139) and she lampoons Dawn Levov (whom she refers to as 'Lady Dawn') as a neurotic snob who is determined to sanitise life: '"I don't want to see anything messy, I don't want to see anything dark." But the world . . . *is* messy, it *is* dark. It's *hideous*!' (136, italics in original). In a similar spirit, she taunts Seymour during their encounter in the Hilton. When he refuses to look at her exposed genitalia, she accuses him of being a man who is 'always averting his eyes because it's all too steeped in reality for him' and then she touches herself, announcing that 'this is what life smells like' (146). Her appalling amorality notwithstanding, Rita's jibes carry some weight, because Seymour – as Zuckerman imagines him[16] – is indeed an escapist, a Utopian dreamer who awakes, during the course of the novel, to what James Joyce's Stephen Dedalus famously calls 'the nightmare of history'.

It is clear throughout *American Pastoral* that Seymour, on one level, inhabits a mythical realm far removed from – indeed specifically conceived as an escape from – the historical realities of American life. The opening page of the novel refers to the 'magical name' of the Swede and to the way in which his 'elevation . . . into the household Apollo of the Weequahic Jews . . . provided a bizarre, delusionary kind of sustenance, the happy release into a Swedian innocence, for those who lived in dread of never seeing their sons or their brothers or their husbands again' (4). From the outset, then, Seymour's humanity is subordinated to his function as a transcendent symbol, the object of 'frenzied adoration' and 'idolatrous adulation' (4,5). Growing up as 'the indestructible hero of the wartime Weequahic section, our neighborhood talisman, the legendary Swede', it is perhaps hardly surprising that the adult Seymour identifies himself with a figure from American folklore, Johnny Appleseed (65). In his guise as the carefree Johnny, Seymour gestures expansively as he roams the fields of Old Rimrock, spreading imaginary seeds as he strides happily through 'the acres and acres of woods he loved with all of a new country dweller's puppy love for nature' that surround his home on the symbolically named Arcady Hill Road, 'making love to his life' (318, 319). Yet Seymour's intoxication with his Arcadian existence is not shared by his father, Lou, who points out that 'this is a narrow, bigoted area [. . .] where the haters live', or by his Jewish neighbour, Bucky Robinson, from whom Seymour learns that this apparently idyllic community has a dark history: '[B]efore the war there'd been a swastika scrawled on the golf-course sign [. . .] the Klan held meetings in Boonton and Dover [. . .] crosses were burned on people's lawns not five miles from the Morristown green' (314). Whereas as a young athlete Seymour had been the means by which his community escaped from the historical reality of wartime America and lived out vicariously a fairy tale of empowerment and assimilation, in Old Rimrock he himself is crushed by the weight of history, whether it be the historical past that makes him feel like an interloper compared to his neighbour, Bill Orcutt ('[h]is family couldn't compete with Orcutt's when it came to ancestors'), or the pressure of contemporary history, in the form of the violent protests against the Vietnam War and the race riots of the 1960s (306).

Seymour is repeatedly represented as a naïve dreamer, whose Utopian vision of a pure pastoral existence is corrupted by the contaminants of ethnicity, sexuality and history. Jerry accuses Seymour of living in 'your old man's dream-world . . . in glove heaven' and when Zuckerman meets Seymour for the first time since they were both boys, he observes that 'd]eath had burst into the dream of his life' (277, 29). Rita Cohen, acerbic as ever, dismisses Seymour's version of harmonious family history as '[a]nother one of your fucking fairy tales' (137). Most poignantly, Merry comments on her father's tendency to idealise her childhood. When she tells him of her years on the run, living in destitution, Seymour cannot reconcile this with the image that persists in his mind of Merry as 'a privileged kid from paradise', so that Merry marvels at '[h]ow strongly [he] still crave[s] the idea . . . of [his] innocent offspring' (262, 248). Just as Seymour stays on in Newark, after all the other businesses have left, 'sitting alone in the last factory left in the worst city in the world', clinging on to an outmoded dream of harmonious worker-management relations, until finally he is forced to abandon the factory after the Newark race riots of 1968,[17] so in his personal life he tenaciously clings to the idea of the family idyll long after it has been exposed as a delusion (268).

However hard Seymour struggles to retrieve a nostalgic idea of history, in which 'the wholesome striving of the past' helped create 'the utopia of a rational existence', the more turbulent, irrational forces of history always intervene (122, 123). So it is that when Merry detonates her bomb, Zuckerman describes it not just as a personal tragedy, but as the destruction of a particular kind of 'mid-century innocence' – a 'longed-for American pastoral' – by the 'fury, the violence, and the desperation of the counterpastoral' (86). Seymour hopes to find shelter in sleepy Old Rimrock from the political storms that rock urban America, only to find that '[h]istory, American history, the stuff you read about in books and study in school, had made its way out to tranquil, untrafficked Old Rimrock, New Jersey' (87). He tries to fortify his home against the dangers of contemporary urban life but 'the decade blast[s] to smithereens his particular form of utopian thinking'; he attempts to preserve a pastoral quarantine but eventually 'the plague America infiltrat[es] [his] castle' (86). On the other hand, these allusions to grand abstractions ('history', the sixties, 'America' itself) should not obscure the fact that two individuals – the two human beings closest to him – destroy Seymour's paradise: Merry by detonating her bomb, Dawn by cuckolding him.

The final irony of the novel is that these serpents in Seymour's Eden are themselves also engaged in their own rituals of purification, their own particular dreams of Utopia. When Merry changes from a charming girl into a gawky teenager, her metamorphosis is figured once again in the trope of the fairy tale: '[L]ike some innocent in a fairy story who has been tricked into drinking the noxious potion, the grasshopper child who used to scramble delightedly up and down the furniture . . . became large, a large, loping, slovenly sixteen-year-old' (100). But set against this parable of the fall from innocence into corruption/experience – another version of paradise lost – is a different sort of fable: that of a girl whose undoing comes not from her loss of innocence, but, paradoxically, from her relentless pursuit of it.

From an early age, Merry is obsessed with what might be termed an iconography of innocence. She moves from an infatuation with the figure of Christ and the Virgin Mary (religious incarnations of uncontaminated humanity) to the idolatrous worship of Audrey Hepburn (rooted in what Zuckerman calls 'an improbable dream of purification'), to a morbid fascination with televised images of Buddhist monks immolating themselves, to a commitment to the 'terrifyingly pure' ideology of militant antiwar groups such as the Weathermen – that 'angry ragtag army of the violent Uncorrupted', as Zuckerman describes them – to a dogmatic adherence to the Jain rituals of self-purification through which the true believer can attain a 'perfected soul' (93–5, 254–6, 244, 232). For Seymour, Merry's incarnation as a Jain is 'absurdly innocent'; he denounces the 'egregious innocence' with which she announces that she has killed four people while at the same time espousing 'the most supercoherent of dreams', whose central tenet is 'a belief in the sanctity of life' (254, 264, 245). With this final pathological version of Merry's quest for absolute purity, articulated with perfect fluency and 'insane clarity' (the oxymoron enacting the perverse, paradoxical logic of Merry's own reasoning), Seymour's idealistic vision of Merry's future takes a bitter twist: 'What he had dreamed about – that his wonderful, gifted child would one day stop stuttering – had come to pass' (250).

Dawn Levov, too, embarks on a project of self-purification in the form of cosmetic surgery. When Seymour expresses reservations about Dawn's dream of recovering her youthful beauty to Sheila Salzman, formerly Merry's speech therapist and briefly his lover, Sheila advises him not to 'be too puritanical about this' (353). However, these words are unwittingly ironic, since it is Dawn whose pursuit of aesthetic perfection conceals an ascetic desire for self-cleansing. By literally acquiring a new skin – and planning, as Seymour begins to suspect, to elope with Bill Orcutt, who has his own Utopian pastoral project of 'keep[ing] Lake Hopatcong from devastation by pollutants' – Dawn hopes metaphorically to purge herself of her sins and begin anew (301). As Seymour sees it, Dawn's plan is, at a stroke, to delete her history: 'Rid of the stain of our child, the stain on her credentials, rid of the stain of the destruction of the store, she can begin to resume the uncontaminated life' (385). These lines anticipate the central image, the image that lends itself to the title, of the third novel in Roth's 'American Trilogy', *The Human Stain*, and the final section of this chapter explores some of the meanings of this phrase.

## *The Human Stain*

On a literal level, the words 'human stain' refer to the skin pigmentation that determines, or at least heavily influences, the ethno-racial identity of human beings. The plot of the novel turns on the fact that Coleman Silk, although by ancestry a black man, is sufficiently light-skinned to conceal this fact. Most critics of the novel refer to Coleman, somewhat misleadingly, as a black man who passes for white. Igor Webb, for example, claims that 'Coleman Silk's big secret [. . .] is that he's black, that he's passed as a white man from the day he signed up for the Navy in the Second World War' (Webb 2003: 234), Bonnie Lyons writes that '[t]he novel presents his passing as white as his precious secret' (Lyons 2001: 90), Elaine B. Safer refers to Coleman as 'a black man passing as white' (Safer 2003: 241) and Robert Alter characterises him as 'a person of mixed race passing for white' (Alter 2002: 29). Even those few critics who point out that Coleman in fact swaps one ethnicity for another (he pretends to be not a WASP, but a Jew) don't pursue the implications of this decision. Mark Shechner describes him as 'a Black man who has made a career for himself in the academy by passing for white, or at least passing for Jewish' but does not elaborate on the distinction hinted at by the qualification 'or at least passing for Jewish' (Shechner 2003b: 171). Similarly, Lorrie Moore asserts that '[b]eing Jewish, for Coleman Silk, means being white', but says nothing further about the suggestion – implicit in her careful attribution of the equation between whiteness and Jewishness to Coleman – that this is not a universal assumption (Moore 2000: 7). Even Dean J. Franco, though he quotes Daniel Itzkovitz's claim that Jews in America were traditionally seen as 'both white and racially other' (Itzkovitz 2001 quoted in Franco 2004: 92), begins his essay on *The Human Stain* with the bald assertion that it is 'a novel about a black man passing as white' (Franco 2004: 89).

This simplistic view is shared by a number of characters in the novel. For Walter, Coleman's brother, Coleman is a 'traitor to his race' who tries to be 'more white than the whites', and Nathan Zuckerman, although he only discovers the truth about Coleman's identity after he has died, decides retrospectively that his friend's 'art was being a white man' (Roth 2000: 342, 345). Certainly, Coleman exploits the opportunity provided by the pale tone of his skin to elude the metaphorical stain (the stigma) that has attached, and that continues to attach, to black citizens in the U.S. However, he never passes as a white man. As a sailor in the U.S. navy, Coleman is generally assumed by his comrades to be 'of Middle Eastern descent', but he spends most of his life masquerading as a Jew (131). He gets the idea in the first place from his boxing coach and mentor at high school, Doc Chizener, who tells him 'not to mention that he was colored' when he takes Coleman to the University of Pittsburgh to audition for a boxing scholarship (98). Chizener instructs Coleman that '"[i]f nothing comes up [. . .] you don't bring it up. You're neither one thing nor the other"' and goes on to explain that '"[y]ou look like you look, you're with me, and so he's [the boxing coach at Pittsburgh] [. . .] going to think that you're Jewish"' (98, 99). As is implied by Doc Chizener's equation of Jewishness with being 'neither one thing nor the other', the identity that Coleman assumes is in fact *not* that of a white man, but rather of an ethnic minority that has, historically, often been identified more strongly with blacks than with whites and that has traditionally fitted comfortably into neither category, occupying an ambiguous, liminal space between the two.[18] Although the choice of a Jewish identity is both convenient (because Coleman attends a school where so many of his classmates are Jewish he is familiar with his material) and timely (this was a moment, Zuckerman tells us, 'when Jewish self-infatuation was at a postwar pinnacle among the Washington Square intellectual avant-garde'), it may also seem somewhat perverse (131). If, as Zuckerman informs us, Coleman 'could play his skin color however he wanted, color himself just as he chose', then surely it would have made more sense to become part of the WASP establishment (109).[19] After all, however fashionable Jewishness might have been among the East Coast intelligentsia, the post-war years in America were hardly free of anti-Semitism: in Coleman's chosen field of academia, for example, unofficial quotas were still enforced to restrict the numbers of Jews entering many colleges, and there were still very few Jews in positions of tenure.[20]

In fact, Coleman cannot 'color himself just as he chose': the stain of his skin may be paler than that of most African Americans, but it is not pale enough for him to join the ranks of the Anglo-Saxon American elite. In an interview with Charles McGrath, Roth himself claims that Coleman's decision to take on a Jewish identity is 'strictly utilitarian', 'a cunning choice that successfully furnishes him with a disguise in the flight from his own "we"', but Zuckerman's description of Coleman's motives is rather more complex than this would suggest (McGrath 2000: 8). Rather than successfully sloughing off his skin – eluding the category of ethnic minority altogether – Coleman becomes, in Zuckerman's phrase, 'a heretofore unknown amalgam of the most unalike of America's historic undesirables' (132).[21] Indeed, if Zuckerman's hypothesis is correct then Coleman's death is at least partly the result of race hatred: when Les Farley runs Coleman and Faunia off the road, he seems to be motivated almost as much by anti-Semitism as by a desire for vengeance on his wife (whom he blames for the death of their children). If the purpose of Coleman's imposture is to purify himself symbolically by removing any tint or taint of colour from his identity, then clearly he fails. On the other hand, it might be argued that it is, paradoxically, the very success of Coleman's project that undoes him: he distances himself so convincingly from his ethnic origins that his students and colleagues have no qualms in convicting him of displaying anti-black prejudice. This is one of the many ironies of Coleman's story: seeking to escape from what Zuckerman calls 'the stranglehold of history that is one's own time' – from the restrictions imposed on him by the history of black Americans – he eventually becomes a victim of the concerted attempt to reverse this history of discrimination often referred to as 'political correctness' (337). The stain of blackness is replaced by the stain of racism.

Like Ira Ringold and Seymour Levov, Coleman is ultimately trapped in the very historical nets that he tries to fly by, but unlike the protagonists of these novels he achieves a kind of redemption in the form of his affair late in life with Faunia Farley. As her first name implies, Faunia in a sense embodies a pastoral ideal of womanhood: one of her jobs is to milk the cows at an organic farm and Coleman admires the way in which she seems entirely at home with these animals and the nature they represent. Yet Zuckerman is also careful to introduce a note of anti-pastoral satire that warns against the dangers of naïvely idealising Faunia's work:

> The farm has a strong following particularly among the numerous people . . . in flight from the pollutants . . . of a big city. In the local weekly, a letter will regularly appear from someone who has recently found a better life out along these rural roads, and in reverent tones mention will be made of Organic Livestock milk, not simply as a tasty drink but as the embodiment of a freshening, sweetening country purity that their city-battered idealism requires. (46)

In fact, Faunia turns out to be anything but the conventional milkmaid of pastoral romance. Far from living out a rustic idyll, we discover that she has endured childhood abuse, the loss of both her children and the violence of her ex-husband. As Zuckerman puts it: 'Rural disaster has squeezed Faunia dry even of her tears' (28).

Although she has the 'severely sculpted features customarily associated with the church-ruled, hardworking goodwives . . . stern colonial women locked up within the reigning morality and obedient to it', she is an independent-minded, sexually adventurous woman whose philosophy of life could not be farther removed from the Puritan tradition (1). It is Faunia who articulates the phrase 'the human stain' in the novel, to explain why Prince, a crow that has been 'hand-raised', is rejected by the other crows. Zuckerman then proceeds to paraphrase her thoughts: '[W]e leave a stain, we leave a trail, we leave our imprint. Impurity, cruelty, abuse, error, excrement, semen – there's no other way to be here' (242). Rather than lamenting the imperfection of life, Faunia embraces it: instead of seeking to purify her existence (as Eve Frame and Dawn Dwyer do), she 'cannot get enough of the toxins: of all that you're not supposed to be' (297). It is with these transgressive 'toxins' that Faunia infects, and paradoxically cures, Coleman. Whereas before the affair, Coleman is sick with self-righteous indignation, consumed by a 'misanthropic exertion of Swiftian proportions', once he begins his relationship with Faunia he is 'contaminated by desire alone' (20). Coleman's preference for 'the great reality-reflecting religion' of the Greeks rather than the 'exquisite unearthliness' of Christianity, with its 'perfectly desexualized . . . man-god and his uncontaminated mother' suggests that, like Faunia, he has always been more of a realist than a Utopian dreamer (243). Yet it is only as a result of his intimacy with Faunia that he is able fully to recognise for the fantasy it is what Zuckerman calls 'the youngest, most innocent of our ideas of life, the indestructible yearning for the way things aren't and can never be' (207). Coleman's disdain for the moral absolutism of his lawyer, Nelson Primus, who allows 'no incriminating impurity [. . .] to breach [his ethical boundaries]', demonstrates that he has, under Faunia's influence (the very influence that Primus warns him against), definitively rejected pastoral idealism in favour of a more worldly engagement with 'life, in all its shameless impurity' (79, 3).

Coleman's and Faunia's realism and humanity (in all senses of that word) are opposed in the novel by Les Farley, the Vietnam veteran whose bitter misanthropy prevents him from experiencing any meaningful communication with others. Farley conforms in many respects to a familiar stereotype of the Vietnam veteran: profoundly traumatised by his combat experiences (particularly by the loss of his closest comrades), he is a paranoid racist psychopath and, so Zuckerman believes (though there is no hard evidence presented in the novel to support his hypothesis), a murderer to boot.[22] Yet the final image of Farley in the novel (the image with which *The Human Stain*, and indeed the 'American Trilogy' as a whole, concludes) could not, on the face of it, be more peaceful, indeed pastoral.

Driving along 'a remote mountain road' en route to East Orange to meet Coleman's family, Zuckerman notices a truck with a POW/MIA sticker that he 'somehow kn[o]w[s]' is Les Farley's. Zuckerman parks his car and sets off to find Farley. Making his way through fields 'thick with high evergreens', he eventually spies 'the shining eye of a frozen lake', surrounded by 'caressable-looking' mountains (344, 345). Startled by the natural beauty of the place, Zuckerman feels that he has 'intruded upon – no, trespassed upon . . . a setting as pristine . . . as unviolated, as serenely unspoiled, as envelops any inland body of water in New England. It gave you an idea . . . of what the world was like before the advent of man' (345). Zuckerman's sense of himself as an interloper, contaminating the prelapsarian environment with his very presence, is contrasted with his description of Farley himself, fishing peacefully, in perfect harmony with nature: 'Only rarely . . . does life offer up a vision as pure and peaceful as this one: a solitary man on a bucket, fishing through eighteen inches of ice in a lake that's constantly turning over its water atop an arcadian mountain in America' (361). Here nature is engaged in a purification ritual. As Farley explains to

Zuckerman, the 'numerous springs underneath the lake' constantly replenish the water supply, so that the lake 'cleans itself' (360). So far, so idyllic. As always with Roth, however, there is a sinister side to this Edenic world: a Sodom and Gomorrah lurking within Arcadia. When Farley confides to Zuckerman that he comes to this 'secret place' as part of his own purification ritual – to get '[a]way from man, close to God' – it serves as a reminder of what I have been arguing is an abiding theme of the 'American Trilogy': namely, the idea that Utopian dreams, pastoral ideas of purity, invariably entail a rejection of humanity (360). This rejection can take the form of a repudiation of your own human stain (as in the symbolic ethnic self-cleansing in which Ira Ringold, Seymour Levov and Coleman Silk, in their different ways, are all implicated), or it can manifest itself in a misanthropic retreat from the company of others (of which both Farley and Zuckerman are guilty). Although at first sight Farley seems to achieve some sort of salvation in his pastoral idyll, it becomes clear in the final paragraph of the novel that his Utopian dream of inhabiting a pure realm can never be realised, since he himself is a symbolic human stain on the otherwise unblemished landscape, a 'tiny spot' in the middle of a vast expanse of white ice, 'the only human marker in all of nature, like the X of an illiterate's signature on a sheet of paper' (361). Unlike his ex-wife, Faunia (whose memory is invoked by the image of the 'illiterate's signature'), Les cannot reconcile himself to his own, or to others', humanity. Ultimately, it is Zuckerman, not Farley, who is saved from the sterility of the pastoral retreat.

It emerges near the beginning of *American Pastoral* that Nathan Zuckerman is 'impotent and incontinent', having to cope with the indignity of wearing diapers, following an operation to remove his prostate, and he returns to this theme in *The Human Stain* (Roth 1998: 28). Early on in that novel Zuckerman spends an evening with Coleman Silk, during the course of which Silk confesses that he is having an affair with Faunia Farley, an apparently illiterate cleaning lady half his age. At one point during the evening, the two friends begin dancing to the old 1940s tunes played on a local radio station:

> On we danced. There was nothing overtly carnal in it, but because Coleman was wearing only his denim shorts and my hand rested easily on his warm back as if it were the back of a dog or a horse, it wasn't entirely a mocking act. There was a semi-serious sincerity in his guiding me about on the stone floor, not to mention a thoughtless delight in just being alive, accidentally and clownishly and for no reason alive [.] (26)

When he returns home, Zuckerman realizes that he has wet himself: 'I discovered . . . that [my] trousers were discolored at the front and that I smelled a little . . . I'd been so engaged by Coleman and his story that I'd failed to monitor myself' (36–7). The urine stains on Zuckerman's trousers, like the infamous semen stains on Monica Lewinsky's dress (one of the many allusions implied by the novel's title), are the result of a failure to exercise restraint, to keep in check the progress of human intimacy, to 'monitor' oneself. They symbolise the failure of Zuckerman's 'self-imposed separation from every last . . . cultural poison and alluring intimacy', the contamination of his monastic existence by the human stain (43).

The novel begins with Zuckerman comparing Coleman Silk's affair with Faunia Farley to Bill Clinton's affair with Monica Lewinsky and condemning the 'purity binge' that leads to the demonisation of the (real-life) President of the United States and of the (fictional) former Dean of Athena College (2). Zuckerman cites, as an example of this 'ecstasy of sanctimony', the words of William F. Buckley, a syndicated conservative newspaper columnist who attributes Clinton's downfall to his 'incontinent carnality' – the use of the word incontinent implicitly linking Clinton's alleged inability to control the sexual function of the phallus with Zuckerman's inability to control its excretory function (2,3).

Zuckerman's response to such moralistic hysteria is to dream of 'a mammoth banner, draped . . . from one end of the White House to the other and bearing the legend A HUMAN BEING LIVES HERE' (3). Whereas for Buckley, Clinton's unrestrained sexuality is a sign of his inhumanity, for Zuckerman it confirms that Clinton *is* a human being with all the normal human impulses and imperfections. The word 'incontinent' is thus rehabilitated, so that Zuckerman's involuntary urination signals, not the degradation or humiliation that we might expect, but rather a form of revitalization, a 'delight in just being alive'. Just as, at the close of *I Married A Communist*, Zuckerman finds himself late at night 'wide awake from the stimulus of all [the] narrative engorgement' provided by Murray Ringold's account of his brother's life, so Zuckerman's encounter with Coleman stirs him up. Although there is nothing 'overtly carnal' in his dance with Coleman, there is an intimacy that rouses Zuckerman from a self-imposed state not just of personal celibacy but of indifference to the sexuality of others.

Zuckerman is at great pains to emphasize that he had 'altered deliberately [his] relationship to the sexual caterwaul' – that is renounced all carnal relations – even before becoming medically impotent, so that '[t]he operation did no more than to enforce with finality a decision I'd come to on my own' (37). However, the dance with Coleman and Coleman's account of his affair with Faunia excite Zuckerman and bring home to him the importance of '[t]he contaminant of sex, the redeeming corruption that de-idealizes the species and keeps us ever mindful of the matter we are' (37). The oxymoron 'redeeming corruption', like the earlier phrases 'ecstasy of sanctimony' and 'purity binge', indicates the paradox at the heart of this novel, and of the 'American Trilogy' as a whole, a paradox encapsulated by the rhetorical question that Zuckerman poses near the end of *The Human Stain*: 'What is the quest to purify, if not *more* impurity?' (242). For Zuckerman (and Roth) to be alive, to be human, *is* to be stained, not simply in the Christian sense of the taint of original sin, but also in a more worldly sense: it is our bodily needs and functions – eating, pissing, shitting, ejaculating, crying, vomiting – that make us human.

To repress these needs or to seek to ignore their reality is to become, at best, less than human, at worst irredeemably inhumane. For the author of *Carnovsky*, to reject carnality, to withdraw altogether from the arena of human sexuality and retreat 'into a two-room cabin set way back in a field on a rural road high in the Berkshires', insulating himself from the conflicts and tensions of adult life, is to betray himself, and subscribe to the very 'fairy tale of purity' that deforms and destroys the lives of Coleman Silk, Seymour Levov and Ira Ringold (10, 341). Ultimately, Zuckerman discovers that nature is no substitute for human nature: he renounces his own Utopian dream of the artist in pastoral isolation dedicated purely to his art – his own self-purification ritual – and (re)engages with the confusion irrationality, incoherence and mess of 'lived reality'.

If history is incorporated into a realist, anti-pastoral discourse in the 'American Trilogy', it serves a rather different function in *The Plot Against America*. In this novel, Roth paradoxically represents conventional history as a comforting illusion, a precariously constructed narrative of teleological progress that a shift of consciousness can suddenly destabilise.

## Notes

1 Though not a conventional trilogy (there is no narrative continuity or chronological sequence across the three books), Roth, in an interview with

Charles McGrath, refers to the novels as 'a thematic trilogy, dealing with the historical moments in postwar American life that have had the greatest impact on my generation' (McGrath 2000: 8).

2 See Brauner 1995: 166–8 and, for a more detailed discussion of the anti-pastoral as a mini-genre, Brauner 2001: 74–112.

3 For a detailed discussion of the place of the pastoral in the American literary tradition, see McDonald 2004. I agree broadly with McDonald's argument that there is a 'collision in *American Pastoral* of Roth's sympathy for innocence and his recognition of experience' (McDonald 2004: 39), but whereas McDonald situates Roth's novel in the context of American intellectual history and political philosophy, I am more interested in Roth's deployment of history as intrinsically antagonistic to a mode of Utopian dreaming (the opposite, in a sense, of rational thinking) that he associates with the pastoral, both as a literary genre and as a loose agglomeration of images of purification.

4 See, for example, Moore 2000 and Gerstle 2001. *I Married A Communist* has received less critical attention than the other two novels in the trilogy and its links with them have consequently been relatively neglected. This neglect may be partly because the novel was assumed by many critics to be, as Robert Alter puts it, 'a transparent exercise in paying off personal scores against Claire Bloom, Roth's ex-wife, and her daughter' (Alter 2002: 28).

5 All three are, for example, closely associated with American Presidents: Coleman is described as a 'great man brought low . . . like . . . Nixon at San Clemente or Jimmy Carter, down in Georgia' (Roth 2000: 18), and the parallels between the attempts by the Athena College authorities to indict him on charges of racism and the attempts in the US Congress to impeach Bill Clinton run throughout the novel; Nathan Zuckerman refers to Seymour as 'another man of glamour exuding American meaning . . . our [that is, American Jews'] Kennedy' (Roth 1997: 83); and Ira first makes his name as an actor by playing Abraham Lincoln.

We are also encouraged to read these novels in this light because of the frequent allusions to the epic and tragic modes in their pages. Ira becomes (at least in the imagination of the young Nathan Zuckerman) one of those 'heroic Americans who fought against tyranny and injustice, champions of liberty for America and for all mankind' whom he plays on the radio (Roth 1998: 25). The titles of the three sections into which *American Pastoral* is divided ('Paradise Remembered', 'The Fall', 'Paradise Lost') invoke Milton's epic poem *Paradise Lost*, and Zuckerman refers to Seymour's fate as both a 'tragic fall' and a 'great fall' (Roth 1997: 88). The epigraph to *The Human Stain* is taken from Sophocles' tragedy *Oedipus Rex* and the rest of the novel is filled with allusions to other classical and Shakespearian tragedies and to the epics of Homer (particularly *The Illiad*).

To quote just one example from among many: 'Out on his lawn, Coleman was seized suddenly with the sort of indignation he had not felt since the day following Markie's outburst . . . He knew . . . that indignation on such a scale was a form of madness . . . He knew from the wrath of Achilles, the rage of Philoctetes, the fulminations of Medea, the madness of Ajax, the despair of Electra, and the suffering of Prometheus the many horrors that can ensue when the highest degree of indignation is achieved' (Roth 2000: 63). In a review of *The Human Stain*, Graham Higgin suggests that 'like the Greek tragic poets, Roth depicts a world in which humans are mixed-up beings, scrambled out of the odds and ends of inherited traits and acquired experience, animal propensities and spiritual aspirations' (Higgin 2000: 8). For a detailed discussion of the network of classical allusions in *The Human Stain*, see Savin 2002.

6 As Ira's brother, Murray, puts it: '[H]is whole life was an attempt to defuse the violent impulse' (Roth 1998: 292).

7 The classic study of the ways in which this pastoral mythology manifests itself in the American literary tradition remains R.W.B. Lewis's *The American Adam* (1955). For an interesting discussion of *American Pastoral* as a novel in this tradition (a discussion that draws heavily on Lewis), see McDonald 2004.

8 The epigraph to *The Human Stain*, taken from Sophocles' tragedy *Oedipus Rex*, quotes Oedipus asking Creon, 'What is the rite of purification?' and the fifth section of the novel is entitled 'The Purifying Ritual'.

9 Much has already been written on Roth's treatment of 'purity' and 'the pastoral' in the trilogy. Ada Savin notes in passing in her essay on Roth's use of classical allusions in *The Human Stain* that the 'generic and metaphoric hybridity' of *The Human Stain* 'stands as a bulwark against the dangers of imposing purity, in life as in art' but doesn't elaborate (Savin 2002: 184). Monika Hogan reads *American Pastoral* as a sequel of sorts to *The Counterlife*, arguing that '[t]he Swede is the product of Zuckerman's melancholic reflection on his own failed "pastoral"' in that earlier novel, and that Seymour Levov's tragedy should be understood in the light of Zuckerman's own attempt to 'assimilate into "whiteness"', an attempt doomed to failure by what she calls 'his hypochondriacal fear of his body's eruption into racialization' (Hogan 2004: 12, 13). Whereas Hogan's argument is that 'the Zuckerman novels expose the "American dream" as being reliant on a fantasy notion of bodily purity and wholeness' (Hogan 2004: 3), I am more interested in tracing the non-somatic, metaphorical meanings of purity in these novels. Laura Tanenbaum concludes her essay on *American Pastoral* by complaining that whereas Merry's version of the pastoral – her 'quest for purity' – is ruthlessly exposed in the novel, Seymour's 'assimilationist dreams' are treated more sympathetically (Tanenbaum 2004: 52). Neelakantan similarly argues that in *American*

*Pastoral* the 'evocation of pastoral is associated with the novelist's nostalgic depiction of a pre-1960s American idyll' (Neelakantan 2004: 62). In contrast, I will argue that it is Seymour's inflexible idealism (which Merry's own dogmatism is arguably both the product of and a response to) that the novel pitilessly dissects. Finally, Derek Parker Royal, in his essay on 'Pastoral Dreams and National Identity', reads *American Pastoral* and *I Married A Communist* as political allegories in which Seymour's 'quest for an unambiguous and uncomplicated life parallels his nation's attempts at retaining the façade of innocence, even in the face of civil and national embroilment' and Ira's 'colorful life' becomes 'a stand-in . . . for an idealized America' (Royal 2005b: 195, 192). I agree with much of what Royal says, but I feel that these novels employ allegorical elements in order to critique the very notion of allegory as itself a pastoral dream: whereas Royal suggests that Ira and Seymour represent the fate of American itself, I see their tragedy as deriving from their deluded belief that they fulfil this mythical role.

10 For a detailed discussion of the role of these father figures in the novel, see Lévy 2002.

11 In *My Life as a Man,* Peter Tarnopol presents his domestic conflict with Maureen Johnson both as a microcosm of the social and political turmoil of 1960s America and at the same time as evidence of his own solipsistic isolation from the 'vivid and momentous history' going on around him: 'In the spring of 1963 . . . when for nights on end I could not get to sleep because of my outrage over Judge Rosenzweig's alimony decision, police dogs were turned loose on the demonstrators in Birmingham; and just about the time I began to imagine myself planting a Hoffritz hunting knife into Maureen's evil heart, Medgar Evers was shot to death in his driveway in Mississippi' (Roth 1985: 269).

12 The 'American Trilogy' has its fair share. The 'high point' of Faunia's marriage to Les Farley, for example, is what she describes as their 'great warm shit fight' (Roth 2000: 29), while the nadir of Murray Ringold's childhood is reached when his father vengefully spreads his own excrement all over the apartment vacated by his wife and two sons (Roth 1998: 293). More metaphorically, Sylphid in *I Married A Communist* resolves to give her mother 'a dose of life's dung' (Roth 1998: 179).

13 He asks himself: 'What *were* the details? Who were these men? Was it somebody who was part of that life . . . was it somebody she knew or was it a stranger . . . What went on? Had they held her down . . . Had they beaten her? What did they make her do? Were there no people there to help her? Just what did they make her do?' (Roth 1997: 267).

14 Early on in the novel Zuckerman speculates that once '[d]eath had burst into the dream of his life', Seymour makes the 'belated discovery of . . . what it is like to ask why' and later Jerry tells him that before Merry's

bombing Seymour had '[n]ever in his life had occasion to ask himself, "Why are things the way they are?"' Once he begins to ask questions of himself and his life, however, Seymour cannot stop. In particular, he torments himself with the question of why Merry turns out as she does: 'Why? . . . Did it have to do with him? That foolish kiss? . . . Why must she always be enslaving herself to the handiest empty-headed idea? . . . What had he done to produce a daughter who . . . refused to think for herself . . . Why did a girl as smart as she was . . . let other people do her thinking for her? Why was it beyond her to strive . . . to be all that one is, to be true to *that*?'; 'How could their innocent foibles add up to this human being?'; 'What then was the wound?'; 'What *is* the grudge? What *is* the grievance? . . . how did Merry get to be who she is?'; '*Is* Merry lying? Is Merry brainwashed? Is Merry a lesbian? Is Rita the girlfriend? Is Merry running the whole insane thing?' He also responds to the other major crises in his life – Merry's rape (see previous note), Jerry's denunciation of Seymour's 'dream-world' and the revelation of his wife's affair with Orcutt with a series of questions (Roth 1997: 29, 70, 240–41, 238, 92, 138, 369, 276, 359).

In addition to these anguished interrogations, the novel also repeatedly poses rhetorical questions – such as 'What does a reasonable man say next?' and 'Where do you look for the cause?' – and indeed finishes with two such unanswered, unanswerable, inquiries: 'And what is wrong with their life? What on earth is less reprehensible than the life of the Levovs?' (Roth 1997: 249, 340, 423).

15 Zuckerman makes this observation in the final page of the novel, when Jessie Orcutt, the drunk wife of the Levovs' neighbour, Bill Orcutt, stabs Lou Levov with a fork.

16 That Seymour is the product of Zuckerman's imagination is something that the novel reminds us of explicitly in its opening section, although from the second section onwards Zuckerman effectively disappears as a palpable presence from the novel. Zuckerman is equivocal, however, on the question of how accurate his portrait of the Swede is (that is to say, how closely his reconstruction of his life adheres to the 'reality' that is posited within the novel's own fictional framework). He concedes that 'of course the Swede was concentrated differently in my pages from how he'd been concentrated in the flesh', but remains non-committal on the question of 'whether . . . I'd imagined an outright fantastical creature, lacking entirely the unique substantiality of the real thing' (77). Later, he introduces the main narrative of the novel with the oxymoronic announcement that 'I dreamed a realistic chronicle' (89). For a detailed discussion of the role of Zuckerman as narrator of the novel, see Royal 2001.

17 Zuckerman represents these riots as yet another of the purification rituals of the novel, observing (satirically?) that in the burning of Newark's streets 'something purifying is happening' (Roth 1997: 268).

18 The African-American novelist James Baldwin notoriously claimed that '[t]he Jew is a white man' but his contemporary Ralph Ellison insisted that 'many Negroes, like myself, make a positive distinction between "whites" and "Jews"' and criticised Jewish intellectuals for 'their facile . . . identification with the "power structure"', diagnosing their presumption as an example of what 'Negroes call . . . "passing for white"' (quoted in Budick 2001b: 201–2). Emily Budick claims that '[f]or Jews their likeness to whites (culturally as well as genetically) . . . forms the basis for their superiority over blacks' (Budick 2001b: 204). For a more detailed discussion of the vexed history of black–Jewish literary relations in the United States, see Budick 1998 and Newton 1999. For a detailed discussion of the ambiguous racial status of Jews in the United States, see Brodkin 1998.

19 A number of commentators have suggested that Roth based Silk on Anatole Broyard, an author and eminent cultural critic who concealed his racial identity from virtually everyone, including his own children. However, Broyard passed as white and did indeed become part of the WASP literary establishment. As a prominent book reviewer for the *New York Times* for many years, Broyard was, as Henry Louis Gates put it, 'one of literary America's foremost gatekeepers' (Gates 1997b: 180).

20 There are some writers who present a very rosy picture of life for Jews in the post-war period. Morris Dickstein, for example, recalls the immediate post-war years as a period 'when the Jew became the modern Everyman, everyone's favorite victim, schlemiel and secular saint' (Dickstein 2001: 61). Dickstein even claims that 'social anti-Semitism in America became virtually a thing of the past' after the war (Dickstein 2001: 58–9). There is plenty of evidence, however, that anti-Semitism, social and institutional, persisted after the war. Although Dickstein is right up to a point when he observes that 'professions like academic life opened to them [Jews] that had always been off limits', this was a gradual process rather than a sudden opening of the floodgates (Dickstein 2001: 58–9, 59). Emily Budick points out that the image of the Jew as everyman was largely the creation of an intellectual Jewish elite, and that it leaned heavily on an identification with the black struggle for civil rights in post-war America: 'Under the guise of universal brotherhood, "Jew" bec[ame] the essential, transcendentalized category of the human' (Budick 2001b: 200).

21 In fact Coleman's movement across ethnic boundaries is by no means unique. In her excellent study of what she calls 'ethnic impersonator autobiographies', published in the same year as Roth's novel, Laura Browder demonstrates that 'ethnic passage from one identity to another is not an anomaly' (Browder 2000: 2). Browder's argument that these autobiographical narratives 'stand as monuments to the tradition of American self-invention as well as testaments to the porousness of

ethnicity' (Browder 2000: 3) fits well with Zuckerman's characterisation of Coleman as following 'in the great frontier tradition, accepting the democratic invitation to throw your origins overboard if to do so contributes to the pursuit of happiness' (Roth 2000: 334). Similarly, Browder's observation that 'there is an audacity inherent in their [the ethnic impersonators'] choices, a refusal to accept essentialist rules of race for themselves that has the transgressive quality of an outrageous joke' (Browder 2000: 11) is echoed in Zuckerman's description of Coleman's reinvention of himself as a Jew as the expression of a 'colossal sui generis score-settling joke' (Roth 2000: 131).

22 Many critics express disappointment at what they see as Roth's recycling of hackneyed clichés in his characterisation of Farley. Lorrie Moore complains that he seems to be a composite of 'every available cliché of the Vietnam vet' (Moore 2000: 7) and Mark Shechner describes Les as 'Brand X Vietnam Vet, all shattered nerves and tripwire aggression' (Shechner 2003: 189). However, Elaine B. Safer argues that such criticism misses the point, namely that Farley's behaviour is supposed to be farcical, while Jeffrey Charis-Carlson argues that 'the novel's narrative is actually dependent on Lester's inability to act like the stereotypical Vietnam vet' since it is his failure to respond conventionally to his visit to the 'moving wall' war memorial that 'sparks the apathetic state in which he . . . forces . . . Faunia and her lover, Coleman Silk, off the road' (Charis-Carlson 2004: 111). For Graham Higgin, the 'description of his [Les's] failure to reconcile himself to the wounds gorged in his life is one of the novel's highest achievements' (Higgin 2000: 8).

6

# Fantasies of flight and flights of fancy: rewriting history and retreating from trauma in *The Plot Against America*

> I wanted nothing to do with history. I wanted to be a boy on the smallest scale possible. I wanted to be an orphan. (Roth 2004: 232–3)

> It is very, very hard to talk about grief. (Jonathan Safran Foer quoted in Mackenzie 2005: 6)

The publication of *The Plot Against America* was attended with more fanfare and controversy than any of Roth's books since *Portnoy's Complaint*. Just as *Portnoy* had been heralded as the publishing event of 1969 long before its actual appearance, partly because of the buzz created by the appearance of two of its chapters in the preceding twelve months and partly as the result of shrewd promotion by Roth's publishers, so *The Plot Against America* was trailed by a carefully orchestrated marketing campaign that exploited rumours that the novel's title alluded to the events of 9/11 and that included the dissemination of extracts from the book prior to its publication.[1] In spite of Roth's own repeated denials that the book was intended as an oblique or symbolic commentary on George W. Bush's 'war against terror', many early reviewers read the novel as, and many readers bought the book anticipating, a political allegory.[2] As Michael Wood noted:

> This book was a runaway bestseller in the US even before it was published; an unusual occurrence for an untopical novel, even one written by someone of Roth's standing and popularity. But surely the novel is topical; isn't that what the title says? Well, this is, perhaps, what

> people have taken the title to mean. Two current plots against America immediately spring to mind. There is the global plot of al-Qaida against the evils of capitalism ... And there is ... the plot of the Bush administration to abolish many civil liberties and concentrate autocratic powers in the hands of the president. (Wood 2004: 3)

Whether accurate or not, these associations undoubtedly contributed to the unusual coverage and prominence that Roth's book achieved. A number of publications on both sides of the Atlantic devoted several different pieces to the book, both before and after its publication, and in the annual 'Books of the year' feature in *The Guardian* it received seven citations, more than any other book, fiction or non-fiction (Various 2004: 4–7).[3] Although judgements about its worth varied considerably, from Alan Cooper's unequivocal statement that it is 'a great novel', confirming Roth's pre-eminence among contemporary novelists (Cooper 2005: 241), to David Herman's damning verdict that it is 'slow, predictable and often lacks surprises or real drama', its impact was undeniable (Herman 2004: 76).

If *The Plot Against America* was the most ubiquitous literary novel of 2004, then the most eagerly awaited novel of the following year was Jonathan Safran Foer's *Extremely Loud and Incredibly Close*. After the euphoric critical reception and spectacular commercial success of his first novel, *Everything Is Illuminated* (2002), published when Foer was just twenty-five years old and turning him virtually overnight into the brightest young star in the literary firmament (as the receipt of the National Book Award for his first book, *Goodbye, Columbus* had done to the twenty-six-year-old Roth four decades earlier), the expectations for his second novel were great.[4] Pre-publication publicity was fuelled, as it had been for Roth's novel in the previous year, by the promise that it would engage with 9/11. When the first reviews began to appear, however, it soon became apparent that the critical bubble of approval for Foer had burst. Although it received a ringing endorsement from Salman Rushdie,[5] there was a general chorus of disapproval, in which condemnation of its perceived aesthetic shortcomings was often accompanied by denunciation of its treatment of 9/11, as at best misguided and insensitive, at worst an unethical appropriation, and opportunistic exploitation, of human suffering.[6] While there may have been a degree of self-pity and self-dramatisation in Foer's observation in an interview that he had become 'the most hated writer in America' (quoted in McInerney 2005: 6), some of the reviews of *Extremely Loud and Incredibly Close* smacked somewhat of *schadenfreude*, their authors apparently relishing the opportunity of putting this young upstart firmly in his place. Even those who were broadly sympathetic tended to qualify their praise with the recommendation that Foer exercise greater self-restraint: Charles Matthews and John Updike conclude their reviews by suggesting that *Extremely Loud and Incredibly Close* 'would have been a stronger . . . book . . . if he had reined in his imagination' (Matthews 2005: n.p.) and that 'a little more silence . . . might let Foer's excellent empathy . . . resonate all the louder' (Updike 2005: n.p.). Or else they damned the novel with faint praise, as in Michael Faber's judgement that Foer is 'as sincere and committed as he needs to be' (Faber 2005: 26), or Jay McInerney's grudging admission that Foer's novel 'is more memorable and psychologically acute than most of the journalism generated by September 11' (McInerney 2005: 6). This last comment comes from 'The uses of invention', an article in which McInerney defended the right of novelists to deal with this material. He suggests that the attacks on Foer are evidence of the fickleness of literary fashion, conforming to a predictable pattern in American letters where feverish hype of a writer's reputation is swiftly succeeded by brutal deflation: 'The culture still seems to require precocious first novelists . . . we tend to over-celebrate them, and then we tend to kill them, figuratively speaking, in part because we expect so much from them after their brilliant beginnings' (McInerney 2005: 5).

Certainly, Foer was not the first, and will not be the last, to suffer a critical backlash of this sort. Roth had seen his second and third books – *Letting Go* and *When She Was Good* – receive distinctly lukewarm reviews after *Goodbye, Columbus* had won the National Book Award when he was the new kid on the literary block. A decade earlier Norman Mailer had been as slated for his second novel, *Barbary Shore* (1951), as he had been feted for his first, *The Naked and the Dead* (1948). Some novelists, such as Ralph Ellison, the author of *Invisible Man* (1952), find the weight of expectation excited by their debut fictions so crushing that they never manage to publish another. To some extent, then, Foer seems to have been the victim of what might be called the difficult second novel syndrome, exacerbated in his case by his youth and the scale of his earlier success.

There is, however, also an ideological dimension to the reception of *Extremely Loud and Incredibly Close* that manifests itself particularly in reactions towards the novel's narrator. Even those critics generally well disposed towards Foer tended to express irritation with Foer's characterisation of his protagonist. Oskar Schell is a nine-year-old 'inventor, amateur entomologist, computer consultant, Francophile, letter writer, pacifist, amateur astronomer, natural historian, percussionist, romantic, Great Explorer, jeweller, origamist, detective, vegan and collector of butterflies' (as the blurb on the back of the paperback edition of the novel puts it).[7] He is variously described as 'more like a mouthpiece than an actual child' (McInerney 2005: 5), 'an unreasonable invention', a 'two-dimensional curiosity' (Barbash 2005: n.p.), and 'a plastic bag crammed with oddities' (Miller 2005: n.p.). Michael Faber observes that 'the best defence of Oskar as a character is to compare him with other precocious juvenile narrators in literature, such as Holden Caulfield and Huckleberry Finn'.[8] However, he goes on to claim that 'Holden and Huck exist in a narrative universe that's intended, overall, to be convincing', whereas 'Foer's characters . . . are constructed not from fleshly materials but embroidered scraps of language, poetic notions, allegorical conceits' (Faber 2005: 26). Laura Miller, similarly, contends that 'Foer could have pulled this off [engaged the reader's sympathies] if Oskar felt alive', but that instead he becomes 'a device serving the author's purposes rather than a fully imagined human being' (Miller 2005: n.p.). Reviewers were equally troubled by what they perceived as the unrealistic nature of the world Oskar inhabits: John Updike confessed to being 'boggled . . . by a nine-year-old boy's being allowed to roam . . . all over the five boroughs' (Updike 2005: n.p.) and Roger Gathman observed, scathingly, that '[t]he city Oskar traverses . . . is inhabited by quirky, gentle and sympathetic folk, and not one mugger' (Gathman 2005: 2). In an interview with Jonathan Birnbaum, Foer argued that expectations of realism were misplaced: 'I am not really writing a nine-year-old kid . . . not in a realistic way . . . sometimes you have to tell certain lies of reality in order to tell certain truths of emotion'. However, his use of actual history (the events of September 11, 2001, the bombing of Dresden and Hiroshima etc.) was always likely to invite what he calls 'judg[ment] by journalist's standards', or at any rate to ensure that readers became exercised by the question of the novel's verisimilitude (Birnbaum 2005: n.p.).

What is perhaps more surprising, given its explicit rejection of historical reality, is that the critical reception of *The Plot Against America* was also characterised by debates about its realism (or lack thereof). In spite of the extravagant fiction on which the novel is founded – the invention of an alternative history in which the famous aviator and infamous anti-Semite Charles A. Lindbergh defeated

Franklin Delano Roosevelt in the 1940 U.S. presidential election – Roth himself insisted, as he had done when promoting *Operation Shylock* a decade earlier, on the autobiographical fidelity of the novel, telling one interviewer that 'People think I have, but I have never written about my family on the nose before like this' (Roth quoted in Grossman 2004: 83). This was a particularly bold and characteristically mischievous claim, given that he had written at length about his family in earlier works of non-fiction (*The Facts* and *Patrimony*). For many critics, the realism of the novel is one of its main virtues: Blake Morrison claims that it is 'a "what if . . . ?" that reads like a "what really happened"' (Morrison 2004: 2); Peter Kemp that Roth's '[a]utobiographical immediacy gives his fictitious reign of terror gritty actuality' (Kemp 2004: 41); and J.M. Coetzee that 'the fantasy of a Lindbergh presidency is only a concretization, a realization for poetic ends, of a certain potential in American political life' (Coetzee 2004: 5). Alan Cooper goes so far as to argue that the imagined events of the novel come 'perilously close to being actual history' and that the 'sureness . . . [of the] characterization makes it irrelevant that the Lindbergh plot against America is a writer's fantasy' (Cooper 2005: 242, 243). According to James Wood, the novel's 'counter-history', though 'wild', is 'presented too plausibly' to incur incredulity (Wood 2004: 5). A. Alvarez believes that Roth's 'voice sounds so spontaneous that the lazy reader might suppose he is listening to confession rather than reading a work of fiction' (Alvarez 2004: 22) and Lev Grossman agrees, suggesting that 'Roth's delivery is so matter-of-fact, so documentary deadpan that when we're 10 pages into the book our own world starts to seem like a flimsy fantasy' (Grossman 2004: 83). Tony Hilfer, on the other hand, found the novel's deadpan tone deadening, so that the 'problem' with Roth's novel is that 'it is not sufficiently fantastical' (Hilfer 2004: 26) and for Bryan Cheyette 'the novel lacks the courage of its convictions and . . . becomes extraordinarily sentimental' (Cheyette 2004b: 27). Finally, Craig Brown is 'always conscious' that the events of Roth's novel 'could never have happened, and that made-up tears are somehow frivolous when set beside tears that were all too real' (Brown 2004: 10).

Brown's comments, like the allegations of tastelessness that some reviewers made against Foer, conflate ethical judgement with literary criticism. Michael Faber seems to feel that Foer evades the actual suffering caused by 9/11, since the novel 'promises to take you to Ground Zero, but helplessly detours towards the Land of Oz, spending most of its time journeying through the Neverlands in between' (Faber 2005: 26). For Faber, the formal failure of the book (its lack of realism and digressive structure) is a consequence of its moral failure (its unwillingness to tackle head on the horror of the attack on the twin towers). Similarly, Brown suggests that *The Plot Against America* is flawed aesthetically because of its implausibility (he claims that the events it depicts 'could never have happened'), and ethically because the suffering that Roth imagines American Jews experiencing ('made-up tears') trivialises the historical suffering ('tears that were all too real') actually experienced by European Jews during the Holocaust.

This strikes the keynote in the reception of *The Plot Against America* and *Extremely Loud and Incredibly Close*. That so many reviewers couched their critiques in terms of the realism, or otherwise, of Roth's and Foer's novels, may reflect the fact that, in spite of the widespread preference for postmodern fiction in academia in the last third of the twentieth century, realism has remained the dominant mode of contemporary fiction, the default template for most readers and reviewers. More than this, however, it reveals an anxiety on the part of the reviewers about the controversial subject-matter of both books, an anxiety apparently shared by their authors. Whereas Roth always carefully distanced himself from his publishers' strategy of implicitly connecting his novel with contemporary political events, Foer was only too happy in interviews to confirm that his novel dealt explicitly with the events of 9/11. When it was put to him that it might be risky to write about the attack on the World Trade Center so soon after the event, Foer responded that 'it's a greater risk not to write about it . . . to avoid what's right in front of you' (Shenley 2005: n.p.). In another interview he stressed that 'novelists have a responsibility, [sic] to pay attention to important things' (Birnbaum 2005: n.p.), echoing (consciously?) the young Roth's argument in 'Writing American Fiction' that for novelists in the U.S. to be unwilling or unable to tackle political realities is 'a serious occupational impediment' (Roth 2001a: 169). Moreover, Foer implied that he had a political agenda when he told Jonathan Birnbaum that one of his reasons for writing the book was because 'the way that the story of Sept. 11 was being told was with absolute certainty' (Birnbaum 2005: n.p.). In fact, the alacrity with which Foer embraced the popular notion that his was a 9/11 novel should be treated with the same scepticism as Roth's eagerness to play down any connection. Whereas Foer sought to legitimise his references to the terrorist attacks on the twin towers in terms of the moral obligations of the writer to engage with the pressing issues of contemporary life, Roth wanted to reinforce his own credentials as a writer whose imaginative faculties operate independently of, and transcend, any particular event or *zeitgeist*. For both novelists, 9/11 is certainly of symbolic importance: for Roth it lends additional resonance to his depiction of a world in which the line between paranoia and reality is hard to draw; for Foer it particularises the themes of absence and loss with which he is preoccupied. Politics (whether topical or historical, actual or imaginary) is, however, peripheral to both novels; instead they explore the ways in which their precocious child protagonists confront – and avoid confronting – trauma, and how that trauma accelerates and distorts their development.

It is tempting to identify *The Plot Against America* as part of a teleological narrative of Roth's career; to see it as a development of themes that have manifested themselves in his writing for many years. Its focus on the intersection between the dramas of domestic life and national politics might seem to align it with the 'American Trilogy'. Nevertheless, Roth had demonstrated a predilection for rewriting history much earlier in his career, in *The Great American Novel* (the mythical story of a third major baseball league), in '"I Always Wanted You to Admire My Fasting"; or, Looking at Kafka' (where he imagines an alternative destiny for Kafka, who survives the war, becoming the young Roth's Hebrew teacher and the suitor of his aunt but remaining unknown as a writer), and in *The Ghost Writer* (in which Zuckerman fantasises that Amy Bellette might be Anne Frank, who has survived the war, preserving the secrecy of her identity in order not to diminish the impact of her *Diary*). There is, indeed, an uncanny premonition of *The Plot Against America* in another of Roth's fictions from the 1970s: *My Life as a Man*. In this novel, published thirty years before *The Plot Against America*, Peter Tarnopol, the protagonist and fictional author, describes one of his short stories, entitled 'The Diary of Anne Frank's Contemporary', in which a young boy is traumatised by moving house. Quoting from the story, which is narrated from the perspective of the young boy, Tarnopol writes:

> For me, being uprooted after a lifetime in the same house was utterly bewildering; to make matters worse, I had gone to bed with the room in a state of disarray that was wholly foreign to our former way of life. Would it be this way forevermore? Eviction? Confusion? Disorder? . . . The day after the move, when it came time to go home from school after lunch, instead of heading off to the new address, I 'unthinkingly' returned to the

> house in which I had lived all my life in perfect safety . . . I was astonished to find the door to our apartment wide open and to hear men talking loudly inside . . . 'It's Nazis!' I thought. The Nazis had parachuted into Yonkers, made their way into our street, and taken everything away. *Taken my mother away.* (Roth 1985: 244–5, italics in original)

Later he cries 'with relief to find that my mother is alive and well . . . and that we are Jews who live in the haven of Westchester County, rather than in our ravaged, ancestral, Jew-hating Europe' (Roth 1985: 245). Whether or not Roth was consciously harking back to this earlier idea during the composition of *The Plot Against America*,[9] it does seem to contain many of the elements of the later novel, notably the sense of disorientation and dislocation that replaces so swiftly, and hence reveals the fragility of, the prior feeling of 'perfect safety' in the child's mind, and that is symbolised by (imagined) loss of the mother. Most strikingly, this story seems precisely to anticipate the 'perpetual fear' of anti-Semitism that haunts the young Philip of *The Plot Against America* – a fear that might be seen as the culmination of a subtle shift in Roth's treatment of this theme over the course of his career (Roth 2004: 1).

In Roth's earlier work, as I have argued elsewhere, any threat to Jewish identity tends to come from within the Jewish community.[10] Many of the stories in Roth's first book, *Goodbye, Columbus*, revolved around tensions between different types of American Jew. 'Defender of the Faith' pits the secular, morally upright, but arguably self-hating and vindictive Marx against the manipulative, opportunistically tribal, but arguably conciliatory and self-accepting Grossbart; 'Eli, the Fanatic' deals with the conflict between the modern, assimilated, well-established and well-heeled Jewish community of Woodenton and the newly-arrived, impoverished Orthodox Jews whose language, culture and religion owes more to nineteenth-century Europe than post-war America; the title-story of the collection centres on the relationship between Neil Klugman, a lower-middle-class Jew from an unfashionable district of New Jersey, and Brenda Patimkin, the daughter of *nouveau riche* American Jews and heiress to a sporting goods empire. Over the ensuing three decades, in novels such as *Portnoy's Complaint, The Ghost Writer, Zuckerman Unbound* and *The Anatomy Lesson*, Roth continued to be more interested in internal Jewish politics than in any external menace to the Jews. This work dramatises the tensions between Jewish fathers and sons, rival brothers, writers and critics – Jews judging, condemning, betraying and undermining one another

– rather than those between Jews and non-Jews. When, in the final two sections of *The Counterlife*, Roth's fiction finally engages with Gentile anti-Semitism (as opposed to Jewish self-hatred), it is depicted very much as a phenomenon specifically associated with the English upper classes.

Earlier in the *The Counterlife*, in the section entitled 'Judea', Nathan Zuckerman had found himself embroiled in an argument with the militant Zionist settler, Mordecai Lippman, over the state of Gentile–Jewish relations in America. Lippman believes that anti-Semitism is rooted deep in the psyche of Gentile America, claiming '[t]here is nothing the American goy would like better than a *Judenrein* [Jew-free] United States' and praying that 'the Jews will leave America before a second Hitler succeeds', but Zuckerman dismisses his apocalyptic prophesies (Roth 1986: 124–5). He insists that 'America simply did not boil down to Jew and Gentile, nor were anti-Semites the American Jew's biggest problem' and furthermore that he 'could not think of any historical society that had achieved the level of tolerance institutionalized in America or that had placed pluralism smack at the center of its publicly advertised dream of itself' (146, 54). At the same time, however, Zuckerman admits to being '"a little idealistic about America"' and concedes that if '"all American values are flushed into the gutter"' then Lippman's prediction that anti-Semitism will destroy American Jewry might turn out to be accurate (54). As Roth pointed out in 'Writing About Jews', however, the fact that 'the barrier between prejudice and persecution collapsed in Germany . . . is hardly reason to contend that no such barrier exists in our country' (Roth 2001a: 206).

In contrast to Zuckerman's optimism about the place of Jews in the United States, his experiences in England persuade him that, as his future sister-in-law, Sarah, puts it, the English aristocracy are '"the sort of people who, if you knew anything about English society, you would have *expected* to be anti-Semitic"'(Roth 1986: 280). Not content with warning him of the prejudice that he should anticipate encountering, Sarah proves adept at practising the genteel anti-Semitism that she has identified as characteristic of her class. First of all, she tells Zuckerman that her mother won't like '"the idea of her languid, helpless Maria [Sarah's sister and Zuckerman's fiancée] submitting to anal domination by a Jew"', then she observes that '"it must be terribly worrying whether you're going suddenly to forget yourself, bare your teeth, and cut loose with the ethnic squawk"' (Roth 1986: 278, 279).

Finally, she treats him to a lecture on the history of anti-Semitism in English literature, which, she claims, is evidence of '"*a shared* consciousness"' between author and reader of the contempt in which Jews are held (281, italics in original). Malicious though Sarah's intentions may be, her suggestion that anti-Semitism is endemic in certain sections of English society seems to be implicitly confirmed by a later incident in the novel (when a woman dining near Zuckerman and Maria at a restaurant complains about a smell, which he takes as a racial insult directed at him).

In *Deception*, published four years later, there is an even stronger sense of English anti-Semitism. In that novel the protagonist Philip has an English lover (she seems to be the model, or at least a fictionalised version of the model, for Maria in *The Counterlife*) who teases him about 'the clippings about Israel that he cuts from the London papers to prove to her that the British are anti-Semitic' (Roth 1990: 38). Philip tells her that '"The way most people say 'shit' in public, you all say 'Jew'"' and he becomes indignant when his interpretation of an enigmatic remark apparently addressed to him by a stranger on the Kings Road in Chelsea ('"You don't even dress right!"') as an anti-Semitic insult is dismissed by English friends as evidence of how 'paranoid' he is (78, 102, 105).

When, in *The Counterlife*, Maria argues that 'there's more [anti-Semitism] in America, actually, just because there are more Jews, and because they're not so diffident as English Jews', Zuckerman is adamant that he has never encountered it in America: '"I didn't run into this stuff there – never"' (Roth 1986: 299). Yet in *The Facts*, published in between *The Counterlife* and *Deception*, Roth recalls that during his childhood '[a]t home the biggest threat came from the Americans who opposed or resisted us – or condescended to us or rigorously excluded us – because we were Jews'. From an early age, he claims to have been aware 'of the power to intimidate that emanated from the highest and lowest reaches of gentile America' and of the way the Gentile managers of his father's employers, the insurance company Metropolitan Life, 'openly and guiltlessly conspired to prevent more than a few token Jews from assuming positions of anything approaching importance within the largest financial institution in the world' (Roth 1998: 20, 22). Although readers of Roth must always resist the temptation to assume that his protagonists (even those who are given his name) are authorial mouthpieces, this must nevertheless have come as something of a surprise to many of those readers, given the consistently dismissive attitude of earlier Roth protagonists to the idea that American Jews might be an embattled minority, suffering the same kinds of discrimination endured by other American minorities. This shift in Roth's work – from representing America as a haven where Jews, for the first time in modern history, were able to enjoy full democratic rights, economic freedom and political protection, to a more equivocal view of America as a country where Jews were expected to know (and stick to) their (lowly) place in the social hierarchy – continues with the publication of *American Pastoral.* In that novel there is an insistent emphasis on the role of anti-Semitism in shaping the lives of American Jews during the post-war years.

Throughout *American Pastoral* there are repeated references to the obstacles to effective assimilation for Jews in America. Sometimes these take the form of explicit expressions of racial hatred. After his daughter, Merry, blows up the local post office in Old Rimrock, a Gentile enclave in which the Levovs' ethnic difference marks them as outsiders, Seymour Levov 'receives anti-Semitic mail . . . so vile it sickens him for days on end' (Roth 1997: 168). At other times it manifests itself as a more subtle form of prejudice, such as the condescension that Seymour detects in his neighbour, Bill Orcutt, who, on the pretext of a tour of the local county, 'for one solid hour . . . got to goyishly regale a Jewish sightseer' about his family history (168, 381). There are also occasional allusions to institutional racism, from the 'notorious Marine Corps anti-Semitism' that Seymour's parents fear he will encounter during his tour of duty in the Second World War to their apprehension of the Ivy League as 'a world of Gentile wealth' that didn't 'admit Jews, didn't know Jews, probably didn't like Jews all that much' (14, 307).

There are also signs that Roth was already thinking, during the composition of *American Pastoral,* about a novel that would deal more directly with the phenomenon of American anti-Semitism: a novel that would feature Charles Lindbergh. When Zuckerman, in his capacity as the narrator of *American Pastoral,* describes the manner in which Merry's bombing is reported in the local press, he points out that 'the papers luridly recall' details of the last local tragedy to achieve national coverage – the Lindbergh baby kidnapping – and that Merry Levov's 'name several times appear[ed] right alongside [the convicted murderer of the child, Bruno] Hauptmann's' (170). Later in the novel, Seymour's father, Lou Levov, denounces Lindbergh (along with several other notorious American anti-Semites – Father Coughlin, Gerald K. Smith, Senator Bilbo – who figure in *The Plot Against America*) as one of a number of pro-Hitler 'so-called patriots . . . [who] would take the country and make Nazi Germany out of it' (289, 287). He goes on to warn that '[t]hese people have taken us to the edge of something terrible' and to praise 'that wonderful book', *It Can't Happen Here,* Sinclair Lewis's novel that imagines, like Roth's, a scenario in which fascism temporarily takes root in America after the election of a charismatic, populist demagogue (287). There are also moments in *I Married A Communist* that seem to anticipate the concerns of *The Plot Against America,* notably Murray Ringold's description of the McCarthyite anti-Communist witchhunts as 'a democratic pogrom full of terror' and Ira Ringold's condemnation of the political prejudices of his fellow army recruits: '"You guys would duplicate the very actions of the Germans if you were in their place. It might take a little longer because of the democratic element in our society, but eventually we would be completely fascist"' (Roth 1998: 266, 47).

It is possible, then, to see the fiction preceding *The Plot Against America* as staking out some of the ground that Roth excavates more thoroughly in this novel. At one point Philip's lover in *Deception* tells him that '"you're of the little pocket of Jews born in this century who miraculously escaped the horror, who somehow have lived unharmed in an amazing moment of affluence and security. So those who didn't escape . . . have this fascination for you"' (Roth 1990: 136) and *The Plot Against America* can be seen as further evidence of this fascination. Whereas in 'Looking at Kafka' and *The Ghost Writer* Roth imagined European Jews miraculously escaping from their historical fate, in this novel Roth turns the tables, imagining what might have happened to American Jews if they hadn't escaped unscathed from the Second World War, but had themselves been subjected to a form of fascist rule. Although the narrator of *The Plot Against America* (to whom I will refer as Philip in order to distinguish him from Roth the author) claims that it was the nomination of Lindbergh as the Republican Presidential candidate that first threatened to undermine 'that huge endowment of personal security that I had taken for granted as an American child of American parents in an American school in an American city in an America at peace with the world', Lindbergh is simply the catalyst for the eruption of anti-Semitic feeling that has been simmering for many years beneath the surface of the America in which the young Philip places so much naïve faith (Roth 2004: 7, 18). These are, after all, the days 'of unadvertised quotas to keep Jewish admissions to a minimum in colleges and professional schools' and of 'the weekly Sunday radio broadcasts of Father Coughlin . . . whose anti-Semitic virulence aroused the passions of a sizeable audience during the country's hard times' (11, 7). Jews at this time found themselves 'by and large obstructed by religious prejudice from attaining public power', victims of 'discrimination of the Protestant hierarchy that kept ninety-nine percent of the Jews employed by the dominant corporations uncomplainingly in their place' (123–4). Although Philip nostalgically recalls a time before the nomination of Lindbergh when '[o]ur homeland was America', he can hardly conceive of a Jew being admitted to the pantheon of American national icons ('"Do you think there'll ever be a Jew on a stamp?"', he asks his mother) and he knows 'that no Jew could ever be elected to the presidency . . . as if the proscription were laid out in so many words in the U.S. constitution' (5, 23, 244–5). His experience, and his father's, growing up as 'an impoverished kid other kids called a kike', exposes the idea of a golden age for American Jewry as a myth (123). Indeed, the older Philip concedes that, in retrospect, the potency of Lindbergh's threat lay in the fact that his 'personal convictions [were] shared . . . by a rabid constituency even more extensive than a Jew like my father, with his bitter hatred of anti-Semitism – or like my mother, with her deeply ingrained mistrust of Christians – could ever imagine to be flourishing all across America' (14). Later, he acknowledges that 'there were . . . ordinary Americans, tens of thousands of them, maybe millions of them' who 'hated Jews' (166–7). Whereas as the novel begins, Philip distances himself from the paranoia of his parents, whose 'atavistic sense of being undefended' he claims 'had more to do with Kishinev and the pogroms of 1903 than with New Jersey thirty-seven years later', by the end he shares their 'assumption that these people [the non-Jewish population of New Jersey] wouldn't require much encouragement to be turned into a mindless, destructive mob by the pro-Nazi conspiracy' (268).

In this sense, the novel seems to go much further than any of Roth's previous works. Indeed, many reviewers saw it not as a logical progression, but as a revision or even inversion, of Roth's earlier representation of American Jewish–Gentile relations.[11] Alternatively, it was interpreted as a symbolic reconciliation with all the Jewish parents and parental figures whose 'generalized mistrust of the Gentile world' the protagonists of earlier novels had satirised and rebelled against (Roth 2004: 41).[12] For Adam Kirsch, this apparent change of heart was a case of Roth clipping his own wings: 'Everything that makes Mr Roth a great novelist – his rage, his subversive comedy, and his slipperiness – is a protest against . . . caution, diplomacy, anxious respectability . . . *The Plot Against America* is a startling book because it shows Mr Roth appearing to agree, for the first time in his career, with all those inner and outer voices of caution' (Kirsch 2004: 14). Brian Morton and Alan Cooper, on the other hand, identify as one of the novel's greatest strengths its endorsement of the values of Bess and Herman Roth, whose 'ordinary decency' (Morton 2004: 32) powerfully 'indicts the deep-seated proclivity in Christians to slide easily into anti-Semitism' (Cooper 2005: 251).

Yet to read the novel in such didactic terms is to misrepresent it. Although Mary McCarthy, in a letter that Roth reprinted in *Shop Talk*, diagnosed 'a severe case of anti-anti-semitism' that she felt contaminated the final two sections of *The Counterlife*, Roth has no more sought to combat anti-Semitism in his fiction than to fuel it, the accusations of some Jewish critics notwithstanding (Roth 2001b: 114). In his essay 'Writing About Jews', written some forty years before the publication of *The Plot Against America*, Roth had suggested that 'repeating . . . "It can happen here," does little to prevent "it" from happening' and in an interview with Alain Finkielkraut in 1981 he insisted that 'however much I may loathe anti-Semitism . . . my job in a work of fiction is not to offer consolation to Jewish sufferers or to mount an attack upon their persecutors' (Roth 2001a: 207, 109). In the same interview, he observes that it was 'in the vast discrepancy between' the 'tragic dimension of Jewish life in Europe and the actualities of our daily lives as Jews in New Jersey' that he 'found the terrain' for his earliest fiction. *The Plot Against America* seems to me to underline rather than erase this discrepancy. After all, the scale of the threat that Roth imagines for American Jews hardly even begins to compare with the magnitude of suffering endured by European Jews. In Roth's novel, anti-Semitic riots, concentrated in the Deep South and the Midwest, claim the lives of one hundred and twenty-two American Jews: a drop in the ocean when measured against the six million European Jews murdered by the Nazis. Far from being products of a lurid imagination, the mini-pogroms that take place in *The Plot Against America* seem to be at least partly based on the real-life sporadic outbreaks of anti-Semitic violence that Roth recalls in *The*

*Facts* taking place during the wartime years when his family vacationed at Bradley Beach:

> [T]here were these 'race riots,' as we children called the hostile nighttime invasions by the boys from Neptune: violence directed against the Jews by youngsters who, as everyone said, could only have learned their hatred from what they heard at home. (Roth 1988: 24)

Roth goes on to recount a rumour that circulated, after one of these episodes, that one of the Jewish boys had been caught by the marauding anti-Semites, who 'held him down and pulled his face back and forth across the splintery surface of the boardwalk's weathered planks', rendering a 'bloody pulp of a Jewish child's face' (Roth 1988: 25). This description – which implicitly undermines the title of the section of *The Facts* in which it occurs ('Safe at Home') – is actually more graphically detailed than any anti-Semitic incident in *The Plot Against America*. In the latter book, anti-Semitic attacks against Jews take place almost exclusively off-stage, as it were. Although Philip 'was able to alarm myself with a nightmarish vision of America's anti-Semitic fury . . . surging . . . straight into our Summit Avenue alleyway and on up our back stairs like the waters of a flood', this premonition proves more ghastly than the reality (342–3). In fact, the worst violence that the young Philip witnesses is not the result of fascist activity but, ironically, a vicious fistfight between two members of his own family (his father, Herman, and his cousin, Alvin). This raises the question of how central the issue of anti-Semitism is to the novel. If Roth's intention had really been, as Cooper argues, to indict 'the deep-seated proclivity in Christians to slide easily into anti-Semitism' (Cooper 2005: 251), he would surely have exposed the Roth family in *The Plot Against America* to a more virulent strain of prejudice than their ejection from a hotel in Washington D.C. and the two taunts of 'loudmouth Jew' directed at Herman Roth (Roth 2004: 65, 78). Moreover, if Roth had wanted to write a novel about anti-Semitism in America in the period leading up to the Second World War, he wouldn't have had to invent the Lindbergh Presidency. Roth is well aware of the real history of American anti-Semitism during this period, as is illustrated by the discussion of Arthur Miller's novel *Focus* (1945)[13] in *I Married A Communist*, and of the Leo Frank case at the end of *The Plot Against America*. When David Herman suggests that 'America in the first half of the twentieth century had enough antisemitism [sic] for a shelf-full of great novels' (Herman

2004: 78), he is overstating the case somewhat. But it is in any case questionable whether Roth's primary intention is to revisit a subject that had already been treated not just in Miller's novel, but in Saul Bellow's *The Victim* (1947) and Bernard Malamud's *The Assistant* (1957), as well as in popular fiction such as Laura Z. Hobson's *Gentleman's Agreement* (1947).[14] In the same way as 9/11 functions heuristically in *Extremely Loud and Incredibly Close*, as a means of examining the impact of sudden trauma on the consciousness and conscience of Oskar, so anti-Semitism in *The Plot Against America* is important not so much in itself but insofar as it provides a pretext for Roth's primary subject: the subjecthood, and subjectivity, of Philip.[15]

Roth's novel begins boldly:

> Fear presides over these memories, a perpetual fear. Of course no childhood is without its terrors, yet I wonder if I would have been a less frightened boy if Lindbergh hadn't been president or if I hadn't been the offspring of Jews. (Roth 2004: 1)

Boldly, because a novel predicated on an alternative version of history actually opens by imagining an alternative to that alternative that is in fact our reality: a world in which Lindbergh never became President of the United States. Boldly, too, because, alongside this articulation of a political history that is, within the framework of the narrative, itself imagined ('if Lindbergh hadn't been president'), Philip imagines a personal history in which his Jewishness is erased. Philip attributes his fearfulness to two accidents of history, one fictional (Lindbergh's presidency) and one reflecting an autobiographical reality (his Jewishness), but the language of this passage subtly suggests that the former is more historically determined than the latter. Whereas the verbal echo of 'presides' in 'president' implies that the imprint of Lindbergh's term of office on Philip's life is indelible, his Jewishness is represented as provisional: he describes himself only as 'the offspring of Jews', rather than as Jewish.

Philip repeatedly attempts during the course of the novel to disown his parents (and thus the Jewishness that they pass on to him) by adopting other identities. At first, Philip's version of the Freudian family romance takes the form of daydreams, flights of fancy in which fear of the unfamiliar is mingled with desire for new experiences. Enlisted by his friend, Earl Axman, into the strange game of 'Following Christians' – in which the two Jewish boys board buses in downtown Newark and trail one of the 'adult Christian men' all the way back to his home – Philip soon falls into the habit of constructing scenarios of more permanent dislocation:

> I was lost, a lost boy – that's what I pretended . . . Will I be arrested and thrown in jail? Will some Christian family take me in and adopt me? Or will I wind up being kidnapped like the Lindbergh child? I pretended either that I was lost in some far-off region unknown to me or that, with Lindbergh's connivance, Hitler had invaded America and Earl and I were fleeing the Nazis. (116)

This curious mixture of lurid paranoia (imagining himself imprisoned, kidnapped, or on the run from Nazi persecution) and whimsical daydream (pretending to find himself in a strange land, or taken in by strangers) characteristically merges fantasies of flight with flights of fancy. Whether being overtaken by hostile historical forces in his homeland (as in the scenario of Hitler invading America), or inhabiting an ahistorical, geographically amorphous realm ('lost in some far-off region'), Philip's visions all involve a radical self-detachment, a situation in which he defines himself as 'lost', literally and figuratively.

Later, Philip graduates to reinventing himself as a child without family ties. He attempts to gain admission to the local Newsreel Theater in the hope that he will see footage of his Aunt Evelyn at the White House, who has been invited (along with her husband, Rabbi Lionel Benglesdorf, archadvocate and co-ordinator of Lindbergh's policy of 'Americanizing' the Jewish population of the United States) to a reception in honour of Hitler's foreign secretary, von Ribbentrop. So that he will be allowed to watch the newsreel, Philip assumes the identity of a child from the local Catholic orphanage sent by one of the sisters 'to do a report on President Lindbergh' (198). Later in the novel, disguised in clothes that he has stolen from his neighbour, Seldon Wishnow (whose attempts to form a friendship Philip interprets as a parasitic 'latch[ing] onto me as his other self'), Philip runs away from home in the middle of the night, hoping to 'be taken in by the nuns as a familyless child' (222, 235). Finally, towards the end of the novel, he orphans himself again, employing the alias 'Philip Flanagan' in the service of a more radical fantasy of flight, vowing to 'run away from everything I'd done and everything I hadn't done, and start out fresh as a boy nobody knew' (346). Philip's scheme is to head for Elizabeth to seek employment at a pretzel factory where handicapped children work: 'I'd tell them in writing that I was a deaf-mute . . . I'd never speak and I'd pretend not to hear, and nobody would find out who I was'

(346). He hopes to save the money he will earn 'to buy a one-way train ticket to Omaha, Nebraska, where Father Flanagan ran Boys Town', a refuge where 'boys from the street . . . were fed and clothed and received an education' (349). Initially, he intends once again to borrow Seldon's name but then decides that he must not 'identify myself as Jewish', but instead claim that 'I didn't know what I was or who. That I was nothing and nobody' (349).

This is not the first time that a Jewish protagonist of one of Roth's novels has Christened/Christianised himself. In *Portnoy's Complaint* an adolescent Alexander Portnoy mentally tries out a number of pseudonyms – Alex Portenoire, Al Port, Al Parsons, Alton Peterson, Alton Christian Peterson – that he imagines using to present himself to the Gentile girls whom he desires, as a boy with a background compatible with their own (Roth 1969: 137, 151). Philip's fantasies are, however, not motivated by opportunism, or pragmatism; rather, they express a disturbing, increasingly nihilistic impulse to erase all traces of his family history and his own identity. If Philip begins by dreaming harmlessly and conventionally enough of adventures in which he becomes a 'lost boy' (with an allusion perhaps to J.M. Barrie), fleeing from the Nazis or being adopted by a kindly Christian family, he ends by plotting in earnest not simply to 'start out fresh' in the spirit of Huck Finn lighting out to escape the confines of his social world, but to renounce entirely his ethnicity, his past and his self; to become a creature isolated from all ordinary human contact, speechless and oblivious to the speech of others, 'nothing and nobody'. Philip's fantasies are not the romantic dreams of rebellion and self-liberation often entertained by older children (and embodied by Philip's older brother Sandy, who initially participates enthusiastically in, and later promotes, Lindbergh's 'Just Folks' programme, in which Jewish boys are 'apprenticed' to Gentile families so as to expose them '"to the traditional ways of heartland life"'), but rather nightmares of self-annihilation; his flights of fancy become flights from the very idea of selfhood (84).

What causes this retreat from everything – family, friends, community, culture, history, the ability to speak and to hear – that ordinarily constitutes, and protects, a child's sense of identity? Trauma. Not the trauma of Lindbergh's election or the subsequent attacks on the cohesiveness of the Jewish-American community carried out under the guise of furthering integration by the Office of American Absorption *per se*; but rather the impact these events have on one particular Jewish-American family, the Roths. From the outset, Roth emphasises Philip's belief that Lindbergh's election as president has changed his family irrevocably. This feeling manifests itself early in the novel in the form of a series of nightmares that cause Philip to roll out of his bunk bed and hit the floor. In one of these bad dreams, Philip finds himself 'walking to Earl's with my stamp album when someone shouted my name and began chasing me' (42). In the process of eluding his pursuer, he drops his precious collection and when he checks its contents to ensure that no stamps have been dislodged or lost, he discovers that his set of 1932 Washington Bicentennials has undergone a sinister metamorphosis: 'instead of a different portrait of Washington on each of the twelve stamps, the portraits were now the same and no longer of Washington but of Hitler' (43).

Once again, Roth incorporates into a novel that rewrites history an episode that imagines the rewriting of *that* rewritten history: in Philip's dream America has become an annex of Nazi Germany, its pluralistic ideals replaced by a totalitarian ideology. In the young Philip's imagination, political iconography, as manifested in the supplanting of Washington's image by Hitler's, reflects a much more personal anxiety: a feeling not only of being overtaken (and taken over) by dark forces beyond his control, but a conviction that these changes are reaching back into the past and undermining the foundations of his life, just as the Nazi influence over Lindbergh's America seems, in Philip's dream, to have seeped backwards through history to contaminate the political landscape of the 1930s.

When the Roths' visit to the Lincoln Memorial in Washington is marred by an argument between Herman and some anti-Semitic Lindbergh supporters, Philip invokes the biblical tale of the Fall to express his sudden alienation from the patriotism that the Memorial had at first inspired in him. He decides that the vista from the Lincoln Memorial to the Washington Monument is 'the most beautiful panorama I'd ever seen, a patriotic paradise, the American Garden of Eden spread before us, and we stood huddled together there, the family expelled' (66). This metaphorical exile anticipates the episode, later in the novel, when the Roth family are on the point of emigrating to Canada, a plan which a dismayed Philip takes as signifying that his 'incomparable American childhood was ended' (301). What emerges clearly from both these moments of crisis, heightened by poetic syntactical inversion ('the family expelled') and archaic diction ('was ended'), is that what disturbs Philip most is not the feeling of being cast out from a Utopian ideal of America that never really existed, but of being thrust suddenly from his own previous state of childish innocence (and ignorance) into the adult world of experience (and corruption). Instead of relying on his mother to provide him with reassurance and security, he must now comfort and console her: 'My mother was trying to act like someone whose panic wasn't running wild within her, and suddenly I felt that it had fallen to me to hold her together, to become all at once a courageous new creature with something of Lincoln himself clinging to him' (66). This epiphany captures perfectly the ambiguity of Philip's postlapsarian condition, in which he is both awed by the responsibility that has now 'fallen' to him and proud of his rebirth as a 'courageous new creature'. It is echoed later in the novel when Philip witnesses for the first time his father shedding tears in distress at the news that Alvin has lost his leg while fighting for the Canadian army against the Germans:

> A new life began for me. I'd watched my father fall apart, and I would never return to the same childhood . . . as Lindbergh's election couldn't have made clearer to me, the unfolding of the unforeseen was everything. Turned wrong way round, the relentless unforeseen was what we schoolchildren studied as 'History,' harmless history, where everything unexpected in its own time is chronicled on the page as inevitable. The terror of the unforeseen is what the science of history hides, turning a disaster into an epic. (113–14)

Having witnessed his mother's 'panic', Philip sees the emotional disintegration of his father: the myth of parental invulnerability – one of the cornerstones of a secure childhood – is shattered forever. This passage, like the others cited above in which the 'harmless' inevitability of history recalled in tranquillity is replaced by the terrifying indeterminacy of history as it unfolds, clearly has a metafictional dimension; it invites us to consider the nature of the novel's enterprise, as well as the nature of events that are occurring within the framework of the novel. It also anticipates what is to become one of the leitmotifs of the novel (the 'great refrain of 1942'), encapsulated in the title of its fifth chapter: 'Never Before' (172). For as the 'relentless unforeseen' rolls onwards, the old certainties of Philip's life unravel, to be succeeded by a 'new life' of vagaries and contingencies. Not only can Philip 'never return to the same childhood' that he had enjoyed prior to Lindbergh's administration; he can never return to any sort of childhood. Now that the vulnerability of both his parents has been exposed, Philip is no longer a child at all in the sense that he has previously understood the term. The 'child's peacetime illusion of an eternal, unhounded now' has been replaced by a recognition that everything is subject to the most violent and radical change (225).

As Philip watches with increasing horror, everything and everyone he thought he knew alters. After a bitter family argument (in which his brother, Sandy, accuses his father of being '"a dictator *worse* than Hitler"') culminates in Bess, Philip's mother, striking Sandy twice, the only way that Philip can reconcile this display of violence with the 'gentle, kindly' mother who has never before dealt a blow to either of her sons is to try to persuade himself that '"She doesn't know what she's doing . . . she's somebody else – *everybody* is"' (193, 194, italics in original). Although Bess herself insists that 'everything is going to get back to normal', Philip knows better (193). When he returns home from school one day to see 'three police cars parked in the front of our house' and the 'women on the block . . . on their front stoops trying to figure out what was going on, and all the kids . . . peering out at the cops . . . from between the row of parked cars', he is filled with foreboding and decides to join the crowd of onlookers rather than entering his home (167). 'Never before', he reflects, 'could I remember them silently gathered together like that, looking so apprehensive' (167). When he sees a body covered with a sheet being removed from the house next door by medics, accompanied by his mother, he becomes convinced that his father has committed suicide because he 'couldn't take any more of . . . what Lindbergh had done to our family' (169). Although it turns out to be Seldon Wishnow's father rather than his own who has died (possibly committing suicide after a long debilitating illness), Philip is profoundly traumatised by the whole episode, reflecting once again on the ways in which his life has changed irretrievably:

> I'd never before looked at my house from a hiding place across the street and wished that it was somebody else's. I'd never before had twenty dollars in my pocket. I'd never before known anyone who'd seen his father hanging in a closet. I'd never before had to grow up at a pace like this. (167)

The emphasis here is on the way in which external events are artificially accelerating Philip's internal development – he has 'never before had to grow up at a pace like this' – and on the strategies that Philip uses to retreat from this traumatic, premature confrontation with the adult world: in this case, wishing that his house 'was somebody else's'. His initial response to the new conditions of his existence is to resolve to improve his own behaviour, 'to make everything turn out right by being the best little boy imaginable . . . better even than myself', but he soon realises that he cannot compensate for everything that is going wrong by creating a self that paradoxically transcends and perfects his own (132). Instead, he withdraws further into – and at the same time away from – himself, emerging from a symbolic period of illness in which he lies 'so weak and lifeless that the family doctor stopped by every evening to check on the progress of my disease, that not uncommon childhood ailment called why-can't-it-be-the-way-it-was' not as the 'courageous new creature' he had had intimations of at the Lincoln Memorial but as a cowed boy living in 'perpetual fear' (172, 66). Instead of aspiring to be 'the best little boy imaginable', a boy who will 'make everything turn out right' for his family and for his country, Philip wants to 'be a boy on the smallest scale possible . . . an orphan'; to remove himself from his family, to retreat from the trauma of the adult world (132, 233).

On the historical level, Roth's novel ends happily. At the lowest point of the penultimate chapter, 'Bad Days', with Lindbergh's vice-president, the *éminence grise* Burton K. Wheeler, apparently beginning to impose totalitarian rule on the United States, Philip's narration is unexpectedly interrupted by the insertion of a series of extracts purporting to be '*Drawn from the Archives of Newark's Newsreel Theater*'. These detail the swift 'restoration of orderly democratic procedures' (largely as the result of the intervention of Anne Morrow Lindbergh, who functions as an unlikely *deus ex machina*) and the subsequent 'landslide victory of Franklin Delano Roosevelt for a third presidential term' (320). If history resumes its familiar course, however, the Roth family does not. The novel does not conclude with the excerpts from the newsreel, or with the ensuing, reassuring narrative of America's belated entry into the war and the eventual victory of the Allied forces. Instead, the final chapter of the novel backtracks, so that the book finishes, as it starts, with an assertion of the 'Perpetual Fear' that is the legacy, for Philip, of the Lindbergh administration. 'Perpetual Fear' is the title of this final chapter, and its last words are a reminder that, while Philip himself becomes an orphan only in his imagination, his 'other self', Seldon, becomes one in reality, his mother having been killed during an anti-Semitic riot in Kentucky: 'There was no stump for me to care for this time. The boy himself was the stump, and . . . I was the prosthesis' (362). Whereas earlier in the novel Philip had dressed the wound left by the amputation of his cousin

Alvin's leg, here he must address the psychological wounds of an emotional amputee: he must parent a boy whose parents have both died. The irony of this situation is intensified because Philip himself has in a sense orphaned Seldon. Seldon and his mother are forced to relocate to Kentucky as a direct result of Philip's intervention when he persuades his aunt Evelyn to use her influence to have the Wishnows moved, hoping that they will fill the place allotted to the Roths in the Office of American Absorption programme of relocation. Having spent much of the novel inventing scenarios in which he would be parentless and get himself adopted, Philip finishes the novel by himself adopting a parentless child.

This tension – between the desire to perpetuate childhood and retreat from the trauma that threatens prematurely to end it, and the need to assume the authority and responsibility of adulthood – is also at the heart of *Extremely Loud and Incredibly Close*. Like Roth's novel, Foer's begins by imagining a world in which reality is radically altered:

> What about a teakettle? What if the spout opened and closed when the steam came out, so it would become a mouth, and it could whistle pretty melodies, or do Shakespeare, or just crack up with me? I could invent a teakettle that reads in Dad's voice, so I could fall asleep [.] (Foer 2005: 1)

What seems at first to be childish whimsy – a harmless, albeit eccentric flight of fancy – soon reveals itself to be something graver. Like Philip in Roth's novel, Oskar is suffering from 'that not uncommon childhood ailment called why-can't-it-be-the-way-it-was': all his 'what ifs' – all his extravagant inventions – are sublimations of his desire to rewrite history so that his father does not die in the attack on the twin towers on 9/11.[16] Imagining a teakettle that would replicate his father's voice and be able to read to him at bedtime (as his father used to) and hence cure the insomnia with which he has been afflicted ever since his father's death, is typical of the strategies Oskar employs throughout the novel to retreat from the trauma he has suffered. Like Philip, who holds himself responsible for the awful events that engulf Seldon and, by implication, his own family (remarking that 'this devastation had been done by me'), Oskar is haunted by a sense of complicity in his father's death, having failed to answer the telephone when his father left the last of a series of messages on the answering machine from inside one of the burning buildings (Roth 2004: 337).

Philip punishes himself metaphorically by imagining different ways of orphaning himself; Oskar literally inflicts pain on himself, pressing his skin until it bruises. Whereas Philip dreams of being adopted, Oskar adopts a series of surrogate fathers: Stephen Hawking (to whom he writes a series of letters and who eventually replies); a centenarian retired war journalist who lives in an apartment on the floor above; his own grandfather (unaware that this man is his father's father, Oskar believes him simply to be his grandmother's lodger); and finally, briefly, a man from whom Oskar's father, shortly before his death, had bought a blue vase which contains a key that Oskar discovers after 9/11. Much of the novel is taken up with Oskar's quest to find the box which the key will open. Ostensibly, this is an attempt to solve a mystery that Oskar hopes will reveal something of significance about his father's life, but in fact it offers Oskar an opportunity to avoid confronting the reality of his father's death. The key, which Oskar discovers by chance when he knocks over the blue vase which contained it, is accompanied by a scrap of paper with the word 'Black' on it and Oskar resolves to track down everyone in New York with that surname, knowing full well that such a mission is unlikely ever to conclude. When, by an unlikely series of coincidences (at one point Oskar himself observes that 'If it weren't my life, I wouldn't have believed it'), Oskar finally comes face to face with the Black whose name he had found scrawled on the bit of paper, it turns out that he too has been hunting for the key. Mr Black tells him that, after his own father died, he had delayed reading a final letter from him 'for a few weeks' because it was 'too painful' (Foer 2005: 297). When he does eventually read it, he discovers that his father had left him the key to a safe-deposit box in a bank in a blue vase; but by then, Black has already sold the vase to Oskar's father. Black's subsequent attempts to track down Oskar's father, like Oskar's attempts to find Black, are motivated partly by guilt associated with a father's death: because Black and Black's father 'weren't exactly close', Black sells all his father's belongings and, after reading the letter, fears that he has rejected the legacy that his father intended to bequeath to him (296). As Oskar listens to Black speak about his father, he realises that 'even though I wanted him to tell me about my dad instead of his, I also wanted to make the story as long as I could, because I was afraid of its end' (297). Just as Black postpones opening his father's letter because he wants to defer for as long as possible the moment when he has to confront the fact of his death, so Oskar deliberately sets himself a potentially endless task because he is in flight from the fact of his father's death. While he is still investigating the mystery of the key, his father's case is still open, as it were. Once he solves the puzzle, he will be left only with his memories.

Like Philip, whose mantra of 'never before' emphasises the absolute rupture between his past and present lives, Oskar is always painfully aware of the irrevocable nature of the changes in his life wrought by his father's death. In the first few pages of the novel, there are continual reminders of the way in which Oskar thinks of his life as divided into two distinct eras: the period before his father's death (which he euphemistically refers to as 'the worst day'), when 'I used to be an atheist', and 'Dad constantly used to tell me I was too smart for retail', and 'Dad always used to tuck me in' and so on; and the period after 9/11, when he 'started inventing things', harming himself, and wearing 'heavy boots' (Oskar's term for feeling sad) (11, 3, 4, 7, 12, 36). Everything in Oskar's life is defined in relation to his father's death, whether a casual reference to 'the ring tone I downloaded for the cell phone I got after Dad died' or the revelation that he 'never used to lie to her [his mother] before everything happened', just as everything in Philip's life falls either into the period before or after Lindbergh's inauguration (3, 6). Both boys try to rewrite the past so as to alter the present. Whereas Philip begins *The Plot Against America* by imagining how different a boy he might have been had Lindbergh not been elected President, Oskar ends *Extremely Loud and Incredibly Close* by imagining a reversal of the sequence of events that leads to his father's death, so that the plane that crashes into the tower 'would've flown backward away from him, all the way to Boston' (325). Flicking backwards through a series of photographs that he has downloaded from the internet of a body falling from one of the towers (a figure who he suspects might be his father), so that 'the last one was first, and the first was last', Oskar is able to make it look 'like the man was floating up through the sky' (325). Here, as in Roth's novel, a flight of fancy becomes a fantasy of flight, except that Philip daydreams of a metaphorical flight (running away from home) and Oskar's fantasy involves his father literally taking flight,[17] in order to return him to the tower. As the events of 'the worst day' continue to rewind in Oskar's mind, he eventually restores him to the home where he can be reunited with his family, who then, in the final words of the novel, 'would have been safe' (326).

The method of Oskar's resurrection of his father alludes to the New Testament ('the last one was first, and the first was last' is a verbal echo of one of the most famous passages from Christ's sermon on the mount) and owes a debt to the inversions of chronology deployed in other postmodern novels, such as Martin Amis's *Time's Arrow* and Kurt Vonnegut's *Slaughterhouse Five*. It also echoes an earlier passage in Foer's novel, which, like Vonnegut's, deals with the bombing of Dresden. This event, in which Oskar's grandfather and grandmother lost many of their loved ones (including the grandmother's sister, with whom the grandfather had been in love), is juxtaposed throughout the novel with the events of 9/11. Oskar's trauma is contextualised by his grandparents'. The grandfather is so damaged by his experiences that he withdraws into silence, communicating only by means of a notepad in which he scrawls messages, and is unable to sustain his relationship with the grandmother, repeatedly taking flight from her, only subsequently to return unannounced (this is why Oskar does not know his real identity when he meets him). The grandmother develops her own, generally more successful, survival strategies. At one point she has a dream in which, like Oskar's back-to-front flickerbook (reproduced in the final pages of the novel), history is inverted, and the destruction caused by the fire-bombing of Dresden is magically undone:

> In my dream, all the collapsed ceilings re-formed above us. The fire went back into the bombs, which rose up and into the bellies of the planes whose propellers turned backward, like the second hands of the clocks across Dresden, only faster. (307)

Although the grandmother knows that her redemptive vision is only a dream, just as Oskar knows that his father's salvation can only take place in his imagination, the intention of these rewritings of history is, like those in Roth's novel, to challenge the conventional view of history as inevitable, fixed, predetermined, objective; to posit, through the imagining of alternative histories, an idea of history as provisional, precarious, indeterminate and subjective. However, they may, paradoxically, have the opposite effect: rewinding and replaying these events might reinforce a teleological view of history by apparently implying that each stage of history is one link in a causal chain that cannot be broken, a linear route from which there are no diversions or exits, only the possibility of reversing.

On the eve of 9/11, Oskar's father tells him a bedtime story about the existence of a Sixth Borough in New York, 'separated from Manhattan by a thin body of water whose narrowest crossing happened to equal the world's long jump record' (217). The holder of this record makes the leap as part of an annual party and '[f]or those few moments that the jumper was in the air, every New Yorker felt capable of flight' (218). The use of the term 'jumper' here implicitly connects the athlete to those who leapt to their deaths from the twin towers; the collective fantasy of flight of the assembled crowd alludes to the crowds of New Yorkers who witnessed the collapse of the towers while fleeing from the scene and also anticipates Oskar's photographic montage in which a jumper from one of the towers miraculously levitates rather than descending. However, the story also functions as a parable about history and storytelling. While he listens to the story of the Sixth Borough, which gradually begins to drift further and further away from its neighbouring island, floating across the planet with 'a gigantic hole in the middle of it where Central Park used to be' (its own ground zero), Oskar repeatedly interrupts his father's narrative to cross-examine him on the authenticity of the narrative: '"Was there *really* a sixth borough?"'; '"You just mean in the story, right?"'; '"I know there wasn't really a sixth borough. I mean, objectively"' (217, 221). The father refuses to concede that his story is not real, remarking instead that '"You won't read about it in any of the history books, because there's nothing – save for the circumstantial evidence in Central Park – to prove that it was there at all"' (217). Later in the novel, Oskar, having received a series of form letters in response to his requests to Stephen Hawking that he adopt Oskar as his protegé, finally gets a personal reply in which the famous physicist reminds him that '*the vast majority of the universe is composed of dark matter*' and that life '*depends on things we'll never be able to see*' (Foer 2005, italics in original). Hawking (or rather, Foer's fictional version of him) goes on to ask, rhetorically:

> *What's real? What isn't real? Maybe those aren't the right questions to be asking . . .*
>
> *What if you never stop inventing?*
>
> *Maybe you're not inventing at all.* (305; italics in original)

The '*Note to the Reader*' in the 'Postscript' to *The Plot Against America* raises similar questions. It begins with the declaration that the book 'is a work of fiction' but then announces that the postscript 'is intended as a reference for readers interested in tracking where historical fact ends and historical imagining begins', thereby implying that the story contains historical fact and also, through the use of the oxymoron 'historical imagining', that what is imagined may in some sense be historical, and that what is historical may in some sense be imagined (364).[18]

Both Foer's and Roth's novels blur the boundaries between what is real and invented, and between history and story. Partly they do this formally, through the fusion of different narrative genres. The juxtaposition in *Extremely Loud and Incredibly Close* of the essentially realistic depiction of Oskar's struggle to come to terms with his father's death with the often surreal treatment of the relationship between Oskar's grandparents might be read as an homage to the magical realism of writers such as Salman Rushdie and Gunter Grass.[19] Foer's novel certainly alludes to *Midnight's Children* (1981) and *The Tin Drum* (1959), and Morley argues that *The Plot Against America*, too, represents 'a new departure for Roth into magic realism', though thematically it 'return[s] to the preoccupations of his earlier fictions' (Morley: unpublished). However, both novels also implicitly redefine the parameters of what is historical by examining the impact of acts of political violence on the lives of individuals who are, in historical terms, insignificant. At one point in Carol Shields' novel *Happenstance* (1991), the protagonist of 'The Husband's Story', a historian by profession, reflects that 'most of life fell through the mesh of what was considered to be worthy of recording' (Shields 1994: 107). Philip's father in *The Plot Against America* makes a similar point, arguing that history ought to be inclusive and democratic: '"History is everything that happens everywhere. Even here in Newark. Even here on Summit Avenue. Even what happens in his house to an ordinary man – that'll be history too someday"' (Roth 2004: 180). However, as Oskar discovers, in *Extremely Loud and Incredibly Close*, history *qua* history is exclusively the province of the rich, the famous and the influential. When the retired journalist Black searches in vain amongst his voluminous collection of index cards recording the significance of world-historical individuals for an entry on Oskar's father, Oskar acknowledges that the absence of a card bearing his father's name signifies that 'Dad wasn't a Great Man . . . Dad was just someone who ran a family jewelry business. Just an ordinary dad' (Foer 2005: 159). Yet in the context of Foer's story it is the history of Thomas Schell (Oskar's father), and of his parents and his son, that takes precedence over the big players on the historical stage: there is no mention in the whole novel of either George W. Bush or Osama bin Laden. Likewise, in *The Plot Against America*, Lindbergh himself remains a peripheral figure; it is the Roth family who loom large. The most important papers in these novels are not political documents, but Philip's stamp album, Oskar's scrapbook (appropriately titled *Stuff that Happened to Me*),[20] and his grandfather's notepad, filled with the most mundane and quotidian utterances. Although both books were, to differing degrees, promoted as '9/11 novels', ultimately they engage with the political realities of the attack on the World Trade Center and its aftermath only obliquely. This might be regarded as a failure of nerve or ambition. They might be said to exhibit a certain timidity masquerading as audacity, making gestures towards grasping the big ideological nettle of our times, while shrinking away from actually doing so. At the same time, Foer's and Roth's paradoxical achievement has been to write what Roth in 1973 called 'a counterhistory, or *countermythology*, to challenge the mythic sense of itself the country had [in the 1950s]'; to rewrite history by eschewing the very stuff of conventional history; and to demonstrate the effect of trauma by dramatising the retreat from that trauma into flights of fancy and fantasies of flight (Roth 2001a: 78).

## Notes

1 These twin strategies were combined in the inclusion of the whole of the first chapter of the novel as a supplement to the 'Review' section of *The Guardian* of 11 September 2004, the third anniversary of the attacks on the twin towers. The 'Review' section itself also devoted its opening four pages to a profile of Roth by his old friend, the British poetry critic A. Alvarez, accompanied by a photograph of Roth with the Stars and Stripes in the background. I am indebted to Catherine Morley for drawing my attention to the iconography deployed in the publicity campaign for the novel.

2 In fact in several interviews Roth claimed that the origins of the novel lay not in the events of 9/11 but rather in 'a chance comment by the historian Arthur Schlesinger Jr., who speculates in his autobiography that in 1940 some right-wing members of the Republican Party considered drafting the pioneering pilot Charles Lindbergh as a presidential candidate' (Roth quoted in Grossman 2004: 82).

3 At the end of each year, the newspaper asks a broad range of writers, intellectuals and broadcasters to nominate their favourite books of the previous twelve months.

4 The novel is reputed to have made Foer a multimillionaire and the 2003 British Penguin paperback edition fills five of its pages with excerpts from reviews that are extraordinarily effusive, as well as printing one judgement, from *The Times*, on the back cover: 'A work of genius. A new kind of novel . . . after it things will never be the same again. It will blow you away'.

5 Rushdie is quoted on the back of the QPD paperback edition in large print, claiming that the novel is 'an exceptional achievement'. This solitary tribute is in stark contrast to the thirty-five tributes that bookend the paperback edition of *Everything Is Illuminated*.

6 Roger Gathman, for example, argues that 'the 9/11 background seems more exploited than explored, a reference that pops up to lend automatic gravitas to the proceedings' (Gathman 2005: n.p.), while Walter Kirn begins his review of the novel by noting, sardonically, that it will become 'known . . . perhaps primarily, and surely intentionally, as that new Sept. 11 novel whose last pages include a little flip-book of video stills arranged in reverse order to create a fleeting, blurry movie of an actual human being careering upward through the sky toward the top of the fiery doomed tower from which . . . the fresh-and-blood [sic] person on the film was – in undoctored, forward-rushing fact – jumping or falling to his death' (Kirn 2005: n.p.). Tom Barbash also takes exception to what he sees as the gimmick of the flipbook ending, complaining that it 'lends to the story a horrific and unearned gravity and . . . cheapens a gorgeous and beautifully sad moment at the end of the final chapter' (Barbash 2005: n.p.). Similarly, Tim Adams suggests that '[b]y the time you get to the end, and flip backwards through the pictures of the falling figure . . . you may feel a good deal of the emotion has been borrowed and not quite earned' (Adams 2005: n.p.).

7 This list appears, slightly altered, in the main narrative in the form of Oskar's business card, which also advertises his talents as a 'jewelry designer', 'jewelry fabricator', 'amateur archeologist' and a 'collector of: *rare coins, butterflies that died natural deaths, miniature cacti, Beatles memorabilia, semiprecious stones, and other things*' (Foer 2005: 99, italics in original).

8 Several American critics did indeed make this connection but more often than not in order to damn rather than defend Foer. Walter Kirn, for example, refers to Oskar as a 'hyperactive impersonation of Holden Caulfield' and concludes his review by wishing (in a parody of the reversal of time that Oskar imagines at the end of the novel) that 'all the Holden Caulfields who aren't Holden were back inside J.D. Salinger's typewriter' (Kirn 2005: n.p.).

9 Or perhaps even to an earlier autobiographical piece published in *Harper's* magazine in 1959, 'Beyond the Last Rope', in which Roth recalls himself as a young child noticing 'a man who looked like Hitler' but deciding to 'let Hitler go free', since he was at an age when 'more and more of my childhood fibs and inventions were being put down . . . by the impatient skepticism of adults' (Roth 1959c: 47).

10 See Brauner 2001: 154–70, 183.

11 James Wood, for example, comments that 'where Roth's fiction often tests American Jews by the standard of their various accommodations with their country, here he tests America by its projected treatment of the Jews' (Wood 2004: 3).

12 David Herman, for example, observes that 'Roth's early books present the Jewish parents as sometimes hysterical, even comic, people with values to be reacted against, to be left behind. Here, they are right' (Herman 2004: 77), while Joan Acocella notes that whereas '[i]n Roth's novels, this relentless cautioning is usually done by the parents', here it is the narrator himself who voices the worst fears of his community (Acocella 2004: n.p.).

13 Roth also mentions Miller's novel in *Reading Myself and Others* (Roth 2001a: 94). The plot of *Focus* is predicated on the phenomenon of deep-rooted and growing anti-Semitic sentiment in America in the pre-war years. See Brauner 2001: 44–51 for a detailed critical discussion of the novel.

14 Roth had written about *The Victim* and *The Assistant* early in his career (in his essay 'Imagining Jews' in *Reading Myself and Others*). In *The Counterlife* Nathan Zuckerman refers to the film version of Hobson's novel, in which Gregory Peck played the role of Hobson's protagonist – a Gentile journalist who assumes a Jewish identity in order to investigate the extent to which anti-Semitism is operating in 1930s America (Roth 1986: 293).

15 There appears to be an autobiographical element to Foer's story. Interviewing Foer for a piece in *The Guardian*, Suzie Mackenzie discusses an incident that took place when the author 'was eight, almost nine . . . when his child world was blown apart' (Mackenzie 2005: 5). The blast turns out to have been literal as well as metaphorical. Foer tells her that one day, while attending a chemistry class at summer camp, there was a huge explosion in the classroom in which he and three other children had been trying to make sparklers. Foer escaped with minor physical injuries but was psychologically severely scarred, having witnessed his best friend's disfigurement. He recalls seeing 'all the skin on his [friend's] face peeling off' (Mackenzie 2005: 5), a description that closely echoes the account, included in *Extremely Loud and Incredibly Close*, of a Japanese man who, in the aftermath of the Hiroshima bombing, watches helplessly as his daughter dies in his arms: 'I tried to clean her up. But her skin was peeling off' (Foer 2005: 188). In the interview, Foer claims to have suffered four years of what would now be diagnosed as Post-Traumatic Stress Disorder, before deciding at the age of twelve to 'become a new person' (Mackenzie 2005: 6).

16 The novel is punctuated by these inventions – some of which, like the 'skyscraper that moved up and down while its elevator stayed in place', address, and attempt to redress, the events of 9/11 explicitly – but the word

invention is also used to refer to Oskar's compulsive (imagined) reconstruction of the circumstances of his father's death (Foer 2005: 3). Hence Oskar's inventions are, paradoxically, both a way of revisiting his father's death and of distracting himself from it.

17 Images of flight are important in the novel. The second of three photographs that precede the narrative text of *Extremely Loud and Incredibly Close* shows a flock of birds taking off and later in the novel Oskar experiences an epiphany of sorts when, from the window of the aged Mr Black's apartment, he witnesses 'a flock of birds [flying] . . . extremely fast and incredibly close. Maybe twenty of them. Maybe more. But they also seemed like just one bird, because somehow they all knew exactly what to do' (Foer 2005: 165, 168). This description is interrupted in the book by the insertion of another photograph of birds on the wing.

18 Catherine Morley makes a similar point in an unpublished article on *The Plot Against America*.

19 This juxtaposition echoes the structure of *Everything Is Illuminated*, in which the mystical and mystifying chronicle of the fictional Jewish ghetto Trachimbrod is framed by the more conventional narrative of (the character) Foer's attempt to reconstruct his grandfather's wartime experiences in the Ukraine.

20 Foer may intend a satirical allusion here to Donald Rumsfeld's notorious explanation for the high incidence of civilian casualties in the Iraqi conflict: 'Stuff happens'.

# Afterword

Writing this book I have felt, at times, rather like Tristram Shandy in Laurence Sterne's novel, who exclaims, paradoxically, that 'the more I write, the more I shall have to write' (Sterne 1986: 286). Whereas Sterne's anti-hero is constantly fighting a losing battle to catch up in his memoirs with the events of his life, I have been struggling as I write to keep up with new developments in the field of Roth studies. So prolific is Roth (publishing on average a book every two years) – and so critically fashionable (there have been ten books and more than one hundred book chapters and journal articles published on his work in the last five years of the twentieth century and the first five of the twenty-first) – that staying in touch with work by him and on him is a full-time job in itself. As I write, Roth's novel, *Everyman*, has just been published, to mixed reviews.

A recurring refrain in many of these reviews has been the idea that the novel reflects the septuagenarian Roth's increasing preoccupation with mortality. Yet Roth's interest in the precariousness of life is not a recent development. On the contrary, his first story, 'The Day It Snowed', published in 1954 when the author was just twenty-one, revolves around the misguided attempts of a young boy's family to hide from him the reality of death (they tell him that deceased relatives have 'disappeared'). It ends with the boy himself, distressed at having finally discovered the truth, running in front of a car and being killed. Three years later, Roth published a brief autobiographical sketch in *Harper's* entitled 'Beyond the Last Rope'. A nostalgic recollection of lazy days spent sun-bathing and swimming on Bradley Beach, the piece nonetheless ends with two intimations of mortality: as Roth 'enters the water with my girl', he realises that 'if I am old enough for her, my parents are suddenly older than I like to imagine'; and in the final words of the story the news that a fellow Bradley summer vacationer has got married and entered the trucking business seems to Roth to contain 'rumours of my own mortality'.

From the outset, then, Roth has shared with Samuel Beckett the sense that we are all 'born astride of a grave', and his fiction has repeatedly explored the fragility of the human body. From the early story 'Novotny's Pain', in which the protagonist is struck down mysteriously during military service with excruciating back pain, to the mid-career novel *The Anatomy Lesson*, in which Roth's perennial protagonist, Nathan Zuckerman, suffers from acute undiagnosed neckache, to the 'American Trilogy' of the 1990s in which Zuckerman is left impotent and incontinent following an operation on his prostate, illness is ubiquitous.

In this respect, as in many others, Roth's new novel, *Everyman*, revisits familiar territory. It tells the story of a Jewish man born in the same year as Roth himself, the 'reliable son' of a jeweller whose 'stroke of genius was to call the business not by his name but rather Everyman's Jewelry Store' (thereby ensuring that he doesn't alienate the 'thousands of church-going Christians' who live nearby).[1] He marries and divorces three times, works in advertising and then, in retirement, takes up painting and finally dies, suddenly, on the operating table. We are never told the protagonist's name and the title of the novel derives not so much from his father's business as from the fifteenth-century morality drama, *The Summoning of Everyman*, in which the allegorical representative of mankind finds himself suddenly required to give a 'general reckoning' or 'account' of his life so that he may be judged and sent accordingly to Heaven or Hell. At first glance, Roth's novel appears to have little in common with its namesake. Whereas the anonymous author of the medieval play makes his didactic purpose quite explicit, announcing at the start that his is 'a moral play . . . [that] shows/How transitory we be' and reminding the audience at the end that only those who provide an 'account whole and sound' will 'in heaven . . . be crowned', Roth's novel resolutely refuses any possibility of an afterlife or a divine governing order, consoling or otherwise, insisting that life is 'given to . . . all, randomly, fortuitously, and but once, and for no known or knowable reason'. The novel's protagonist, though he is given a Jewish burial in accordance with tradition, has no belief in an eternal soul, insisting on the contrary that '[t]here was only our bodies, born to live and die on terms decided by the bodies that had lived and died before us' (51). It is precisely because death is final and absolute, the novel implies, that it is so shocking.

For all the obvious differences of form and sensibility, however, the two *Everymans* share certain structures. For example, the medieval Everyman's anguished exclamation when he realises that his time on earth is up – 'O Death, thou comest when I had thee least in mind' (described by Roth in interviews as 'the first great line in English drama') – is echoed in the description of his modern counterpart's state of mind as he is anaesthetised prior to the operation that kills him: 'He went under feeling far from felled, anything but doomed, eager yet again to be fulfilled, but nonetheless, he never woke up'. If the morality play is solely concerned with the fate of its protagonist at the point of death, Roth's novel is similarly relentless in its emphasis on the decline, depression and decrepitude that accompany ageing, although it zigzags between past and present, juxtaposing recollections of the hero's earlier years with his experiences as a retired septuagenarian. At one point Roth's anonymous third-person narrator wryly observes that the conversation among the elderly students whom the protagonist teaches in his art class 'invariably turned to matters of sickness and health, their personal biographies having by this time become identical with their medical biographies and the swapping of medical data crowding out nearly everything else'. This parochial preoccupation with illness and death is as true of Roth's hero as it is of his pupils. Like Mickey Sabbath, the anti-hero of *Sabbath's Theater* who, Roth's narrator remarks with characteristically paradoxical, mordant wit, 'only had a life at the cemetery', the hero of *Everyman* also finds that 'his deepest pleasure was now at the cemetery'. Furthermore, he realises that his mind is becoming 'steadily . . . dominated by medical thoughts to the exclusion of everything else' and, in another Rothian paradox, that 'eluding death seemed to have become the central business of his life and bodily decay his entire story'. Though clearly aware of the irony, the novel itself comes perilously close at times to sounding like the *kvetching* of an elderly man with too much time on his hands and too many medical textbooks to hand: *Everyman's Complaint*, perhaps?

More moving than the detailed descriptions of various ailments and medical interventions is the increasing sense of loneliness that envelops Roth's hero. Just as Everyman finds himself gradually forsaken by all his worldly allies – Fellowship, Cousin, Kindred, Goods, Strength, Discretion, Five-Wits and Beauty – and has to face death armed only with his Good-Deeds, Roth's modern-day everyman finds himself increasingly isolated as he approaches the end. Estranged from his wives, from his two sons (who blame him for the break-up of his marriage to their mother), and finally from his brother, Howie (whom he worships as a boy but whose rude good health he comes to resent), Roth's protagonist finds himself unable or unwilling to forge new friendships with his fellow residents at the Starfish retirement village and fantasises about moving into an apartment with his daughter, Nancy (the one member of his family with whom he has maintained a loving relationship) and her twins.

Finally, Roth's *Everyman* borrows from its medieval precursor a spare, elliptical quality that is both its greatest strength and weakness. *The Summoning of Everyman* is a short drama, its brevity contributing to and enacting the sense of urgency felt by its protagonist, who must prepare himself for his day of reckoning hurriedly. *Everyman* is one of Roth's shortest books – more a long novella perhaps than a novel – and at its best this results in episodes of distilled, concentrated intensity. One example is the scene in which Millicent Kramer, the star pupil in the art class, begins to tell the protagonist of the pain that is depriving her of all that she values in life, only to pull herself up short, exclaiming, '"I'm terribly sorry. Everybody here has their ordeal. There's nothing special about my story and I'm sorry to burden you with it. You probably have a story of your own"'. This is affecting in itself and becomes even more so when we are told soon afterwards that '[t]en days later she killed herself with an overdose of sleeping pills'. Yet less is not always more. Kramer's dignified restraint packs a more powerful punch than the garrulous self-pity of her peers but too often Roth's novel, in its attempts to represent the attenuated, weary resignation of its protagonist – who announces, peremptorily, '[t]his is the man I have made. This is what I did to get here, and there's nothing more to be said!' – risks appearing attenuated, weary and resigned itself. For example, in the middle of an angry dialogue between the protagonist and his second wife, Phoebe, who has finally confronted him with her knowledge of his infidelity, Roth's narrator abruptly aborts the scene, observing that 'these episodes are indeed well known and require no further elaboration'. This reticence is certainly a deliberate strategy on Roth's part: it serves to emphasise the loss of 'that sharp sense of individualization . . . that is the opposite of the deadening depersonalization of serious illness', to render the protagonist a representative figure whose experiences are universal enough to carry the symbolic freight that goes with the novel's title. Yet just as the protagonist himself sometimes uses his unexceptionality as an alibi – a way of avoiding responsibility for the choices that he has made – as when he attributes the failure of his second marriage to larger social trends ('He was one of the millions of American men who were party to a divorce that broke up a family'), so Roth sometimes seems to stint on the sort of social and psychological detail that might have made the novel truly memorable, in the interests of retaining his allegorical framework.

The overall tone of the novel is curiously muted; comedy and rage are in short supply – and comedy and rage are what Roth does best. There is, as always with Roth, some sparkling prose in *Everyman* (a particularly brilliant passage is the one in which the narrator recalls 'licking his forearm to taste his skin fresh from the ocean and baked by the sun', 'the taste and the smell intoxicat[ing] him so that he was driven to the brink of biting down with his teeth to tear out a chunk of himself and savour his fleshly existence') but it is, in the end, a minor Roth novel. Lesser Roth is still greater than the best of most of his peers and perhaps, at this late stage of his career, we should be grateful for anything we get, but I like to think that, unlike Everyman, Roth still has the time and vitality left to produce at least one more masterpiece.

Certainly, given the trajectory of his career to date, it seems quite possible, even probable, that Roth's journey as a novelist may yet contain a number of twists and turns. For this reason, this book cannot be definitive one; this afterword will not be the last word (or even my last word) on Roth. Yet it is possible, after a career spanning almost half a century, and an *oeuvre* of twenty-six books, to take stock and assess Roth's contribution to American letters in general and to the development of the post-war American novel in particular.

Roth's place in the canon now seems assured; there is a general consensus that he is the most important living American novelist and a growing body of opinion that he is the best post-war American writer. The only major literary prize that has so far eluded him is the Nobel Prize for Literature, and if I were a gambling man I would place a bet on him winning that before long. I must confess to feeling a certain ambivalence about this state of affairs. When I began writing on Roth in 1990 (as part of my doctoral thesis) his critical reputation was still rather insecure. Although *Goodbye, Columbus* had established itself as something of a classic, being widely taught in American high schools, Roth was otherwise known primarily as the author of a novel (*Portnoy's Complaint*) to which the whiff of scandal still clung. At that time, the reaction of many of my academic colleagues when I mentioned my enthusiasm for Roth was either facetious or condescending, or both. There was a general sense that Roth had had his fifteen minutes of fame (or notoriety) as a novelist and that he was now somewhat *passé*. Part of me therefore feels vindicated by Roth's subsequent renaissance; I take (whether justifiably or not) a certain pride in the fact that my judgement then – that Roth, far from having written himself out, was as dynamic and vibrant as any living novelist – has prevailed. At the same time, I feel something of the proprietorial jealousy that often attaches to admirers of artists whose genius is initially acknowledged only by a select few, but who later become widely celebrated for their achievements. Co-existing with the temptation to say 'I told you so' is the inclination to say 'you're not a genuine connoisseur – you're just jumping on the bandwagon'. There is also often a sense among her or his original followers that the artist has received recognition by sacrificing his or her integrity, or at least by moving more into the mainstream: 'You're admiring him for the wrong reasons – or for the wrong books; his earlier work was better'.

In my view, Roth has consistently improved as a writer as his career has developed. *Portnoy's Complaint* (1969) deserves to be well-known for more than its taboo-breaking treatment of masturbation and, *pace* Irving Howe,[2] the novel rewards rereading; *My Life as a Man* (1974) is rather underrated. However, of his five finest novels – for me *The Ghost Writer* (1979), *The Counterlife* (1987), *Sabbath's Theater* (1995), *American Pastoral* (1997) and *The Human Stain* (2000) – four have been written in the second half of his career, three of them in the final five years of the twentieth century. There have been some disappointments in Roth's later work – *The Dying Animal* (2001) is, along with the other Kepesh books (*The Breast* (1972) and *The Professor of Desire* (1977)), among his weaker work, and *Operation Shylock* (1993), though it contains some brilliant writing, is finally rather less than the sum of its parts. However, in general Roth has pulled off a rare and remarkable trick. Rather than simply reprising old themes, reliving former glories or resting on his laurels, Roth has repeatedly reinvented himself as an author, driving himself on with increasing urgency. Far from running out of steam, or ideas, as he gets older, he has instead powered on to new territory, firing on all pistons.

My objective in this book has been both to make the case for Roth's distinctive strengths as a novelist (strengths which were certainly evident in his earlier fiction but which have been demonstrated most effectively in the second half of his career) and also to suggest that making such a case does not necessarily entail removing him from his literary-historical context. My hope is that this book will encourage old devotees to return to, and new readers to discover, Roth's work, and will ensure that future scholarship on Roth pays greater attention both to the particular, paradoxical rhetorical gifts that set him apart from his contemporaries and to the formal and thematic concerns that he shares with them.

## Notes

1 All quotations from *Everyman* are taken from uncorrected proofs and consequently I have not included any page numbers. *Everyman* was published by Jonathan Cape (London) in 2006.

2 Howe famously observed that 'the cruelest thing anyone can do with *Portnoy's Complaint* is to read it twice' (Howe 1982: 243).

# Works cited

## Works by Philip Roth

1959a. *Goodbye, Columbus.* London: Andre Deutsch.
1959b. 'The Love Vessel'. *The Dial* 1:1, 41–68.
1959c. 'Beyond the Last Rope'. *Harper's* (July): 42–8.
1960. 'The Good Girl'. *Cosmopolitan* 148 (May): 98–103.
1962. *Letting Go.* London: Andre Deutsch.
1967. *When She Was Good.* London: Jonathan Cape.
1969. *Portnoy's Complaint.* London: Jonathan Cape.
1971. *Our Gang.* London: Jonathan Cape.
1972. *The Breast.* London: Jonathan Cape.
1978 [1977]. *The Professor of Desire.* London: Jonathan Cape.
1980a. *A Philip Roth Reader.* London: Jonathan Cape.
1980b [1962]. 'Novotny's Pain' (revised). In Roth 1980a: 261–80.
1981 [1973]. *The Great American Novel.* Harmondsworth: Penguin.
1985 [1974]. *My Life as a Man.* Harmondsworth: Penguin.
1986. *The Counterlife.* New York: Farrar, Straus, Giroux.
1988. *The Facts.* London: Jonathan Cape.
1989. *Zuckerman Bound: A Trilogy and Epilogue.* Harmondsworth: Penguin.
1990. *Deception.* London: Jonathan Cape.
1991. *Patrimony: A True Story.* London: Jonathan Cape.
1993a. *Operation Shylock: A Confession.* London: Jonathan Cape.
1993b. 'A Bit of Jewish Mischief'. *New York Times Book Review,* 7 March: 1, 20.
1995. *Sabbath's Theater.* London: Jonathan Cape.
1997. *American Pastoral.* London: Jonathan Cape.
1998. *I Married A Communist.* London: Jonathan Cape.
2000. *The Human Stain.* London: Jonathan Cape.
2001a [1975]. *Reading Myself and Others* (revised). New York: Vintage.
2001b. *Shop Talk: A Writer and His Colleagues and their Work.* London: Jonathan Cape.

2004. *The Plot Against America*. London: Jonathan Cape.
2005. 'It no longer feels a great injustice that I have to die' (interview with Martin Krasnik). *The Guardian* ('G2'), 14 December: 14–17.

## Secondary sources

Acocella, Joan. 2004. 'Counterlives' (review of *The Plot Against America*). *The New Yorker*, 20 September: http://www.newyorker.com/critics/books/?040920crbo_books.
Adams, Tim. 2005. 'A nine-year-old and 9/11' (review of *Extremely Loud and Incredibly Close*). *The Guardian*, 29 May: http://books.guardian.co.uk/reviews/generalfiction.
Alexander, Marguerite. 1990. *Flights from Realism: Themes and Strategies in Postmodernist British and American Fiction*. London: Edward Arnold.
Alsen, Eberhard, ed. 1996. *Romantic Postmodernism in American Fiction*. Amsterdam: Rodopi.
Alter, Robert. 1982 [1967]. 'When He Is Bad' (review of *When She Was Good*). In Pinsker 1982: 4–6.
Alter, Robert. 2002. 'Philip Roth's America'. In Lévy and Savin 2002: 25–33.
Alvarez, Al. 2004. 'The long road home' (interview with Roth). *The Guardian* ('Review'), 11 November: 20–3.
Amis, Martin. 1986. *The Moronic Inferno and Other Visits to America*. London: Jonathan Cape.
Anshaw, Carol. 1993 [1992]. *Aquamarine*. London: Virago.
Baker, Nicholson. 1992. *Vox*. New York: Random House.
Barbash, Tom. 2005. 'Mysterious key sends boy sifting through his life's wreckage after 9/11' (review of *Extremely Loud and Incredibly Close*). *San Francisco Chronicle*, 3 April: http://www.sfgate.com/.
Barth, John. 1967. 'The Literature of Exhaustion'. *Atlantic Monthly* 220: 29–34.
Baudrillard, Jean. 1983. *Simulations* (tr. Paul Foss, Paul Patton and Philip Beitchman). New York: Semiotext(e).
Bellow, Saul. 1966 [1953]. *The Adventures of Augie March*. Harmondsworth: Penguin.
Biale, David, Michael Galchinksy and Susannah Heschel, eds. 1998. *Insider/Outsider: American Jews and Multiculturalism*. Los Angeles: University of California Press.
Birnbaum, Jonathan. 2005. 'Birnbaum v. Jonathan Safran Foer' (interview with Jonathan Safran Foer). *The Morning News*, 14 April: http://www.themorningnews.org/archives/personalities/birnbaum-v-jonathan-safran-foer.
Bloom, Claire. 1996. *Leaving a Doll's House: A Memoir*. Boston: Little Brown.
Bloom, Harold. 1993. 'Operation Roth' (review of *Operation Shylock*). *New York Review of Books*, 22 September: 45–8.

Bloom, Harold, ed. 2003. *Philip Roth*. Philadelphia: Chelsea House.
Boyers, Robert. 1997. 'The Indigenous Berserk' (review of *American Pastoral*). *The New Republic*, 7 July: 36–41.
Brauner, David. 1995. 'Explaining the Self: A Contextual Study of Saul Bellow, Philip Roth and Joseph Heller'. Ph.D. dissertation, University of London.
Brauner, David. 1998. 'Fiction as Self-Accusation: Philip Roth and the Jewish Other'. *Studies in American Jewish Literature* 17: 8–16.
Brauner, David. 2000. 'Masturbation and its Discontents; or Serious Relief: Freudian Comedy in *Portnoy's Complaint*'. *The Critical Review* 40: 75–90.
Brauner, David. 2001. *Post-War Jewish Fiction: Ambivalence, Self-Explanation and Transatlantic Connections*. Basingstoke: Palgrave/Macmillan.
Brauner, David. 2004. 'American Anti-Pastoral: Incontinence and Impurity in *American Pastoral* and *The Human Stain*'. *Studies in American Jewish Literature* 23: 67–76.
Brauner, David. 2005. '"Getting In Your Retaliation First": Narrative Strategies in *Portnoy's Complaint*'. In Royal 2005a: 43–57.
Brauner, David. 2006. 'Everyman Out of Humour' (review of *Everyman*). *Jewish Quarterly* 202: 80–2.
Brent, Jonathan. 1992 [1988]. 'What Facts? A Talk with Roth' (interview with Philip Roth). In Searles 1992: 230–6.
Brodkin, Karen. 1998. *How Jews Became White Folks and What that Says about Race in America*. New Brunswick, New Jersey: Rutgers University Press.
Browder, Laura. 2000. *Slippery Characters: Ethnic Impersonators and American Identities*. Chapel Hill: University of North Carolina Press.
Brown, Craig. 2000. 'Sex, spooks and the fierce wrath of Roth' (review of *The Human Stain*). *The Mail on Sunday* ('Review'), 7 May: 67.
Brown, Craig. 2004. 'Fiction that betrays the awful facts' (review of *The Plot Against America*). *The Mail on Sunday* ('Review'), 3 October: 69.
Budick, Emily Miller. 1998. *Blacks and Jews in Literary Conversation*. Cambridge: Cambridge University Press.
Budick, Emily Miller. 2001a. *Ideology and Jewish Identity in Israeli and American Literature*. New York: State University of New York Press.
Budick, Emily Miller. 2001b. 'The African American and Israeli "Other" in the Construction of Jewish American Identity'. In Budick 2001a: 197–212.
Charis-Carlson, Jeffrey. 2004. 'Philip Roth's Human Stains and Washington Pilgrimages'. *Studies in American Jewish Literature* 23: 104–21.
Cheyette, Bryan. 2004a. 'On Being a Jewish Critic'. *Jewish Social Studies* 11: 1, 32–51.
Cheyette, Bryan. 2004b. 'In flight from history' (review of *The Plot Against America*). *The Jewish Chronicle*, October 8: 27.
Coetzee, J.M. 2004. 'What Philip Knew' (review of *The Plot Against America*). *The New York Review of Books*, 18 November: 4–6.

Cohen, Joseph. 1992. 'Paradise Lost, Paradise Regained: Reflections on Philip Roth's Recent Fiction'. *Studies in American Jewish Literature* 2: 1, 196–204.

Coleridge, Samuel Taylor. 1985. *Samuel Taylor Coleridge* (*The Oxford Authors*), ed. H.J. Jackson. Oxford: Oxford University Press.

Cooper, Alan. 1996. *Philip Roth and the Jews.* Albany: State University of New York Press.

Cooper, Alan. 2005. 'It Can Happen Here, Or All in the Family Values: Surviving *The Plot Against America*'. In Royal 2005a: 241–53.

Cowley, Jason. 2001. 'The Nihilist: Philip Roth's hard, isolate – and heroic – vision'. *The Atlantic Monthly* (May): 41–2.

Daleski, H.M. 2001. 'Philip Roth's To Jerusalem and Back'. In Budick 2001a: 79–94.

Dickstein, Morris. 2001. 'The Complex Fate of the Jewish American Writer'. In Budick 2001a: 57–78.

Dickstein, Morris. 2002. *Leopards in the Temple: The Transformation of American Fiction 1945–1970*. Cambridge, Massachusetts: Harvard University Press.

Diski, Jenny. 2005. 'Your dinner is the dog'. *The Guardian* ('Review'), 15 January: 35.

Doctorow, E.L. 1972. [1971]. *The Book of Daniel.* Basingstoke: Macmillan.

Duban, James. 2002. 'Being Jewish in the Twentieth Century: The Synchronicity of Roth and Hawthorne'. *Studies in American Jewish Literature* 21: 1–11.

Durante, Robert. 2001. *The Dialectic of Self and Story: Reading and Storytelling in Contemporary American Fiction.* New York: Routledge.

Elkin, Stanley. 1990a [1966]. *Criers and Kibitzers, Kibitzers and Criers* (revised). New York: Thunder's Mouth.

Elkin, Stanley. 1990b [1966]. 'The Guest'. In Elkin 1990a: 92–126.

Ellis, Bret Easton. 1986 [1985]. *Less Than Zero.* Basingstoke: Picador.

Ellis, Bret Easton. 1987 [1986]. *The Rules of Attraction.* Basingstoke: Picador.

Ellis, Bret Easton. 1988 [1987]. *The Informers.* Basingstoke: Picador.

Ellis, Bret Easton. 1991 [1990]. *American Psycho.* Basingstoke: Picador.

Ellis, Bret Easton. 1998 [1997]. *Glamorama.* Basingstoke: Picador.

Ellis, Bret Easton. 2005. *Lunar Park.* Basingstoke: Picador.

Ellison, Ralph. 1992 [1952]. *Invisible Man.* New York: Modern Library.

Faber, Michael. 2005. 'A tower of babble' (review of *Extremely Loud and Incredibly Close*). *The Guardian* ('Review'), 4 June: 26.

Foer, Jonathan Safran. 2003 [2002]. *Everything Is Illuminated.* Harmondsworth: Penguin.

Foer, Jonathan Safran. 2005. *Extremely Loud and Incredibly Close.* Bath: QPD.

Franco, Dean J. 2004. 'Being Black, Being Jewish, and Knowing the Difference: Philip Roth's *The Human Stain*; Or, It Depends on What the Meaning of "Clinton" Is'. *Studies in American Jewish Literature* 23: 88–103.

Furman, Andrew. 2000. *Contemporary Jewish American Writers and the Multicultural Dilemma: The Return of the Exiled.* New York: Syracuse University Press.

Gates, Henry Louis. 1997a. *Thirteen Ways of Looking at a Black Man.* New York: Random House.

Gates, Henry Louis. 1997b. 'The Passing of Anatole Broyard'. In Gates 1997a: 180–214.

Gathman, Roger. 2005. 'Novelist trapped in post-9/11 tale' (review of *Extremely Loud and Incredibly Close*). *Chicago Sun-Times,* 3 April: http://suntimes.com/output/books/sho-Sunday-foer03.

Gerstle, Ellen. 2001. 'Philip Roth's *The Human Stain*: An American Tragedy' (review essay on *The Human Stain*). *Studies in American Jewish Literature* 20: 95–9.

Girgus, Sam B. 1992. 'Between *Goodbye, Columbus* and *Portnoy's Complaint:* Becoming a Man and a Writer in Roth's Feminist "Family Romance."' *Studies in American Jewish Literature* 2:1, 143–53.

Gitlin, Todd. 1997. 'Weather Girl' (review of *American Pastoral*). *Nation,* 12 May: 63–4.

Goldman, Albert. 1969. 'Wild Blue Shocker'. *Life* (February): 58–64.

Grant, Linda. 2001. 'Breast man' (review of *The Dying Animal*). *The Guardian* ('Review'), 30 June: 10.

Grass, Gunter. 1964 [1959]. *The Tin Drum* (tr. Ralph Manheim). New York: Vintage.

Greenberg, Robert M. 2003. 'Transgression in the Fiction of Philip Roth'. In Bloom 2003: 81–100.

Gross, John. 1982 [1962]. 'Marjorie Morningstar Ph.D.' (review of *Letting Go*). In Pinsker 1982: 41–3.

Grossman, Lev. 2004. 'The Reign of Roth' (interview with Roth). *Time,* October 4: 82–3.

Halio, Jay L. 1992. *Philip Roth Revisited.* Boston: Twayne.

Halkin, Hillel. 1994. 'How to Read Philip Roth'. *Commentary* (February): 43–8.

Hardwick, Elizabeth. 1997. 'Paradise Lost' (review of *American Pastoral*). *New York Review of Books,* 12 June: 12–14.

Hawthorne, Nathaniel. 1986 [1850]. *The Scarlet Letter and Selected Tales.* Harmondsworth: Penguin.

Hensher, Philip. 1993. Untitled review of *Operation Shylock. The Guardian* ('G2'), 20 April: 11.

Herman, David. 2004. 'What if his Parents were Right?' (review of *The Plot Against America*). *Jewish Quarterly* 196: 75–9.

Higgin, Graham. 2000. 'The gripes of Roth' (review of *The Human Stain*). *The Guardian* ('Review'), 27 May: 8.

Hilfer, Tony. Untitled review of *The Plot Against America. Austin-American Statesman,* 10 September: 26.

Hoffman, Matthew. 2003. 'An ascetic chronicler of America's post-war excesses'. *The Independent*, 30 August: 19.

Hogan, Monika. 2004. '"Something so Visceral in with the Rhetorical": Race, Hypochondria, and the Un-Assimilated Body in *American Pastoral*'. *Studies in American Jewish Literature* 23: 1–14.

Horace. 2003 [1729]. *Horace's Satires, Epistles and Art of Poetry* (tr. S. Dunster). New York: RA Kessinger.

Howe, Irving, ed. 1977. *Jewish American Stories*. New York: Mentor.

Howe, Irving. 1982 [1972]. 'Philip Roth Reconsidered'. In Pinsker 1982: 231–43.

Hutcheon, Linda. 1988. *A Poetics of Postmodernism: History, Theory, Fiction*. New York: Routledge.

Isaac, Dan. 1982 [1964]. 'In Defense of Philip Roth'. In Pinsker 1982: 192–204.

Itzkovitz, Daniel. 2001. 'Passing Like Me: Jewish Chameleonism and the Politics of Race'. In Sanchez and Schlossberg 2001: 38–63.

Jacobson, Dan. 1982. *The Story of the Stories: The Chosen People and Its God*. London: Secker & Warburg.

Jacobson, Howard. 1997. *Seriously Funny: From the Ridiculous to the Sublime*. Harmondsworth: Viking.

Jacobson, Howard. 1999 [1998]. *No More Mister Nice Guy*. London: Vintage.

Jones, Judith Paterson and Guinevera A. Nance. 1981. *Philip Roth*. New York: Ungar.

Kafka, Franz. 1953 [1925]. *The Trial* (tr. Willa and Edwin Muir). Harmondsworth: Penguin.

Kakutani, Michiko. 2004. 'A pro-Nazi president, a family feeling the effects' (review of *The Plot Against America*). *The New York Times*, 21 September: http://www.nytimes.com/2004/09/21/books/21kaku.

Karl, Frederick. 2002. *American Fictions 1980–2000: Whose America Is It Anyway?* Xlibris Corporation. No place of publication specified.

Kelleter, Frank. 2003. 'Portrait of the Sexist as a Dying Man: Death, Ideology, and the Erotic in Philip Roth's *Sabbath's Theater*'. In Bloom 2003: 163–98.

Kemp, Peter. 1997. 'Once upon a time in America' (review of *American Pastoral*). *Sunday Times* ('Books'), 1 June: 13.

Kemp, Peter. 2004. 'Master of shock and awe' (review of *The Plot Against America*). *Sunday Times* ('Books'), 3 October: 41.

Kermode, Frank. 2001a. *Pleasing Myself: From Beowulf to Philip Roth*. Harmondsworth: Penguin.

Kermode, Frank. 2001b. 'Philip Roth'. In Kermode 2001a: 256–65.

Kirn, Walter. 2005. 'Everything is included' (review of *Extremely Loud and Incredibly Close*). *The New York Times*, 3 April: http://query.nytimes.com/gst/fullpage.

Kirsch, Adam. 2004. Untitled review of *The Plot Against America*. *New York Sun*, 27 September: 14.

Kitaj, R.B. 1989. *First Diasporist Manifesto.* London: Thames and Hudson.

Klinkowitz, Jerome. 1980 [1975]. *Literary Disruptions: The Making of a Post-Contemporary American Fiction* (revised). Urbana and Chicago: University of Illinois Press.

Kremer, Lilian. 2002. 'Philip Roth: Writing Jews in Newark, Prague, and Jerusalem'. In Lévy and Savin 2002: 35–50.

Larner, Jeremy. 1982 [1960]. 'The Conversion of the Jews' (review of *Goodbye, Columbus*). In Pinsker 1982: 28–32.

LeClair, Tom. 1989. *The Art of Excess: Mastery in Contemporary American Fiction.* Urbana and Chicago: University of Illinois Press.

Lee, Hermione. 1982. *Philip Roth.* London: Methuen.

Lévy, Paule and Ada Savin, eds. 2002. *Profils Américains: Philip Roth.* Montpellier: CERCLA.

Lewis, R.W.B. 1955. *The American Adam: Innocence, Tragedy and Tradition in the Nineteenth Century.* Chicago: University of Chicago Press.

Lewis, Sinclair. 2005 [1935]. *It Can't Happen Here.* New York: Signet.

Lyons, Bonnie. 2001. 'Lies, Secrets, Truthtelling and Imagination in *The Human Stain*' (review essay on *The Human Stain*). *Studies in American Jewish Literature* 20: 90–5.

Macarthur, Kathleen L. 2004. 'Shattering the American Pastoral: Philip Roth's Vision of Trauma and the American Dream'. *Studies in American Jewish Literature* 23: 15–26.

McDaniel, John N. 2003. 'Distinctive Features of Roth's Artistic Vision'. In Bloom 2003: 41–56.

McDonald, Brian. 2004. '"The Real American Crazy Shit": On Adamism and Democratic Individuality in *American Pastoral*'. *Studies in American Jewish Literature* 23: 27–40.

McGrath, Charles. 2000. 'Zuckerman's Alter Brain' (interview with Roth). *The New York Times Book Review*, 7 May: 8, 10.

Mackenzie, Suzie. 2005. 'Something happened' (interview with Jonathan Safran Foer). *The Guardian* ('Review'), 21 May: 5–6.

McInerney, Jay. 2005. 'The uses of invention'. *The Guardian* ('Review), 17 September: 4–6.

Mailer, Norman. 1949 [1948]. *The Naked and the Dead.* London: Wingate.

Mailer, Norman. 1952 [1951]. *Barbary Shore.* London: Jonathan Cape.

Malamud, Bernard. 1968 [1966]. *The Fixer.* Harmondsworth: Penguin.

Marcus, Greil. 2004. 'Lindbergh at America's helm' (review of *The Plot Against America*). *Los Angeles Times* ('Book Review'), 22 September: 1.

Matthews, Charles. 2005. '9/11 trauma spurs brainy boy's quest' (review of *Extremely Loud and Incredibly Close*). *San Jose Mercury News*, 3 April: http://www.broward.com/mld/mercurynews/entertainment/books/11300753.

Menand, Louis. 1997. 'The Irony and the Ecstasy: Philip Roth and the New Atlantis' (review of *American Pastoral*). *The New Yorker*, 19 May: 88–94.

Milbauer, Asher Z. and Donald G. Watson, eds. 1988. *Reading Philip Roth.* Basingstoke: Macmillan.

Miller, Laura. 2005. 'Terror Comes to Tiny Town' (review of *Extremely Loud and Incredibly Close*). *New York Magazine Book Review,* 3 April: http://www.newyorkmetro.com/nymetro/arts/books/reviews/11574

Milowitz, Steven. 2000. *Philip Roth Considered: The Concentrationary Universe of the American Writer.* New York: Garland.

Moore, Lorrie. 1987 [1986]. *Anagrams.* London: Faber and Faber.

Moore, Lorrie. 2000. 'The Wrath of Athena' (review of *The Human Stain*). *The New York Times Book Review,* 7 May: 7–8.

Morley, Catherine. 'Memories of the Lindbergh Administration: Plotting, Genre and the Splitting of the Self in *The Plot Against America*'. Unpublished.

Morrison, Blake. 2004. 'The relentless unforeseen' (review of *The Plot Against America*). *The Guardian* ('Review'), 2 October: 2.

Morton, Brian. 2004. 'Memories of the Lindberg [sic] administration, Philip Roth imagines the Nazi-sympathizing aviator in the White House – and dark years for American Jews' (review of *The Plot Against America*). *Newsday* ('Culture'), 3 October: 32.

Nabokov, Vladimir. 1971a [1955]. *Lolita.* New York: Berkley Medallion.

Nabokov, Vladimir. 1971b [1956]. 'Vladimir Nabokov on a book entitled LOLITA'. In Nabokov 1971a: 282–8.

Neelakantan, G. 2004. 'Monster in Newark: Philip Roth's Apocalypse in *American Pastoral*'. *Studies in American Jewish Literature* 23: 55–66.

Newton, Adam Zachary. 1999. *Facing Black and Jew: Literature as Public Space in Twentieth-Century America.* Cambridge: Cambridge University Press.

O'Brien, Tim. 1995 [1973]. *If I Die in a Combat Zone.* London: Flamingo.

O'Brien, Tim. 1991 [1979]. *Going After Cacciato.* London: Flamingo.

O'Brien, Tim. 1991 [1990]. *The Things They Carried.* London: Flamingo.

O'Donnell, Patrick. 1988. '"None other": The Subject of Roth's *My Life as a Man*'. In Milbauer and Watson 1988: 144–59.

O'Hagan, Sean. 2004. 'One angry man' (review of *The Plot Against America*). *The Observer,* 26 September: http://observer.guardian.co.uk/print/0,3858,5024572–102280,00.html

Parrish, Timothy. 2000. 'The End of Identity: Philip Roth's *American Pastoral*'. *Shofar* 19:1, 84–99.

Parrish, Timothy. 2003. 'Imagining Jews in Philip Roth's *Operation Shylock*'. In Bloom 2003: 119–44.

Pinsker, Sanford. 1975. *The Comedy that 'Hoits': An Essay on the Fiction of Philip Roth.* Columbia, Missouri: University of Missouri Press.

Pinsker, Sanford. 1982. *Critical Essays on Philip Roth.* Boston: G.K. Hall.

Pinsker, Sanford. 1990. *Bearing the Bad News: Contemporary American Literature and Culture.* Iowa City, Iowa: University of Iowa Press.

Pirandello, Luigi. 1995 [1921]. *Six Characters in Search of an Author* (tr. Mark Musa). Harmondsworth: Penguin.
Posnock, Ross. 2001. 'Purity and Danger: On Philip Roth' (review essay on *The Human Stain*). *Raritan* 21:2, 85–101.
Pughe, Thomas. 1994. *Comic Sense: Reading Robert Coover, Stanley Elkin, Philip Roth.* Basel: Birkhäuser Verlag.
Pynchon, Thomas. 1979 [1966]. *The Crying of Lot 49*. Basingstoke: Picador.
Rodgers, Bernard F. 1978. *Philip Roth.* Boston: Twayne.
Royal, Derek Parker. 2001. 'Fictional Realms of Possibility: Reimagining the Ethnic Subject in Philip Roth's *American Pastoral*'. *Studies in American Jewish Literature* 20: 1–16.
Royal, Derek Parker. 2004a. 'Introduction: Philip Roth's America'. *Studies in American Jewish Literature* 23: ix–xii.
Royal, Derek Parker. 2004b. 'Philip Roth: A Bibliography of the Criticism, 1994–2003'. *Studies in American Jewish Literature* 23: 145–59.
Royal, Derek Parker, ed. 2005a. *Philip Roth: New Perspectives on an American Author.* Westport, Connecticut: Praeger.
Royal, Derek Parker. 2005b. 'Pastoral Dreams and National Identity in *American Pastoral* and *I Married a Communist*'. In Royal 2005a: 185–207.
Royal, Derek Parker. 2005c. '"Critical Unmoorings": An Introduction to Philip Roth Studies'. *Philip Roth Studies* 1:1, 4–6.
Rubin-Dorsky, Jeffrey. 2003. 'Philip Roth and American Jewish Identity: The Question of Authenticity'. In Bloom 2003: 205–32.
Rushdie, Salman. 1981. *Midnight's Children.* London: Jonathan Cape.
Safer, Elaine B. 1999. 'The Tragicomic in Philip Roth's *Sabbath's Theater*'. In Siegel and Halio 1999: 169–79.
Safer, Elaine B. 2003a. 'The Double, Comic Irony, and Postmodernism in Philip Roth's *Operation Shylock*'. In Bloom 2003: 101–18.
Safer, Elaine B. 2003b. 'Tragedy and Farce in Roth's *The Human Stain*'. In Bloom 2003: 239–58.
Sanchez, Maria Carla and Linda Schlossberg, eds. 2001. *Passing: Identity and Interpretation in Sexuality, Race, and Religion.* New York: New York University Press.
Sarnoff, Alvin P. 1992 [1987]. 'Writers Have a Third Eye' (interview with Philip Roth). In Searles 1992: 209–13.
Savin, Ada. 2002. 'Exposure and Concealment in *The Human Stain*'. In Lévy and Savin 2002: 181–97.
Searles, George J. 1985. *The Fiction of Philip Roth and John Updike.* Carbondale: Southern Illinois University Press.
Searles, George J. 1992. *Conversations with Philip Roth.* Jackson, Mississippi: University of Mississippi Press.
Shechner, Mark. 2003. *Up Society's Ass, Copper.* Madison, Wisconsin: The University of Wisconsin Press.

Shenley, Joshua Wolf. 2005. 'Living to Tell the Tale' (interview with Jonathan Safran Foer). *Mother Jones* (May/June): http://www.motherjones.com/arts/qa/2005/05/Safran-Foer.

Shields, Carol. 1991 [1980]. *Happenstance*. London: Flamingo.

Shostak, Debra B. 1991. '"This Obsessive Reinvention of the Real": Speculative Narrative in Philip Roth's *The Counterlife*'. *Modern Fiction Studies* 37: 2, 197–215.

Shostak, Debra B. 2004. *Philip Roth: Countertexts, Counterlives*. Columbia: University of South Carolina Press.

Siegel, Ben and Jay L. Halio, eds. 1999. *American Literary Dimensions: Poems and Essays in Honor of Melvin J. Friedman*. Delaware: University of Delaware Press.

Smyth, Edmund, ed. 1991. *Postmodernism and Contemporary Fiction*. London: B.T. Batsford.

Sterne, Laurence. 1986 [1759–67]. *The Life and Opinions of Tristram Shandy*. Harmondsworth: Penguin.

Stone, Robert. 1998. 'Waiting for Lefty' (review of *I Married A Communist*). *New York Review of Books*, 5 November: 38–40.

Stoppard, Tom. 1968 [1967]. *Rosencrantz and Guildenstern Are Dead*. London: Faber & Faber.

Tanenbaum, Laura. 2004. 'Reading Roth's Sixties'. *Studies in American Jewish Literature* 23: 41–54.

Tanner, Tony. 1976 [1971]. *City of Words: American Fiction 1950–1970*. London: Jonathan Cape.

Taylor, D.J. 1997. 'The nightmare of the American Dream' (review of *American Pastoral*). *The Independent* ('Night and Day'), 1 June: 36.

Turlin, Jean-Louis. 2001. 'I feel like saying: "Stop, that's enough"' (interview with Roth). *The Independent* ('Arts'), 16 October: 4–5.

Updike, John. 2005. 'Mixed Messages' (review of *Extremely Loud and Incredibly Close*). *The New Yorker*, 14 April: http://www.newyorker.com/printables/critics/05031crbo-books1.

Various. 2004. 'Season's readings'. *The Guardian* ('Review'), 4 December: 4–7.

Vonnegut, Kurt. 1973 [1969]. *Slaughter-House Five or The Children's Crusade: A Duty-Dance with Death*. New York: Dell.

Wade. Stephen. 1996. *The Imagination in Transit: The Fiction of Philip Roth*. Sheffield: Sheffield Academic Press.

Webb, Igor. 2003. 'Born Again'. In Bloom 2003: 233–8.

Whitman, Walt. 1996. *The Complete Poems*. Harmondsworth: Penguin.

Wilde, Alan. 1987. *Middle Grounds: Studies in Contemporary American Fiction*. Philadelphia: Pennsylvania University Press.

Wood, James. 1997. 'America berserk' (review of *American Pastoral*). *The Guardian* ('Review'), 5 June: 9.

Wood, James. 1998. 'The Sentimentalist' (review of *I Married A Communist*). *New Republic*, 12 October: 38–43.
Wood, Michael. 2004. 'Just Folks' (review of *The Plot Against America*). *London Review of Books*, 4 November: 3–6.
Yardley, Jonathan. 2004. 'Homeland insecurity' (review of *The Plot Against America*). *Washington Post*, 3 October: 2.
Zucker, David J. 2004. 'Philip Roth: Desire and Death'. *Studies in American Jewish Literature* 23: 135–44.

# Index

Note: 'n.' after a page number indicates the number of a note on that page.